W9-BSL-550

Sam Kashner

When I Was Cool

My Life at the Jack Kerouac School

A Memoir

HarperCollinsPublishers

HarperCollins books may be purchased for educational, business, or sales promotional use. For information, please write: Special Markets Department, HarperCollins Publishers Inc., 10 East 53rd Street, New York, NY 10022.

Frontispiece of Allen Ginsberg by Gordon Ball; copyright © Gordon Ball.

An extension of this copyright page appears on p. 323.

FIRST EDITION

Designed by Nicola Ferguson

Printed on acid-free paper

Library of Congress Cataloging-in-Publication Data
Kashner, Sam.
When I was cool : my life at the Jack Kerouac School / Sam Kashner.—1st ed.
p. cm.
ISBN 0-06-000566-1 (acid-free paper)
1. Kashner, Sam.   2. Jack Kerouac School of Disembodied Poetics.
3. Kashner, Sam—Homes and haunts—Colorado.   4. Poetry—Authorship—
Study and teaching—Colorado.   5. Poets, American—20th century—Biography.
6. Kerouac, Jack, 1922–1969—Influence.   7. Beat generation.   I. Title.
PS3561.A697Z468   2003
811'.54—dc21
[B]   2003047822

04 05 06 07 08 NMSG/RRD 10 9 8 7 6 5 4 3 2 1

"The world is full of renunciations and apprenticeships,
and this is thine: thou must pass for a fool
and a churl for a long season."
—RALPH WALDO EMERSON, "THE POET"

Caveat Emptor

Please don't read this book if you're looking (as I was in the early 1970s) for a history of the Beat Generation. When I got hooked on *Howl* and *On the Road*, when I was ga-ga for *The Dharma Bums* and Gregory Corso's poem "Bomb" (which folded out of the book as if dropped from an F-15; and it looked like a bomb, too, the way the words were arranged on the page), there weren't many books on the Beats. Now there's a tower of Babel. Ginsberg, Burroughs, Kerouac, Corso—they've become the Rat Pack of literature. Anne Waldman is their Angie Dickinson.

In truth, there are many wonderful books on the Beats. Ann Charters, an old friend of Ginsberg's who wrote one of the first and still one of the best biographies of Kerouac, is supreme. There's Gordon Ball, Allen's Boswell, who knew Ginsberg as well as anyone and helped put together *Allen Verbatim* and all the published journals and correspondence; and you should read Barry Miles, Ginsberg's biographer, and Steven Watson, who wrote a wonderful book called *The Birth of the Beat Generation*. Ed Sanders wrote *Tales of Beatnik Glory;* he, too, knew them all, as did John Tytell, who was there almost before anyone. Also, Diane di Prima and Hettie Jones, for their remarkable memoirs of the Beat life, as well as Michael Schumacher's epic life, *Dharma Lion: A Critical Biography of Allen Ginsberg.* And then there's Gerald Nicosia, and

C

O

O

L

Kerouac's other fine biographers and chroniclers, such as Tom Clark, John McNally, and of course Barry Gifford. Not to mention Joyce Johnson, whose mighty *Minor Characters* is a great book about her life with and without Jack Kerouac. These are the historians of the era, and these wonderful books and a few others I've used as an *aide de memoire*, and am deeply grateful to the authors.

I wasn't there at the beginning or even the middle. I was there for the ending. Or, maybe, the beginning of the end. I wasn't a beatnik; I wasn't even a hippie. But I wanted to write poetry and have cool friends and thumb my nose at the establishment; at the same time I wanted to make my parents proud of me. How was I going to do all that?

These are letters from camp. Beat camp. My counselors happened to be former Beats: Allen Ginsberg taught me swimming and Swinburne; William Burroughs took us deep into the forest and then told us which one of us was probably an alien; Gregory Corso taught us how to sing—only the camp song was an aria from *Pagliacci* and his philosophy was strictly jail yard: "Never rat on a friend."

When I left the south shore of Long Island for my Beat experience at the Jack Kerouac School of Disembodied Poetics in 1976, I didn't know who I was. I just knew what I didn't want to be. After arriving, I was initially afraid of the Beats; I even tried to stay away from them. But they were my teachers, so I couldn't avoid them for long. I had nothing to offer them. I wanted them to make me an artist. I wanted the noble calling of literature. There was nothing I could do but enter the hive.

Some people may think this book is an act of heresy. Maybe it is. Maybe it isn't. Maybe it's an answer to Gregory's last phone call to me: "Tell me the truth," he barked, without even saying hello. Maybe all you need for heresy is an opportunity. Someone once said that the past is a kind of prison. You don't always get the chance to open a window in jail. This is my chance.

When I Was Cool

Prologue: Naked Brunch

I wanted to be in the picture. I just can't remember where I first saw it: the photograph in front of City Lights Bookstore of Allen Ginsberg, Peter Orlovsky, and Neal Cassady. They had their arms around each other. They looked happy. They looked like friends. They looked like they understood each other. And Allen Ginsberg—he looked like me.

In the photograph Allen was thin, he had short dark hair, and he wore glasses. Everyone in the picture—even Neal Cassady, the tough guy in the white T-shirt—seemed to like Allen. The photograph projected a feeling of bonhomie. But I can't remember where I first saw it. It might've been at Philip Weiner's house. He was two years older than I. He was fifteen. The Weiners lived next door, around the corner on Shore Drive in Merrick, a prosperous little town on the south shore of Long Island, about an hour from New York City on the Long Island Rail Road. Our split-level houses were so close that I could see the Weiners' bathroom shelf from the window of my father's downstairs office.

Philip's parents were swingers. They went into New York City a lot. Irving Weiner had an office in the garment district. He made children's pajamas. (That was before we knew pajamas could catch on fire.) He took his clients to the Copacabana. The Weiners had framed photos of themselves sitting with other couples at the

C

O

O

L

Copa, looking very glamorous. My mother was always commenting on Shirley Weiner's glorious figure. Every summer she would lie out in the sun on a lawn chair in her backyard in a bikini, smoking a cigarette and sipping a drink. She wore high heels around the house. This was in the late sixties, when the suburbs were supposed to be a safe refuge from the big city.

As soon as I hit puberty, I longed for the big city.

Philip's bedroom was in a converted attic. He had a chemistry set. He said he was working on some kind of formula that would make him invisible. (I always looked to see how I could escape from Philip's attic if I had to. I didn't want him to make me drink the invisibility potion he was cooking up.) He was also the first guy I knew who listened to Bob Dylan records. He showed me one. It was *Bringing It All Back Home*. Philip pointed out all the interesting things thrown around the room in the picture on the album cover, such as a copy of *Sing Out!* magazine and a Dave Van Ronk album. I didn't know what they were. We looked at the song titles and the numbers next to them. I wanted to sound like I knew something, so I told Philip that the numbers next to the songs were the time of day each song was recorded. He said that was impossible. He said we should time the songs and then I'd see how they were only the length of time of each song.

Philip then asked me if I knew about Allen Ginsberg or if I'd ever heard of William Burroughs. He said that Burroughs, best known for his mind-boggled, heroin-laced novel *Naked Lunch,* had gone into the jungle to look for a rare hallucinogenic drug called yagé. Philip said we should go and search for this drug near Camman's Pond in Merrick. We did, but we didn't find it. We found only a few crushed beer cans and a used condom.

Back then, Bob Dylan's voice scared me a little, but the picture of Allen Ginsberg meant something to me. Philip had cut out of the *Village Voice* another picture of Allen wearing a scarf and glasses, a long, unkempt beard, and an Uncle Sam hat. I didn't know why, but I just wanted to take that picture home with me. When Philip started talking about the Beat Generation, I suddenly felt the enthusiasm of the liberated. Something new had crossed my path.

I soon realized I had much to learn. Philip took out one of Allen's City Lights books and read one of the poems to me. I think it was about running into Walt Whitman at the supermarket. At the time (seventh grade), I didn't know who Walt Whitman was. I thought it might've had something to do with food—maybe the Whitman Sampler box of candies. It didn't matter. A new world with its own planets, its own creation, its own myths had just come swimming into my brain. Philip's stories about Burroughs and Ginsberg and their friend Jack Kerouac were like tombstones kicked over in the dark. It was joyfulness in the face of junior high school desk death.

I suddenly felt part of some sublime truth that most of the other creeps in my school would never understand, like our principal, Mr. Grebenauer, who once kept me waiting in his office for an hour before he tore the American flag tie I was wearing off my neck. (My mother wondered where the neck burn had come from. "Gym," I told her. Gym was a great excuse for everything. Melancholics lined up everywhere in school to blame gym.)

After hearing Philip's descriptions of the Beats, I wanted to go back to my own, safe house. Philip knew too many things, and it confused me. I didn't have far to go to get home, for we lived next door, so I walked around the block a few times, thinking things over. I decided to look up the word "Beat" in the *Random House Dictionary*. I dashed into our house on Lowell Lane and ran downstairs to where we kept the big dictionary and I looked up the word.

I didn't know at the time that it was pretty much Kerouac's definition I would find there: "Members of the generation that came of age after World War II, who, supposedly as a result of disillusionment stemming from the Cold War, espouse mystical detachment and relaxation of social and sexual tensions." I don't know how long that definition was in use—it was an old dictionary. My parents kept it in the basement along with *Fanny Hill*, *The Hundred Thousand Dollar Misunderstanding*, and *Candy*, three forbidden books.

Another early picture I saw of Allen Ginsberg was on the cover of an old copy of the *Evergreen Review*. He was bearded and wearing

C

O

O

L

his Uncle Sam hat, his arms akimbo. And he was jumping into flames. It turned out to be two pictures put together: his image juxtaposed over a movie still from a film Allen and Peter had been in together called *Chappaqua*. Then, when I turned sixteen, *Don't Look Back* opened. It was playing in only one theater in Lynbrook, a few towns away from Merrick, and I went to see it with my father. It was a black-and-white documentary about Bob Dylan's 1965 tour of England. The movie starts with Dylan, wearing a vest, holding up cards with the words to his song "Subterranean Homesick Blues" written on them. After each lyric he casually throws the card away. It looked like it was filmed on Clinton Street, or some street in lower Manhattan. But what struck me was the man way in the background, with a long dark beard, wearing a shawl or a tallis over his shoulders. He looked like he was davening—like the old men in my grandparents' temple in the Catskill Mountains— praying while rocking back and forth. At the end of the song, when Dylan has thrown away all the cards, he walks away, and the man in the background walks away after him. It is Allen Ginsberg, Bob Dylan's favorite poet.

In 1969, the world was filling up with forbidden things. Suddenly the houses on Shore Drive, across from the bay, stood out more sharply as something to leap over in order to find *real life*, but night was coming, and I couldn't even see the walls that seemed so hard to get over. The night would take hold of the world I knew; soon I wouldn't recognize it anymore.

I never got to be really close friends with Philip. He went off to college a few years before me. I liked to think he perfected his invisibility formula and just disappeared. I, too, wanted to disappear. By the time I hit sixteen I felt like a displaced person in the suburbs.

To my parents, though, the suburbs were the Garden of Eden. They had come from Brooklyn and the Grand Concourse in the Bronx, and Merrick was like a little bit of heaven. Our front lawn was a pasture. You could shop every day at Waldbaum's and never get hungry again.

My father remembered growing up in the Bronx, and he told us about a woman who had come to his mother to read a letter she'd just received from her brother in Poland. The woman was illiterate, but my paternal grandmother, Gertrude, knew Polish, as well as Russian and English, so this woman had come to ask her to read the letter out loud. As she read the letter, she came to a part where the writer talked about how "we killed a Jew today," and how much happier the village was now that he was dead. That was read in my father's house, when he was a boy. He must have wondered if life in America was really going to be any different from wartime Poland.

How much like Eden, though, or some trembling cup of good fortune, was the house on the corner of Lowell Lane in Merrick! Still, you can get used to anything, luxury as well as hardship.

Because my parents kept their Depression-era hard times a secret from me, I never knew why our house and town seemed like paradise to them. They came to Long Island, our parents, to welcome happiness and prosperity, whereas Jack Kerouac and his friends saw freedom in poverty—the kind of poverty my parents had escaped from.

The essence of "Beat," Allen Ginsberg used to tell people, can be found in *On the Road,* in the phrase "everything belongs to me because I am poor." And all this time my poor parents were killing themselves to make it to the suburbs, to get me and my sister away from want.

The Beat Generation should've been my uncle Joe's heroes. He was still young when he returned from the Second World War. He was a painter. He read *Civilization and Its Discontents.* He knew from Camus. He lived at 410 Central Park West. He stood on line at Carnegie Hall for an entire day for a ticket to see Horowitz come back from his nervous breakdown. He should've been interested in the Beats, but he wasn't. He was too much of a loner. The Beats were first and foremost a group of friends. That's what I liked

Naked Brunch

about them. That's why, later on, I wanted to go to the Jack Kerouac School. I thought it would be like the re-creation of the Columbia University friendships that Allen and Kerouac and their friend Lucien Carr had when they were eighteen years old, drawn together by a love of literature and smoking joints in their dorm room.

It was Lucien who introduced Allen to the poetry of Arthur Rimbaud in college. Even long-dead poets were a part of this family. This was a movement that seemed to be created by kids in college, although they didn't seem like kids. By the time I entered high school two years later, I had become infatuated with the Beats. They had transformed their own lives into myth and legend, made up of the details of their days, their fragments of conversation, the habits of their friends. Burroughs narrated his earliest years as a heroin addict in *Junky*, taking his brief job as an exterminator and giving it a comic voice. Kerouac set everything down in his "spontaneous bop prosody": the story of his life written in marathon sessions fueled by weed and endless Benzedrine. He had turned his life and the lives of his friends into a kind of epic.

When it came time for me to apply to colleges, my high school guidance counselor didn't think I'd be able to get into regular college. She wanted me to go to a school in Iowa that was practically a vocational school. She said my only good grades were in English. She had me on the BOCES bus with kids who hated to read. But I fought back. I wrote a lot of poetry and I got into Hamilton College, although she had discouraged me from applying. She said I was fooling myself. I had only applied to Hamilton College because my high school girlfriend, Rosalie, was going to Kirkland, the women's school across the road from Hamilton, which was still an all-male college. When the acceptance letter came, Miss Nickel, the guidance counselor, pulled me out of class and started dancing with me in the hall. No one from my school had gotten into Hamilton in a long time.

I, too, was surprised I had gotten in. I told her this must have been how it felt for Kerouac to get a football scholarship to go to Columbia. She had no idea what I was talking about.

Kerouac had hated playing football for Columbia, the way I hated my six weeks at Hamilton. We both dropped out. But Kerouac went into the Merchant Marine during the Second World War, and I went to the Jack Kerouac School of Disembodied Poetics.

But once upon a time they weren't so disembodied. Just as the rich live together, their neighborhoods gently touching elbows, so, too, the miserable of the world stick together. Kerouac's weariness of the world made sense to me, as did his furtiveness. They could've called themselves the furtive generation, as they seemed to possess some hidden, inner knowledge of the world that 1950s America didn't share. That's what I wanted. That's what I came looking for.

Six years after Kerouac's death, I sent in my application to the Jack Kerouac School of Disembodied Poetics, a subset of Naropa, the first Buddhist college in the country.

I had been restless at Hamilton College, the strict, all-boys' school in Clinton in upstate New York, where I started my college career. There weren't many Jews at Hamilton, and fewer still in Clinton. Hamilton was the only school to give Ezra Pound an honorary degree *after* the war, after he was convicted of treason. That was enough reason for me to go there. But I was unhappy and I wanted out. Then I saw the brand-new Naropa catalogue: its purple cover with the wheel of the dharma stamped on the front. Ginsberg, Burroughs, Corso, Whalen, Kesey—the core faculty, it promised, all in one place. *Pull My Daisy* with the sound. I was going to be schooled by the Beats. I'd be brought up by them. The son they never wanted. It was going to be nirvana (it wasn't a band yet). I'd tolerate the Buddhist stuff, the meditation practice they talked about. I was there to join Allen Ginsberg's reindeer army of skittish

C

O

O

L

boys who wanted to sit at the same table with the only man who could call William Burroughs "Bill." And, as it said at the back of the catalogue (in very small type), the school *had* applied for certification.

By the time I was filling out my application—there really was one, an essay that I answered with quotes from the Ramones—the Beats were legends. By 1975 some of them had known each other for more than thirty years. That was the thing about them that I really liked: the camaraderie of these men who had tried so hard to avoid society, or at least to separate themselves from it.

In my last year of high school, my parents were hoping my grades would be good enough for me to go to Hofstra. But I didn't want to stand on the overpass and look down on Hempstead Turnpike. I wanted to burn like a roman candle, or at least a *shabbas* candle. I wanted to feel myself burning up with life. I wanted the Beat experience, but I didn't want to get hurt. I wanted *Naked Brunch*.

My parents read through the Jack Kerouac School of Disembodied Poetics catalogue. They saw the picture of the core faculty sitting on a bench: Allen, Bill, Peter, Gregory, and Anne. My mother asked what kind of bathroom facilities the dormitories had. She knew that one of the reasons I didn't want to go to a conventional college was the shared toilets. "Where will you go *pishen?*" she asked. "What about *gayen cocken?*" Just as the Eskimos are said to have two hundred different words for "snow," the Jews have about eight hundred words for going to the bathroom. I knew them all.

I told her I'd have my own apartment. It was agreed. I would go to the Jack Kerouac School. I would become a poet. I would join the Beat Generation.

The day I was going to leave, my parents said they had a surprise for me before they took me to the airport for the flight to

Denver (the school was located in nearby Boulder, Colorado). I went upstairs and closed the door to my room. I looked out the window above the radiator, and I said farewell to my sea of roofs— the Birnbaums, the Goldbergs, the Weiners, already composing in my head the dramatic masterpiece of my future life—like the Beats, like Allen in "Howl," fusing life and literature and legend. I was already anticipating my complicated love life, its joys and ineffable sorrows, the straw of my life on Long Island woven into the gold of Denver. What will the weather be like when I get there? I wondered. Will my first girlfriend be dark or fair? Will Allen come on to me? What would I do if he does? In one instant a thousand terrible and wonderful thoughts came over me like a shower of arrows over a covered wagon.

What I didn't quite realize as I packed my bags for the Kerouac School was that Ginsberg, Burroughs, and the rest of the Beats were on the downward slope of their fame. Eleven years earlier, Allen had been crowned King of the May in Czechoslovakia. William Burroughs's *Naked Lunch,* considered a classic novel of nightmare comedy, was nearly twenty years old. Because the core faculty had turned their autobiography into art, their fictional selves lived on in a kind of perpetual youth. But, as I would soon discover, they themselves had grown old. The Beats I would encounter at Naropa were long in the tooth, cranky, full of bowel complaints and the perils of advanced age.

I came downstairs. My parents had a present for me, waiting for me in the car: it was my father. Seymour Kashner. He would be coming with me to Boulder, to see that I got settled in okay.

My father going with me to the Jack Kerouac School? In the midst of my happiness—another crisis. I felt the cold hand of embarrassment on my shoulder. "Just for the weekend," my mother said. With so many secret fears of what life among the Beats would be like I was secretly relieved. I'd have my "naked brunch," at last. But it would be with my father at the other end of the table, eating Baskin-Robbins.

On the drive to the airport, Seymour asked me about the

C

O

O

L

school's unusual name. Why Jack Kerouac? I wondered about that, too—after all, he was the first among them to die. His presence was marked by his absence. And in some ways he had tried to out-run the idea of being "Beat" and had become more politically con-servative in the years before his early death. He even showed up on William Buckley's old TV show *Firing Line*, bloated and drunk, defending the war in Vietnam. Jack was an old-fashioned American patriot who wanted to put as much distance between himself and the emerging hippie culture as he could. Even his friends had a hard time figuring out why he had run out on them like that. Now that Kerouac had gone, disappearing into Florida and then, as Allen put it, "on the express elevator to heaven," the three remain-ing core Beats—Gregory, Bill, and Allen—contemplated Jack's importance to them and to American literature. Without Kerouac in the room, great claims were made for his work by Allen and his friends.

Allen described Kerouac as the new Buddha of American prose. He said that his friend had "spit forth intelligence into eleven books written in half the number of years (1951–56)—*On the Road, Visions of Neal, Dr. Sax, Springtime Mary, The Subterraneans, San Francisco Blues, Dharma Bums, Book of Dreams, Wake Up, Mexico City Blues,* and *Visions of Gerard,*" a heartbreaking little book about the short life and death of his younger brother, Gerard, the one the nuns of Lowell thought was a saint. Allen would tell us that Jack had created "spon-taneous bop prosody" that also happened to be original classic lit-erature. Several key phrases and the title "Howl" were taken "from his mouth to my ear," Allen said. (I doubt Kerouac would have made such claims for his own work.)

When age and booze started to demolish Kerouac's youth, he simply removed himself from his friends' lives. They were left with the feelings he had inspired in them—they were left, in effect, with his soul. Kerouac removed himself, for the sake of his honor. I started to think that he was embarrassed by the spectacle of people dropping out of society clutching a copy of *On the Road*, which all along was just supposed to be the story of his friends.

But let me tell you what I found out: by the end of Kerouac's book, it seemed to be the story of how he came to his vocation, the noble, serious work of being a writer. It made me like the book even more. All of a sudden I couldn't stand to see those late pictures of Kerouac looking so sad; it was starting to drive me nuts, all that pain and misery painted on his face. It was as if he were bringing back a bad dream that I'd been unable to shake off.

I liked the fact that Allen had encouraged Kerouac to take his writing seriously, to treat it as a calling—I wanted encouragement from Allen too! Going to the Kerouac School would put me right there in the lineage with Kerouac and with Burroughs, the line continuing. But what did I know? I was intoxicated by my numb-skull love of *Howl* and *On the Road*. I wanted to eat of that luminous cake! Later, Kerouac would describe his group of friends as "the most evil and intelligent buncha bastards and shits in America but had to admire in my admiring youth."

If Kerouac had lived longer and gotten to write out his endless Duluoz legend, he would have seen what I saw: the Beat Generation in a weird retirement phase. Not quite ready for assisted living, but famous enough to need assistants. I was going to be one of them. I had grown up wanting to be "Beat"—to eat death and live poetry. And my parents, in their generous good hearts, let me do it, they let me go, though a dangerous if not terrible world awaited me.

1. A Postcard from Allen

Growing up on Long Island, my father used to tease me. He said that I knew John F. Kennedy's birthday but that I didn't know his. May 29, 1917—that was Kennedy's; my father was right. But I knew the year John Kennedy was born only because Seymour was born the same year. My mother, Marion, was younger. She grew up

C

O

O

L

in her own house in Brooklyn, my father in a cramped apartment on Jerome Avenue in the Bronx. My parents met in the Weiss & Klau building on Grand Street in lower Manhattan. They had a four-year courtship. My grandmother, my mother's mother, Lilly Greengrass, used to call my father "the undertaker" because he always looked so serious and wore dark suits.

They got married in 1950. Only recently did that start to sound like a long time ago. We lived in Brooklyn on Avenue J, in my grandmother's old apartment. She had since moved to South Fallsburg, up in the Catskill Mountains, with my grandfather, a retired furrier. They rented rooms and little apartments in an old house they bought. Eventually, my father moved us to Long Island, around 1960. I remembered watching television on a rolling stand in our new house empty of furniture, our front lawn just sand and rock. Our house stood on filled-in swampland before it was a town named for a tribe of Indians called Merokes (translated as Merrick).

I watched John Kennedy being sworn in as president on television that year, but all I remember is that you could see his breath when he spoke, and I liked how his hand chopped the air as if he were chopping through ice so I could see him better.

My sister was two; I was five. As we watched America's youngest president chop the air, I sat in my fire chief's car and she stood in her crib. My mother was upstairs with the first friend she had made in Merrick, Mary Stamler. Like Mrs. Weiner, Mrs. Stamler was very glamorous looking. I didn't know it at the time but my mother was also beautiful. I do remember that I wouldn't let her get old. When I started to notice her gray hair (I was about seven years old), I asked her to get blond hair. So she went to the beauty parlor and had her hair dyed. She looked like television and the things on it that caught my eye. I never really *saw* my mother then, in those days. But I can see her now.

My sister is named Gella. It had been my father's mother's name before she came to America. They called her Gertrude in America, but Marion thought "Gertrude" was too old-fashioned and it would be a burden in the playgrounds of Merrick, where we kids played baseball and climbed the monkey bars over the burial grounds of the Meroke Indians. So the name Gella came back to America, as everything comes back, one way or another.

My sister was a smart, dark-haired little girl with cheeks like Dizzy Gillespie blowing his crooked trumpet. She always made the honor roll. I did not. She was always a good girl. She cried the first time she cursed in front of my parents. She hit her elbow and said "shit," and then looked at our parents and the tears came. They thought it was funny and told her nothing bad would happen just because she had said "shit." This was only a moment, but it shows what the rest of her life might be like.

I wasn't that way. I was more of a contrarian. If my life was easy, I wanted it to be hard. When it was hard, I wanted it to be easy. Before I knew what the word meant, I wanted life to be "beat," but I also wanted a hot towel waiting for me when I got out of the shower. Maybe my parents sheltered me with too much love, too much affection—is that possible? Maybe they should have made me go to a conventional college. Maybe I should I have brought my laundry home every weekend. Instead, I sent home Allen Ginsberg's laundry once a month. I started sending Allen's laundry home because when he gave it to me to do, I didn't know how to work the machines.

After Philip Weiner went to college, my two best friends on Long Island were Fred Mollin and Neal Warshaw. Fred lived in the older part of Merrick, called North Merrick because it was north of the Long Island Rail Road tracks. Fred's father worked as the manager of a Key Food store. He was a grumpy guy with three children. Fred was the youngest. He had long, long red hair. He loved music and was something of a genius on the guitar. He wrote songs. I was his manager. I wrote a letter to John Hammond, the record producer who had "discovered" Bob Dylan; he must have taken pity on my terrible handwriting and guessed that what I wanted was for him

A
P
O
S
T
C
A
R
D

from Allen

C

O

O

L

to hear my friend. So he invited us to come into the city and play for him in his office at the CBS building.

We took the day off from school. Fred carried his guitar in a big black case. He had his song titles Scotch-taped to the side of the guitar. He played a few songs for Mr. Hammond, who sat behind his desk with the shortest gray-haired crew cut I had ever seen. He liked Fred's songs, but he said he wanted a second opinion, so he called for someone to come into his office. He introduced us to Al Kooper.

Al Kooper had played organ on "Like a Rolling Stone" for Bob Dylan. Fred, who was already pale and nervous, started playing for Kooper. Both men looked at each other and smiled. It was the kind of smile mothers have for their children, watching them play in the park. But somehow I knew Fred wasn't going to get his record contract.

Mr. Hammond told me to take Fred to Gerde's Folk City in the Village on West Fourth Street. "It's where Bobby started," he said. A week later I found out when Gerde's had an open-mike night, and we snuck out of school and took the Long Island Rail Road to Gerde's. You never know who might be in the audience.

Fred said I should get up and read one of my poems. I said no, that it was his night, but I had stuffed a few poems in my pocket, just in case.

There we were, sitting backstage at Gerde's. Fred was tuning up, I was muttering my poems to myself, just in case. Suddenly Fred's father stood there, backstage. He had a murderous look in his eye. I'm sure he was angry about having to drive back into New York City after coming home to Merrick and figuring out where we were. He made Fred put away his guitar and leave with him.

Mr. Mollin drove home with Fred in the front seat. I sat in the back. We couldn't look at each other. Fred looked like he was going to cry. I felt like we had been caught stealing rabbits or something. I leaned over and whispered in his ear. I wanted him to know we would be back and that he was a great songwriter. I hated his father. I thought he was cruel. Fred, who usually talked back to his parents in a way that inspired awe in us, didn't say a word. (It was always amazing to us how Fred would tell his parents to go fuck themselves, and they didn't punish him for it.) Maybe Fred never got over the humiliation of being dragged out of Gerde's by his father, because at sixteen Fred left school to become a musician. His parents told him he was making a mistake, that music was a nasty business for him to be getting into. He told them they didn't know what the fuck they were talking about. Then he made them buy him an electric guitar. They did. He became even more of a god to us than before. Ten years later, Leonard Cohen came to Fred's wedding.

My other friend was Neal. He wore a cape and smoked a pipe. He read Marianne Moore and wrote poetry and took pictures of his girlfriends naked. He was sixteen. But even Fred and Neal were surprised that my parents had let me go to the Jack Kerouac School.

I had been accepted as a "summer apprentice," so there we were, Seymour and I, flying to the Denver, Colorado, airport in the late spring of 1976.

Allen and Peter were supposed to meet us—the manufacturer's rep and his son, the might-be-first graduate of the Jack Kerouac School of Disembodied Poetics. But when we arrived, Allen and Peter hadn't shown up. My father said under his breath, "This is a great beginning," but he rented us a car and we drove the sixty miles to Boulder, climbing in elevation the closer we got.

"You can't expect Allen Ginsberg to greet every student at the airport," I said, secretly relieved. Of course, at the time, I didn't know I was the *only* poetry student, so far, of the Jack Kerouac School of Disembodied Poetics. As the mountains of Boulder loomed in the distance, I looked over at my father and felt a sudden surge of loneliness, and I was grateful that Seymour had come with me. I knew it was going to be hard to say good-bye.

We moved my few belongings into a small, semifurnished

A
P
O
S
T
C
A
R
D

from Allen

C

O

O

L

student apartment on Broadway (making me more than a little homesick for New York City). It would prove an ideal location, however, as Allen Ginsberg and Peter Orlovsky's apartment was in the same complex: a three-story, slightly down-at-heels apartment complex with outdoor walkways that made it look like a prison compound. It's where many of Naropa's students stayed.

I said good-bye to my father, fiercely biting back tears, and he drove back to the Denver airport alone, dressed, as usual, in dark jacket and trousers suitable for funerals.

When I met Ginsberg, his beard was missing. My first meeting with Allen Ginsberg and his beard was gone! It was by that beard—that magnificent untidy brisket that appeared in Fred McDarrah's photograph of Allen wearing an Uncle Sam hat—that I had irritated my uncles, upset my parents, and made a name for myself at John F. Kennedy High School. And now it was gone.

On my first official day at the Naropa Institute in Boulder, Colorado, I was told to go to Allen Ginsberg's apartment and introduce myself to him. He was wearing a T-shirt with Naropa's logo on it: an image of the karmic wheel. It looked to me like the wheel of a great ship, the kind of wheel you'd tie yourself to during a storm at sea, like the sea captain had on the ship Dracula used to cross the ocean from Transylvania to Carfax Abbey. All these thoughts swam through my brain as I crossed the threshold, my heart racing, to meet my hero—the author of *Howl*, Bob Dylan's mentor, Jack Kerouac's champion and best pal.

The first summer of Naropa, all the poets, writers, and musicians lived in the Varsity Apartments, down the hill from the University of Colorado, where I was staying. Dancers sunned themselves on the catwalk terraces in front of the apartments. Most of the doors were open. I always hated sandals, so I was dressed in shiny black Beatle boots and a short-sleeved madras shirt on my first day at the Kerouac School. At least I was dressed.

Allen was sitting in his living room at a round glass table fit for all meals. My appointment was for lunch. He was wearing a T-shirt and boxer shorts, white socks, and his shoes were off. He had wire-rimmed glasses that looked silver. His eyes were red. He kept his hair long, though he had already lost a lot of it. I wondered how anyone could think of him now as Sasquatch, a great hairy mess, a brunette Whitman. With his long hair pulled back and his shaved face, he looked more like the manager of the Stage Delicatessen in New York. (I would go there with my friend Roger Lemay one night in the early 1970s after Allen, Peter Orlovsky, and Gregory Corso had all read together at Columbia University. I remember I had the Danny Thomas.)

I was so nervous to be sitting at Allen Ginsberg's table that dust came out of my mouth. It felt as if someone with a shovel was turning ashes over in my stomach. And then Orlovsky came through the front door, carrying two bags of groceries.

Peter looked like childhood drawings I had seen of Hercules. He had a long gray ponytail and a chest that looked like it was full of brine and pickles. He also wore shorts and sandals. Where was his chariot? So this was Allen's lover. His literary wife. I had heard that Allen first fell in love with Peter in a painting. That is, a painting of Peter that Allen had seen in Robert LaVigne's apartment in San Francisco. Peter's fate was sealed when Allen first clapped eyes on him in that painting, and before long they were pledging their life's love to each other late one night in a twenty-four-hour cafeteria. Much later in the summer, I asked Peter about that night. He was drunk, and happy, stepping into a hot tub with a girl. He said he could remember only the coffee and the macaroni and cheese. He said that he and Allen held hands over their dinners. Someone nearby thought they were saying grace. It cracked them up.

Peter put the groceries on the counter. Allen introduced me as a young poet, here to help him. This was what I had come to Naropa for: to become Allen's apprentice. (I remember going to a Young People's Concert, given by Leonard Bernstein. He was introducing "The Sorcerer's Apprentice." He said, "Being an apprentice to a sorcerer, how exciting that would be, but leaving the sorcerer to go out on your own, that would be tricky!" Leave it to Leonard Bernstein to scare children at a Young People's Concert.) I was

A P O S T C A R D

from Allen

C

O

O

L

going to be Allen's apprentice, I was going to learn to become a poet, to become great, which really meant he was going to teach me to live an epic kind of life. I was nineteen years old.

Peter, in a voice that would always remind me of Lenny in *Of Mice and Men,* asked me if I wanted any tea.

"I just bought Swiss Kriss if you need it," he said, in those flat tones that made me think—if just for a minute—of brain damage. "Keeps you regular. I told that to Bill. He hasn't moved his bowels since he got here."

"It's the smack," Allen said to me, with a tiny giggle. "After fifty years, heroin's given Bill impacted bowels." The author of *The Nova Express* had trouble moving down the line. Peter didn't wait for me to answer. He simply brought over a pot of tea for us, served on a tray with a peacock painted on it. He put his hands together and bowed. It suddenly dawned on me: Peter Orlovsky was Allen Ginsberg's geisha.

Allen must have thought I was scrutinizing him—I was just in awe to be in his presence—so he apologized for his mouth being tilted to one side, as if he'd had a stroke.

"I was on an airplane," he told me, "and I was taking two different kinds of medicine. They interfered with each other and when I went into the bathroom on the plane, I saw that my mouth was crooked. The doctor says it will go away eventually. I hate the way it looks. It's hard to kiss." (I remembered that *Kaddish and Other Poems* had been dedicated to Peter Orlovsky, "in Paradise," it read, and, "Taste my mouth in your ear.")

Peter was still puttering around the kitchen, putting the groceries away. He had a big belly. The rest of him was quite lean. Allen began to explain the work to me, what he required of his apprentices, when Peter threw his long mane of gray hair back like a wet horse and gathered it together into an elastic holder. Until then, I had only seen girls do that in school or on the bus. I always thought it was beautiful. I didn't know what to think about Peter's doing it. Allen stopped to look also. I looked at him admiring Peter. I think he was still in love with him then. They didn't speak much when I was there. I'm sure Peter was staying out of our way, simply being polite, because "Allen was working." But they also reminded me of my parents, their silences, the way they sometimes became annoyed with each other.

When I thought about it, it seemed fitting that I was spending the summer of the bicentennial—our nation's two hundredth birthday—with the man who had told America to "go fuck yourself with your atom bomb" in his poem "America." Allen Ginsberg was the father of my country. Throughout my youth, I always saw a different kind of Mount Rushmore—Ginsberg's bearded head was there, and Jack Kerouac's, whose handsome profile already looked carved out of rock. Gregory Corso, the shaggy-haired poet-thief, the François Villon of the Lower East Side, looked out on the clouds where Teddy Roosevelt was for everybody else, and William Burroughs's death's-head rictus formed the narrow slope at the end of my Mount Rushmore. I loved poetry and especially Rimbaud, or at least the idea of Rimbaud, the nineteenth-century French poet who had written all his masterpieces by the age of seventeen and renounced poetry to run guns out of Africa, who had to have one of his legs amputated, who spent the rest of his short life being cared for by his sister, playing the guitar and making up songs under a Belgian, Magritte-blue sky.

So when Allen, between sips of steaming tea, asked me what I knew about Arthur Rimbaud, I had an answer.

"The derangement of the senses?" I said, aware only that the phrase appeared in Rimbaud's poetry. If only I could've said it in French, I thought. That would have been *très cool*.

"Rimbaud is in the pantheon," Allen said. "There are others. Mayakovsky." (*Knew it*, I thought, and said a silent prayer of thanks.) "Breton and Tristan Tzara."

"Sammi Rosenstock," I said.

"Who's Sammi Rosenstock?" asked Allen Ginsberg.

"That's Tristan Tzara's real name." I thought this would impress him. I prayed it would impress him, this great man with the slightly crooked mouth who had just come back from traveling

from Allen

C

O

O

,

L

in New England with Bob Dylan in the Rolling Thunder Revue (that's what I really wanted to ask him about, but I was too shy).

"Sammi Rosenstock" fell on Allen's bad ear. No reaction. Worse than no reaction. He looked bored. I felt my nerve slipping away. The tea felt like battery acid at the back of my throat. There was now a serious possibility, even without the heat, of passing out. Where, oh, where were the other students? The other "poetics" students?

Just two months earlier, Allen's postcard had reached me at my grandmother's house in South Fallsburg, New York, in the Catskills, up the road from Brown's Hotel (that billboards for fifty miles along the thruway advertised as "My Favorite Hotel" with a gigantic picture of Jerry Lewis on them). It had read: "Dear Mr. Kashner, You have been accepted as one of the Naropa summer apprentices. Here is my telephone number. Please call to arrange for an appointment. I look forward to meeting you. I hope you can type. Sincerely yours, A. Ginsberg." On the other side was printed a small poem of Allen's about sitting under a tree and reading a book when a bug of some kind lands on the page and Allen blows the "tiny mite into the void."

My happiness at getting Allen's postcard, his phone number and his signature, was more than I could bear. It never occurred to me what being an apprentice might mean, why it mattered whether or not I could type. I could, but not very well. The treasure was the postcard. Hadn't Allen sent Kerouac a postcard every day for a year in the early stage of their friendship? This was my diploma, even before attending a single class. I read it over and over again at the kitchen table in the old boardinghouse my grandmother ran in the mountains. Suddenly, I remembered that I had failed typing in high school.

Allen had written one other thing in his postcard. His father was very ill. He would be late in coming to Naropa. He and Peter had gone to take care of him. "We're reading to him from 'Tintern Abbey,' " he wrote. I looked it up. Allen was telling his father that all souls return to God. It didn't sound like him. I didn't want to think about death that summer. After all, I was about to leave home and enroll in the Jack Kerouac School of Disembodied Poetics. I had never heard of someone going to care for a dying parent. Whenever someone got sick in our family, they went into the hospital and we never saw them again. Already, Allen Ginsberg's "Golden Book of Life," as he called it, was opening up to me, whether I liked it or not.

2. Allen Can't Find His Poems

The Jack Kerouac School of Disembodied Poetics and the Naropa Institute were established in 1975 by Allen Ginsberg and a Tibetan Buddhist meditation teacher named Chogyam Trungpa Rinpoche. They met arguing over a taxicab. Trungpa was heading downtown, so was Ginsberg. They got in the cab together. It changed both their lives. Allen said that Trungpa (as they called him) had saved his life. "I was like Dylan before the motorcycle accident," Allen told me, referring to the time in 1966 when Bob Dylan had injured himself riding his Triumph motorcycle in upstate New York, and how his recovery forced him to slow down, to reconsider things in his life. Even Dylan's voice seemed to change after the accident, as revealed on his 1969 album *Nashville Skyline,* into the voice of a laconic cowboy.

To get to the Jack Kerouac School of Disembodied Poetics you had to get to the mall on Pearl Street in downtown Boulder, and then climb the stairs next to the New York Delicatessen, a deli, by the way, started by two hippies from Brooklyn who missed their grandmother's babka and matzoh ball soup. I knew I'd come to the right place when I saw three Buddhist monks in saffron robes sit-

C

O

O

L

ting at a table outside the New York Deli, scrutinizing their matzoh balls. I went upstairs.

Naropa, named by Rinpoche after an ancient Buddhist teacher, existed in a long series of rooms that Rinpoche's young followers had taken over, polishing the floors and painting the walls bright yellow and red (the colors of Buddhist shrine rooms). Rinpoche's framed calligraphy hung on the brightly colored walls. There were mandalas and tanka paintings hung throughout the sparsely furnished rooms. I got the feeling that the meager furnishings had come from the University of Colorado in Boulder—stuff that had been put out on the street. Except for Rinpoche's office. His room was exquisitely furnished with plush leather chairs and a beautiful couch. I also noticed that Rinpoche's door was different from all the others: it was a thick, beautiful wooden door that looked as if it had been carved in the Middle Ages and had come from a monastery. Maybe it did. Someone told me that the doorknob was a religious object that had once been held by a *tulku,* or religious teacher. Whenever that door was closed, it meant that Rinpoche was in the building. To me, Rinpoche was as elusive as Elvis.

By the time I arrived at Naropa, Allen Ginsberg had been famous for a long time. Two obscenity trials had made Allen and his friend William Burroughs famous: those of *Howl* and *Naked Lunch.* I knew those books the way an earlier generation knew *Catcher in the Rye,* with its all-maroon cover with the yellow letters. But I never saw *Catcher in the Rye* in my sleep the way I saw the City Lights copies of *Howl* and *Kaddish and Other Poems,* with their black borders and the words "The Pocket Poets Series" at the top, as if it were just another broadside you could take with you to work on the thirty-eighth floor of an unfinished office building and read it while sitting on a girder eating your lunch, then stuff into your back pocket and wait for the foreman to send you home. The books were small, no bigger than your hand, and Allen told me he loved them that way, because it made him think of the railroad handbook that Jack and Neal used to read—*The Brakeman's Handbook*—when they were getting ready to go to work for the railroad. Allen had taken a picture of Jack Kerouac with handbook in his jacket pocket, smoking on the fire escape outside Allen's apartment on the Lower East Side. I noticed there was a copy of the photograph torn from a magazine Scotch-taped to Allen's desk in his apartment. I remember thinking, How weird is that? He was the one who took the picture, but he gets his copy out of a magazine.

Allen couldn't find his poems. The day before, Peter had apparently moved them to give a massage to Barbara Dilley, one of the heads of the dance department at Naropa. She had danced with Merce Cunningham and everyone talked about "The Union Jack" as one of the famous dances she had participated in. She had short hair and looked like pictures of Joan of Arc. She didn't move like a dancer, she moved like a boxer, a very good middleweight. Peter had moved Allen's poems when Barbara came in. Allen was mad.

"I have apprentices coming all day," he barked to Peter, still bustling around the kitchen. "I have to know where things are!"

I saw the poems, a stack of paper on a bar stool near the kitchen. I went over to get them. I brought Allen's poems back to him. I felt like I had found the holy fucking grail. My first job as an apprentice was complete—and a success! I was going to call my parents and tell them. Maybe the *Daily Camera*, Boulder's only newspaper, would interview me on finding the poet's poems.

"I have a lot of work," Allen told me. "I'm putting together my collected poems, I need help. I have to finish poems I haven't written yet! Take this one, for example, it's a long poem about Neal." (He must mean Neal Cassady, I thought, but what if I'm wrong and he means Neil Armstrong, the first man to walk on the moon?) I didn't know Allen well enough to know.

After an hour or so in Allen's presence, I didn't have a sense of who I was dealing with, except that it was really *him*, that he had really lived this life that I *did* know something about, and that by putting himself in a kind of lineage with Walt Whitman, I felt Walt Whitman's breath passing over me. Though it was really Allen's and he was eat-

C

O

O

L

ing a tuna salad sandwich on whole wheat bread that Peter had prepared for him, one that I had refused out of sheer nervousness.

The poem Allen handed to me was interesting, but scary, about
two men lying on a cot. It sounded like they were in a flophouse, or
maybe just a cheap hotel, in Denver, where I think Neal's father, a
drunk, had lived and worked as a barber, though it sounded like he
was a bum or at best a hobo, which is how Allen described him.
Anyway, the two men are getting ready for bed, and if I'm reading
Allen's handwriting correctly, Allen gives Neal a blow job. As Allen
watched me reading the poem, his eyes seemed to say, Are you getting to the good part? The poem stops with Neal throwing his head
back in the throes of ecstasy.

"I haven't been able to finish it," Allen said. "That's where you
come in, that's your first assignment, finish the poem for me. I
want to know what happens," Allen said.

He wasn't laughing. I had to finish Allen Ginsberg's poem about
giving Neal Cassady a blow job. I wasn't sure that I had ever had one
myself, even from my girlfriend, Rosalie, and we were together all
through high school. I would have remembered it. Where do I go for
advice, for help, for inspiration? I didn't know anyone else at
Naropa. Maybe the Naropa librarian could help me? I was still
thinking about the epigraph in *Kaddish*: "Taste my mouth in your
ear." Maybe it was a test, I thought, a test to see if I was interested
in Allen. In Allen giving me a blow job. All of a sudden I didn't feel
very good. Maybe I should've gone to Nassau Community College
after all. Why had Allen given me this assignment? I wasn't gay. At
least I didn't think I was. Maybe Allen knew something about me
that I didn't know myself. After all, at the beginning of my life at the
Kerouac School, I thought Allen Ginsberg could see through walls.
Then certainly he could see through me.

I remembered Allen's beautiful poem about Cassady's cremation. He described Neal's ashes, "anneal'd, and all that muscle and
strength and beauty reduced to ash." I could pretend to know what
that would feel like, but giving Neal a blow job? My first task as
Allen's first apprentice might turn out to be my last. I might be

banished from the kingdom of Shambhala. It's a good thing I didn't unpack.

"You're a sweet boy," he said. "So unborn."

You could say that Neal Cassady was Jack Kerouac's muse. He's the main figure, the central character in *On the Road*. Cassady seemed like Kerouac's "true brother," the lost brother. What is it he called him? A "western kinsman of the sun," or something like that. Cassady was a great talker and driver and cocksman. "Holy Cassady," is how Allen described him.

Cassady was the only one of the Beats to actually be born "on the road." He was the ninth child, born in a charity hospital in Salt Lake City, when the Cassadys were driving to California from Des Moines in a Ford House Truck. Once they arrived after their brief stop in Salt Lake City, Neal's father opened up a barbershop on the corner of Hollywood and Vine. He was a volcanic drunk and the marriage broke up, so Neal Jr. and his father moved to Denver. They lived in a one-dollar-a-week cubicle, sharing it with a double amputee named Shorty, in a five-story flophouse called the Metropolitan.

My father once drove me through the Bowery in New York— the windows rolled up—in our Chevrolet, and the men would come out of thin air and lean over to wipe the windshield, making it dirtier and asking for change. My father never gave it to them; instead, he just turned on the windshield wipers.

I never had to wake up on a naked mattress among men having the d.t.'s. Cassady seemed to thrive in the flophouse. "For a time I held a unique position. Among the hundreds of isolated creatures who haunted the streets of lower downtown Denver, there was not one so young as myself . . . I alone as the sharer of their way of life, presented the sole replica of their own childhood." Neal thought of his childhood as a castle. Eventually Neal moved in with his mother and a twelve-year-old half brother, a sadist named Jimmy. Jimmy had drowned cats in toilets, and he liked to trap Neal in the family Murphy bed, keeping him wedged between the mattress and the wall. Neal felt

ALLEN

C

O

O

L

like he couldn't yell out because that would only make Jimmy angrier, and he would torture him more. Neal's mother was no help. Neal turned his terror of being buried alive in the Murphy bed into a kind of visionary experience where he saw time being speeded up, vibrating like a Vornado fan, blurring and fluttering, fluttering and blurring. Years later he would recall the image of the fan as it emerged from his subconscious while he was tripping on LSD.

Cassady's sexual initiation was no less traumatic. At the age of nine he accompanied his father to the home of a drinking buddy, whose oldest son led his brother and Neal in sexual intercourse with as many sisters as they could hold down. After that experience, all boundaries of sexual decorum evaporated. Neal "sneak-shared" women with his father, and he slept with grandmothers and prepubescent girls in abandoned buildings, barns, and public toilets. Cars, theft, and sex dominated Cassady's adolescence, all linked in what he called "Adventures in Auto-eroticism." Between the ages of fourteen and twenty-one, he stole some five hundred cars. Neal was well read for a car thief, a kind of Grand Theft Auto-didact. He was arrested ten times and convicted six. This impressed me as I never really learned to drive.

Neal was sent to reform school, but as soon as he got out he would catch a glimpse of a car showroom and pick up where he left off, with the "soul-thrilling pleasures" of joyriding through the streets of Denver in a hot car.

It was Kerouac who said that, for Neal Cassady, "sex was the one and only holy and important thing in life." The one area in which Neal Cassady and I shared similar interests—at least when I was a teenager—was in masturbation. There I was as great as Neal. Maybe greater. He masturbated and also had sexual intercourse. I hoped to give up one for the other. Cassady was a good-looking guy, described as thin-hipped and hard bellied, a champion chin-up artist who could throw a football seventy yards. I couldn't get my hand around a football, and found it too hard when it hit my chest. It made a noise. Kerouac compared Neal's face to a young Gene Autry—green eyes, a strong jawline, and a jutting chin. Orlovsky said of Neal's profile, if he wasn't a man "his face would have made a beautiful shoe horn." I think I know what he means. He always bought secondhand clothes, his one suit from a secondhand clothing shop in Chinatown. Kerouac noticed how even Neal's "dirty work clothes clung to him so gracefully, as though you couldn't buy a better fit from a custom tailor but only earn it from the Natural Tailor of Natural Joy."

Neal liked to seduce men and women. It was part of his con man's persona. It was like a sexual swindle. He was flattering, he was manic. He was a car salesman of sex. He sounded like a 33⅓ rpm record played at 45. Allen talked about Neal's penis the way my Israeli cousins used to talk about the Empire State Building. Eight inches long and thick. Before I arrived at the Kerouac School I wondered how Allen could know such a thing. I got myself (with the help of my parents) excused from gym—asthmatoid bronchitis was what it said on the note—but not wanting to shower with other fifteen-year-old boys was the real reason.

I wondered how was I going to get along with my hero, Allen Ginsberg, who had, long ago, put "his queer shoulder to the wheel."

I took several of Allen's poems home. They were written out in longhand, in Allen's tiny scrawl. I studied his handwriting. It looked like the ink from a squid that someone had used to write his name in. He had written poems in a notebook on unlined paper. These new poems seemed to be about death, about his failing powers as a lover. More often than not the love poems ended with Allen's head on the hairless chest of a young boy.

I had come to Naropa to meet girls. I didn't know what to make of poems like "Love Returned" ("Come twice at last / he offers his ass").

I panicked. I left Allen's notebooks on the floor beside my bed, my asthma inhaler on top of the notebooks. I walked out into my first Boulder evening, the mountains pressing up against my eyes. I walked down Pearl Street, which was Boulder's main Rialto. There, in a metal box with the daily paper inside, I saw the banner head-

A
L
L
E
N

Can't Find His Poems

C

O

O

L

line: "John Wayne Is Dead." I thought of Keats's wonderful line "great spirits on earth are now presiding," and pondered the departing ghost of John Wayne. What would Allen Ginsberg think about the Duke's death, a guy who represented everything about America that Allen seemed to stand in stark contrast to?

I looked at the people streaming toward me along the mall. How many of these backpacked strangers were going to wind up at Naropa? What raven-haired girl playing her guitar on the grass in front of the Boulder courthouse was waiting to be a muse, or at least amused by my lonesome self? I had yet to meet any of the other students.

I looked down at my watch (the one my grandfather had sold me on his deathbed, I liked to say, which of course wasn't true. My mother had given it to me as a going-away present). It was getting close to seven P.M. Oh no! Dinner at Ginsberg's! I had almost forgotten.

I ran up the impossible hill toward Allen and Peter's apartment on Broadway. I had forgotten the apartment number, but Bessie Smith's voice led me to them. The door was open. Would other students be waiting there as well? Shy and in awe, as I was?

I looked around the room. No one was remotely my age. Every face in the room I knew from books. If there was a way to die then, I wanted to know what it was. William Burroughs sat under the lamp that hung above the dining room table. He was dressed in a suit and looked as if he had just been interrogated by the customs bureau. I recognized him as the man who had written *Naked Lunch*. (I knew that Donald Fagen had taken the name of the dildo in that book for the name of his band, Steely Dan.) I also knew that William Burroughs had accidentally shot his wife after she had goaded him into shooting an apple off her pretty head in Mexico. Burroughs missed. Joan died. Whoever she really was vanished into myth.

I hoped I lived through dinner.

I still had my backpack with me, and in it was an album I wanted to play for Allen on an old hi-fi that he and Peter had brought from

New York. It was Gene Vincent, the blue-jeaned, hillbilly rocker who died young and was incredibly popular in England, much more so than he ever was in the States. I told Allen how Vincent, on his way to England, had only two things in his suitcase when the airport official opened it up: a teddy bear and a gun.

"That's how I'd like to travel if I could get away with it," Burroughs drawled. "Instead, I have to bring a velvet-lined suitcase full of vials and victuals, just to keep alive."

Other people have commented on William Burroughs's voice, how it could grind gravel, or how it sounded like the bark of a borzoi, the elegant dog on the spine of books published by Alfred A. Knopf. Allen said Burroughs's voice sounded as if it came up from under the sea, from a kingdom of mermen armed with Kalashnikov rifles.

There was something of T. S. Eliot about Burroughs, I thought. Dressed like a toff in a three-piece suit, Burroughs looked like an undertaker taking night classes. His long face was white as a candle and he smelled of talcum powder and Noxzema.

After listening to Gene Vincent for a while, Burroughs suddenly turned to me and asked me what the meaning of "disco" was. I guess he thought that since I was the youngest person in the room, I would know.

"You mean the word 'disco'?" I asked, a little embarrassed at being spoken to. "It's from 'discothèque.' "

Burroughs now had his back to me. He was hammering a nail into the wall in order to hang a picture. I thought to myself that this was how Jesse James got killed, turning his back on Robert Ford while he was hanging a picture on the wall. I thought about the song, about the dirty rotten coward who shot Mr. Howard and laid poor Jesse in his grave.

I handed the Gene Vincent album cover to Allen, who liked Gene Vincent's looks—the pompadour and Vincent's skinniness. A long discussion ensued about skinny men with big cocks, the skinnier, the bigger.

A
L
L
E
N

Can't Find His Poems

"I haven't seen a cock in so long," Burroughs growled. "I wouldn't care if it looked like a hedgehog run to ground." He went back to hanging his picture.

I had absolutely nothing I could add to this conversation. I was conversationally busted. The night might end right here for me. I was saved by Gene Vincent singing "Be-Bop-a-Lula."

"It's not the kind of music I like," Allen remarked. "I prefer blues, like Elmore James, Bessie Smith, Victoria Spivey, do you know that music?" Allen asked. "Dylan loves this music," Allen added. It didn't sound like name-dropping. It just put the discussion out of reach.

"No, I don't." It was my first lie to Allen Ginsberg. I *did* know some of that music. In fact, in junior high school, I was crazy about Son House. When I heard he was living in Rochester, New York, I called information and got his number. His wife answered the phone. "Hello, Mrs. House. Is Mr. House at home?" I asked.

"No, he's out at the Woolworth's," she said. "He went out there to get some foolishness, should I tell him whose call came in?" I could've listened to her talk all day. I had wanted to invite Son House to be the entertainment for our school dance. I must have been out of mind (my schoolmates would have preferred disco), but my heart was in the right place. I could've told Allen that story, but I didn't. I didn't want to sound like I knew anything about anything. I wanted—needed—Allen to be the oracle. I wanted to learn everything there was to know from him, even the things I already knew.

Later that night, after a fascinating but strained evening trying to eat dinner in the company of legends, I tried to finish Allen's poem about Neal. I read some of the other poems Allen had written about blow jobs, tracking phrases that appeared and making use of them. I was stealing from Ginsberg to write a poem he would later claim as his own. (Was "Howl" written this way? Was "Kaddish" written by somebody else for his (or her) mother?) I didn't know whether to stay or to pack up and go home to Long Island. Instead, I just cried.

3. Psychic Surgeon

I stayed. A few days later, the core faculty of the Kerouac School held its first faculty meeting, which was also another dinner in Ginsberg's apartment. William Burroughs took the minutes.

Everyone in Allen's living room was a great talker. (Anne Waldman, the tall, glamorous poet and a core faculty member at Naropa, had been billing herself as "Fast Talking Woman" after her long poem, which she recited in a breathy rush to adoring crowds.) But I noticed that they all stopped talking and listened to Burroughs whenever he spoke. How could anyone ignore that voice, that ruined patrician's face, that T. S. Eliot on smack?

There was something enchanted about Burroughs, in a midsummer night's dream kind of way. It looked as if someone had put a spell on him and he had been changed into a woman, then a man, and then back again, as if they couldn't quite make up their mind.

I saw he was missing a finger. Well, not an entire finger. Just the top of it. I felt like Robert Donat in that Hitchcock movie my father loved, *The 39 Steps,* when Donat thinks he's found sanctuary in the Scottish highlands with the High Sheriff and his family, but then he sees that the High Sheriff is missing a finger, which identifies him as the ringleader of a dangerous group of spies. I wasn't in the Scottish highlands, I was in the Rocky Mountains, but seeing Burroughs's left hand silhouetted in the window made me wonder about how safe I was.

Burroughs, I would soon discover, seemed to save his affection for a select few. He had a simple philosophy of friendship: not to spread his good cheer "all over hell in a vile attempt to placate sulky, worthless shits." When I heard that, I crossed Bill's name off

C

O

O

L

my Chanukah party guest list, the one I was mentally preparing to have when December came around.

I would later learn from Anne Waldman the story of Bill's missing finger. It seems that Burroughs, in his youth, had been in love with a young man named Jack Anderson, who did odd jobs in an office and, on the side, hustled both men and women. Anderson knew of Burroughs's infatuation and tortured him with his other affairs. They lived next to each other in a shabby apartment building, and Bill could hear his boyfriend having sex with other people. He was miserable and angry about these infidelities, or at least the feelings they created, so one day he bought a pair of poultry shears. He later said they reminded him of his Thanksgiving dinners.

"He looked in his dresser mirror, all the while composing his face into the supercilious mask of an eighteenth-century dandy," Burroughs later wrote about the incident, and then he severed the tip from the little finger of his left hand. He watched the blood rushing out of the wound, eventually bandaged the finger, and put the offending digit into his vest pocket, as if he were putting away a handkerchief or returning a fountain pen to his pocket. "I've done it," Bill said to himself. After that, Burroughs noticed, "a lifetime of defensive hostility had fallen away."

That was when Burroughs gave up his dream of becoming a psychoanalyst. Smart move, I thought. It was hard to imagine this silent man, tall and pale, as having been Allen's and Jack's teacher and therapist. (Kerouac had taken one look at Burroughs's mad, bony skull and described him as a Kansas minister.)

I wonder if that missing finger was the reason Allen sent me over to do some typing for Bill the following week. I knew that Kerouac had been Bill's favorite typist. It was Kerouac who typed up the manuscript for what would become *Naked Lunch*. Kerouac was like a one-man secretarial pool, an almost mystical typist, Allen thought, really fast and accurate. I, on the other hand, had failed the Regents exam in typing. Not only did I make Abraham Lincoln look like Sigmund Freud, I typed out John F. Kennedy's silhouette but ran out of time and left a big hole in the back of his head. The teacher thought I had done it on purpose. I didn't. I just messed up.

When I arrived at Burroughs's apartment one week after the first faculty meeting, I wanted to impress him with my efficiency, so I marched right over to his electric typewriter and tried to turn it on. I couldn't find the power button.

"Use your brains, dammit," Burroughs snarled at me. While he watched my distress, he began telling me how to catch a rabbit for food, in case I ever needed to do that. "Start by building a contraption with a shotgun," he explained, "but be careful it doesn't go off in your face." His point was: Think clearly when you're going to kill something, and not act like I did now—the paragon of butter-fingered incompetence.

I would soon learn that Burroughs liked words no one really used in conversation. His small talk sent you to the dictionary. Words like "jeremiad." Burroughs no longer cultivated the role of the dandy, but he still seemed to be playing a part. The part of the man with a virulent strain of something he'll never get rid of. He seemed perfectly happy with his old age. Whereas Allen seemed to want to be young, Burroughs seemed to find a way to defeat death by never stopping to believe in his own death; it was in this way that he seemed to come alive. He had found the perfect role to play in this theater of the Beats—as not death's, but life's avenger.

Burroughs talked while I typed; he liked to tell stories about his youth, as if I were too young to hear anything else. Or maybe my own youth made him think about the past. He liked talking about being eight years old. At that age Burroughs had a little hiding place under the back steps of his parents' house, a secret place where he kept a box, and in the box was a spoon, a candle, and some type of instrument for investigating the forging of hard metals for weapons. It was also around the time he said that he shot off his first gun and wrote his first story. It was called "Autobiography of a Wolf," a ten-page story about an animal who lost his mate and was killed by a grizzly bear. Burroughs said his parents had listened politely to the story. "Surely you mean *biography* of a wolf," his father had told him. "No," Burroughs insisted. "I mean the autobiography of a wolf." They sent him to Harvard. Now he was, he said, "the Payne-Whitney Professor of Bellevue Studies at the Jack Kerouac School."

It dawned on me, leaving Burroughs's apartment and walking home in the cool night air that held the hint of autumn, that Burroughs had just named two psychiatric hospitals for his college chair.

During my first summer at Naropa, Ginsberg had a lot of dinner parties at his apartment. Any visiting writer, any important decision that had to be made, any problem that arose was presented at one of his long, shambling, informal dinners. I went to most of them, sure of a chance to listen to Allen or Burroughs hold forth on whatever was obsessing them that week. For much of that summer, Burroughs was preoccupied with space travel and with unexplained voices that suddenly appeared on tape recordings. He was also enthralled with the literary collages that he and his collaborator, Brion Gysin, had created, called "cut-ups." Burroughs's conversation was in fact a kind of verbal cut-up, consisting of references to Shakespeare, the Bible, Rimbaud, Kohut, Freud, and Jack London. He referred to hustlers in Tangier and to the dying words of Dutch Schultz, to Goethe and the parables of Jesus Christ in the same tone of voice—and it was how he would order his dinners. Milk shakes with scotch. Egg creams and tequila. I loved to hear him talk.

His cut-ups, he said, were a way to alter the meaning of words and ideas. Burroughs claimed he had been doing them for so long that sometimes his cut-ups actually anticipated future events.

"I cut up an article written by John Paul Getty," Burroughs explained at one of Allen's dinners, "and the sentence that came up was, 'It is a bad thing to sue your own father.'" Burroughs claimed that a year later one of Getty's sons did sue him. Then Allen asked Burroughs to tell the story of the air-conditioner.

I looked blankly at my hosts. They all knew what was coming.

"In 1964 I made a cut-up and got what seemed at the time to be a totally inexplicable phrase: 'And there is a horrid air-conditioner.' Ten years later I moved into a loft with a broken air-conditioner, which was removed to put in a new unit. And there were three hundred pounds of broken air-conditioner on my floor—a behemoth—a horrid disposal nightmare, heavy and solid. It had all emerged from a cut-up I did ten years before."

I found out later that Allen, Anne, and Peter had heard Burroughs's fairy tale about his air-conditioner at least a hundred times before. But they enjoyed hearing it, like children who ask to hear their favorite bedtime story and catch you every time you leave something out. It was a deeply weird pleasure to listen to that snarling, midwestern voice. The word "disposal" coming out of Burroughs's mouth was a great pleasure. It was like listening to John Wayne say the word "pilgrim." We all loved listening to Bill.

It reminded me of a scene I had read, maybe it was in *On the Road,* when they stop at "Old Bull Lee's" place. Old Bull Lee was Burroughs, at least that's what we all thought. And Jack and his friends liked to visit Old Bull Lee and his wife, and just listen to Old Bull, sitting out on the porch with a shotgun laid across his lap, talk about what he'd just read in *The Handbook of Psychic Discoveries.*

I noticed that Burroughs didn't say anything for shock value. His life had absorbed too many body blows for that. His *life* had shock value. Like Kerouac's Old Bull Lee, Burroughs was always an old man to them, and a kind of teacher. Even Allen felt that way. Although I never saw Allen Ginsberg afraid, the wrong look from Burroughs and Allen was like a little boy sent to stand in the corner and contemplate the peeling plaster. Burroughs was their oracle.

I, however, wondered what kept him out of the mad house. He seemed to hear voices. There seemed to be no line between

P
S
Y
C
H
I
C

Burroughs's daily life and his dreams. He seemed to walk through his dream life the way we walk through our daily lives. How does he do it? I wondered. How does he avoid getting killed crossing the street?

Bill, as they called him, had brought dessert. Apple pie. "They say it makes you sterile," Burroughs said, after Peter had asked whether or not the pie should be heated up. Burroughs's son, Billy Jr., was to bring the ice cream. "It goes on top of the pie," Burroughs explained, as if it were Dr. Heidegger's experiment.

Peter went into the kitchen to heat up the apple pie. The phone rang and Peter answered it. He called Burroughs to the phone. Burroughs listened for a moment, then put the phone down. "Heat the bathroom, company is coming," was all he said.

Later, I would figure out this code. I would learn what he wanted from the refrigerator, or when it was time for me to lay out the hypodermic needle, like some underage Dr. Watson preparing the needle for Sherlock Holmes after a particularly tough case. "Heat the bathroom, company is coming" was, apparently, an old Latvian custom. When expecting guests in Latvia, someone makes the trek into the bathroom and lights the stove. Burroughs was expecting his son to drop by.

Billy Burroughs Jr. arrived, bringing coffee ice cream in a soiled backpack that looked as if it had been through a war, which, in fact, it had. He had bought it from an army-navy store in Denver; he said it had been to Korea on the back of an American soldier. It even had a bullet hole in it—of which Billy Burroughs was very proud. "Straight from the back of his heart to mine," Billy said.

There was nothing darling about this Billy. At least at first, at least to me. I had never been around a lot of alcohol. My parents still called it "schnapps." Billy Burroughs was finishing out his twenties, and he looked just like Elisha Cook Jr., the character actor who played the gunsel Wilmer in *The Maltese Falcon*. Like Wilmer, Billy wore an overcoat frayed at the sleeves. It was made of camel hair, and it smelled of the unfiltered Camels he smoked. He looked like a dying youth who had come to say good-bye.

Billy came over to his father and they shook hands. Billy looked at his father as if he were looking at Hemingway in a dream, with a bullet hole in his head talking about the Far Tortugas. He asked for a glass with ice in it. His mouth was dry. He kept his overcoat on, though it was hot in the apartment. The two didn't seem to have a lot to say to each other.

Billy Jr. was a good writer, I knew that much. He wrote a book called *Kentucky Ham.* It made me laugh. If the book was any indication, Billy lived to get stoned. His father, along with Anne Waldman, had thought it would be a good thing for Billy to come to Boulder. They hoped that he would fall under the influence of Rinpoche, maybe even start meditating. Give up cigarettes and drinking. Try some food.

Allen made a place for him at the glass table, around which the usual suspects sat on wrought-iron chairs with wicker seats— Anne, Peter, Bill, Allen. Peter had made dinner for the whole crew, a vast, vegetarian lasagna sprinkled with oregano that looked like pot (halfway through the dinner, Peter announced that it really *was* pot). Billy sat hunched over in his overcoat, staring at his plate as though, if he looked at it long enough, his dinner would simply get up and leave. He had a few days' worth of blond beard; his hair was dirty and fell into his eyes.

Billy started talking about Rinpoche, whom he called "the professor," or "the professor of nonexistence." During a lecture, he'd asked Rinpoche whether or not "the far-away" really existed. "Is the future packed away in salt, somewhere? Is the body evidence of the spirit, Professor?" he asked, to the delight of his friends, a hard-core group of young, mostly Irish street kids, some with gold teeth, who were part of Billy's all-white gang. Allen and Burroughs referred to them as "the Westies." They revered Billy. One of them came by that night and whispered something in Billy's ear, and then left. I think they spent a lot of their time scoring drugs and

C

O

O

L

listening to music in the Naropa rooming house on Arapahoe Street.

Burroughs asked me to hang Billy's overcoat up in the closet. I did. I was happy to get away from their father-and-son reunion. I guess I shouldn't have been surprised to discover that there was a pistol in Billy's coat pocket.

I closed the door and went back to the table. Burroughs asked his son if he had been to see Dr. Shringwaym. "He was a CIA man at one time," Burroughs said. "He worked in the pickle factory. So telephone with restraint, Bill. Watch what you say over the phone— remember, the cucumbers are listening in."

I got it. It was beginning to sink in, like a foreign language. If the CIA was "the pickle factory," and pickles are made from cucumbers . . .

I didn't know why Burroughs wanted Billy to call Dr. Shringwaym, or even who Dr. Shringwaym was. Allen then turned to me and asked if I would call the doctor for Billy.

I said that I didn't think the doctor would tell me anything about another patient.

"He's not that kind of doctor," Burroughs said. "He performs psychic surgery." It was the first time that night that Burroughs addressed me directly.

"Go up and call now," Anne said from the other side of the table, her silver bracelets tinkling as she flipped her long dark hair over her shoulder.

"Obey Death. Blind Death," Burroughs chanted as I went up the stairs to Allen's telephone in the bedroom. My lungs felt like all the air had been pressed out of them. How dangerous will this phone call be? Was he really a CIA operative? Dangerous to whom?

I had never been upstairs before. I felt like the only one left on a deserted space station, the one non-astronaut, the scientist who goes up with the pilots to study plant life on Mars but who now has to steer the ship, alone.

As I climbed the stairs, I listened in on the grown-ups—that's how it felt to me—talking quietly downstairs. I could hear parts of their conversation drifting up the stairs. I heard Burroughs raise his voice: "Remember Dutch Schultz's last words!"

"What's that?" I shouted through the walls of the space station, relieved that I was still connected to the mother ship. "What were his last words?"

"I don't want harmony. I want harmony." I heard Anne Waldman's laughter. It made me feel stupid. I had no idea what they were talking about.

I dialed and a voice at the other end answered.

"Dr. Shringwaym," I said. "I'm calling for Billy Burroughs. I'm supposed to tell you—it's time."

4. Billy the Kid

William Burroughs was starting to remind me of Dr. Moreau—you know who I mean, the evil scientist who has his own island and conducts weird science on it, like the making of a half panther, half woman who wants to escape with the hero who finds himself stuck there. Like Dr. Moreau, Burroughs conducted weird experiments in his apartment. Dr. Moreau had a half man, half dog valet, and Burroughs had a young assistant who called himself Jubal. He was from a long line of Southern generals, going back to the Confederacy. Including one, Jubal told me, who shot his own men occasionally for slacking off. He was about twenty-five years old and wore expensive, tailor-made suits. He and his master wrote stories together, *High Noon*–type Westerns that climaxed in fantastic shoot-outs, with great carnage on both sides. When I was introduced to Burroughs he was obsessed with two things—

C

O

O

L

extraterrestrial life and the shoot-out at the OK Corral. *Westworld*, which had opened that summer, was his favorite movie.

Billy had to go see the surgeon. His Irish friends, the Westies, were going to pick Billy the Kid up and drive him into Denver for his date with Dr. Shringwaym. Billy's surgeon gave him an evening appointment, which I thought was pretty strange. Like Freud, the doctor would see him in his "consulting room," which was attached to his house in a suburban part of Denver.

I made that appointment for him, I thought proudly to myself. Since I was terrified of taking drugs, serving the Beats was my "Henry" and my "Charly." Burroughs taught me that: names for heroin and cocaine. At first I couldn't keep the names straight, until I found a mnemonic method that seemed to work. I was a slow learner. But I was soaking up Beat knowledge like a sponge— a sponge off the coast of South America.

I didn't go into Denver very often. I wondered how much thought had gone into establishing the Jack Kerouac School just an hour or so away from Laramie Street and the once-upon-a-time hobo jungles of Denver, where Neal Cassady's father drank and itinerantly practiced his barber trade. "A real Sweeney Todd," is how Burroughs described Neal's father. As it turned out, it was Trungpa, not the Beats, who had settled on Boulder, because the dark mountains reminded him not so much of Tibet but of Elsinore Castle and the mountains of Scotland, where he had gone to establish one of the first meditation retreats for practitioners of the Kagyu lineage of Tibetan Buddhism.

It was while driving his sports car in Scotland that Rinpoche crashed into the window of a shop and nearly killed himself. He had crashed into a joke-and-magic shop. The accident paralyzed him on the left side. Whenever he entered a room (usually wearing a beautiful silk suit that shimmered like mermaid skin) Rinpoche carried his arm as if it were in an invisible sling, his palsied hand held in front of his solar plexus. Someone always helped him to get dressed. He loved jewelry and he always wore a Rolex watch. I could see it on his wrist, even from the back of the auditorium, when he gave his public talks. He had a lovely moon face with dark-rimmed glasses, and he spoke in a high whisper, which always made me think that somehow his vocal cords might have been damaged in the car crash. He always began by saying, "Ladies and gentlemen," and he was always two or three hours late for his talks.

Rinpoche's talks always made people laugh. Like any prince, he loved his own jokes. My teachers—Anne, Allen, Burroughs—all adored Rinpoche. They said he was enlightened. They liked to tell stories about how drunk he would get on sake during dinner, before his lectures. There was always talk of his court, of the women he liked to have around him. In fact, I would soon discover that one problem with having a girlfriend who was a Buddhist at Naropa was that, if she was really attractive, Rinpoche might ask to see her and then, well . . . no self-respecting student of Rinpoche's would turn him down. So don't even bother asking her to choose. I would later come to know about this form of suffering.

Joan Burroughs, William's wife, was a legend by the time I came to Boulder. She had been dead a long time. So long, in fact, that Burroughs had become one of the most famous and outspoken homosexuals of his time, his brief, heterosexual life long forgotten. But there was a time when William Burroughs had become a father, although he didn't seem like one now. He and Joan had slept together, at least once, in a motel in Times Square, and Joan had become pregnant with Billy Jr.

After I had worked for Allen for a couple of weeks, he trusted me enough to let me work not just on the verse that would go into his *Collected Poems*, but on the extensive, ongoing files he loved to keep. This man who hated the CIA and the FBI to the point of obsession kept files on everyone he knew. I saw his file for Billy— "William Burroughs III." He was born on July 21, 1947. I read how

C

O

O

L

Joan, in a very calm voice, had told her husband that it was probably time to go to a hospital and have her baby. They got into
Burroughs's jeep, driving off their farm in Texas to find the nearest
hospital. It was not close by. Joan knew that she could never
breast-feed the baby, as her breast milk was laced with amphetamines from the inhalers she refused to stop using during her
pregnancy. Doing the dishes after dinner one night in Allen's
apartment, he told me about the "Birthday Ode" he had written to
Billy, and how after he was born he hoped that Billy would be more
of a brother to him than his own, rather straight-laced brother,
Eugene, was. But it didn't happen that way. Billy was too wretched,
too sad, to make Allen feel any brighter about his own life. After
Joan had given birth she would put the baby on the porch for her
husband to hold while she would check herself for "worm-like
filaments," the first symptoms, as Burroughs had described for her,
of postnuclear contamination.

Billy Burroughs was born a drug addict, according to Allen's
file, and spent his "first days on earth in withdrawal." The first
time I met him I just saw a sad and quiet young man.

After a week at Naropa, Allen asked me to keep an eye on Billy,
who had been diagnosed with a cirrhotic liver, due to his heavy
alcohol intake. It was one of my new tasks, to try to keep him away
from the bottle, and to keep his Irish gang members from supply-
ing him with booze.

By then I had moved into a nicer apartment in a nearby complex where many University of Colorado students lived. It had a
swimming pool, which I never used, but sometimes I sat by the
pool dressed in long black pants and a black turtleneck sweater. I
had never liked leisure clothes, but I preferred living in the slightly
more upscale Canyon Street apartments, as opposed to the student
apartments on Broadway. And maybe I needed the added distance
from Allen and Peter.

One evening, Billy came by my new apartment and we sat and
watched TV. He was drinking straight out of the bottle and smoking a lot of tobacco and marijuana. I knew it was part of my job as

an apprentice to keep him from drinking, but I was too shy to say anything about it.

Billy told me that in a couple of days he was going to go up into the mountains of Boulder where he and his father were growing marijuana in a hidden spot. He explained that Burroughs had told him, "Maryjane can grow in dry soil. The thing to do is cultivate a few other crops as a kind of beard." Burroughs had turned his apartment into a chemistry lab, developing weed concentrates. (He was also developing tape-recording experiments to investigate life on other planets. "Not on the planets themselves," Burroughs explained, "but between planets. In the space, the distance between planets, that's where the life, though not as we know it, would be.")

"I'll take you up there sometime," Billy said between swigs of Bombay gin. "You can help me cultivate the crop, we'll need help harvesting. We do it only at night, under a full moon. Harvest moon, like the Neil Young song." He laughed, and then he started to fall asleep in front of the television set. Suddenly, Billy sat upright on the couch, in a mood to talk.

"My father never said anything to me about his life," Billy announced. "I learned it all from other people. He refuses to talk about anything real. He cultivates speaking to me in the clichés of parenthood. Things about being on the right track, and advice about how to drive around armadillos when it's late at night on the highway to Denver. Practical advice. He would play Hungarian waltzes and watch me, unblinking, for hours. I would ask him what he was thinking and he would tell me that he was trying to imagine what was going through Lincoln's brain when he was shot."

"A bullet?" I said.

Billy laughed. For the first and only time, I saw him laugh. But that same night I saw him cry. We were watching the James Cagney movie *Angels With Dirty Faces*. In the movie, Cagney pretends to lose his cool on the way to the electric chair, so that the Dead End Kids who look up to him will see him as a coward and reject a life of crime. Billy was a kind of sweaty, unhappy, dead-end kid. I could imagine him reading the morning paper with the headline "Rocky

B

I

L

L

Y

the Kid

Dies Yellow." But as we watched the movie, Billy couldn't stand it when Rocky started screaming his head off on the way to the hot squat.

Suddenly, he jumped up off the couch and ran out of my apartment and into the street. The cars go very quickly up and down the Canyon Street hill, and late at night you can't see anyone crossing the road. I knew Billy could be hit like one of those armadillos on the drive into Denver. And he was my responsibility!

I ran out after him, into the dark Boulder night.

Allen was walking Bill and Anne back to their apartments, and they saw the whole thing: Billy running like a crazed man into the street with me chasing him in hot pursuit. Anne looked at me. Her look said, You can't take care of him, can you? I didn't think you could. She put her arm around Billy, who was by now lying in the street, and she easily led him away. Burroughs watched impassively and never said a word about seeing his son curled up like a fetus in the middle of the road. Allen thought I looked like I was going to pass out. I was.

"What did you say to him?" Burroughs asked me. "What caused him to act so irrationally?"

"He's very shy," Allen said to Burroughs, defending me. "I don't think he's right for telling Billy what to do."

"I should get him analyzed," Burroughs said. "Oh, damn. I'll do it myself."

"We were watching James Cagney on television," I tried to explain. "And on Cagney's way to the electric chair, Billy just ran outside!" My answer seemed only to make things worse, to deepen the impression that I wasn't up to the job.

"I knew little Jimmy Cagney," Burroughs said, ignoring my explanation. "He's queer. Buggered very selectively in Hollywood." And then he walked away, Allen skipping to keep up, even though Burroughs walked with a cane and looked like he carried his head under his arm, Ichabod Crane–style. I slunk back upstairs to my small, one-bedroom apartment.

My living room now looked like it belonged on the Bowery:

empty Bombay gin bottles (with its portrait of Queen Victoria in a cameo on the label), cigarette stubs and ashes over every surface, and a tumescent, silver-domed Jiffy-Pop still sitting on the stove. Billy had run out before we could cut it open. He loved popcorn. I cleaned up a little. My heart was still racing. You could see the mountains from the tiny balcony at the back of my apartment. Where was the Burroughs family marijuana farm? What did they do with it all? Was the "psychic surgeon" some kind of code? Was it all in some Greyhound locker in Denver? They had all gone to the Neal Cassady School of Business. Would I soon be at the wheel, hauling a trunkful of weed for the Burroughses? "Mother Nature on the run in the 1970s." Indeed.

The next day, Billy canceled his appointment with Dr. Shringwaym.

5. Notorious

I holed up in my apartment for a few days after that, embarrassed that I was so inadequate to the job of looking after Billy. Then Allen called and, in a husky voice, asked me to drop by the apartment.

I stopped by around eight P.M. and found Allen propped up in bed with a bad cold and a fever. Nonetheless, he was going over some work and he wanted my help. With his shirt off and with his beard, which Allen grew back whenever Rinpoche left town, he looked like some Western desperado holed up in a barn. I could hear the big clock on the mantelpiece downstairs ticking off the time. When we weren't talking, each ticking of the clock sounded like a gong.

I noticed a sponge and a big bucket of water beside the bed, which Peter was using to bring Allen's fever down. For the first time, Allen reminded me of his own poetry—his sad poems about

C

O

O

L

dressing his sick father, the "don't grow old" poems. Maybe it was the wrong time to ask. I'm sure it was. But when you're young, you're either too shy to ask any questions or you pick the wrong time to ask them.

I thought the best time to ask questions of the Beats was while I was still a somewhat fresh recruit. I remember my father telling me not to be shy about asking questions. "They're supposed to be your teachers," he said.

I had mostly illusions about the Beats when I first arrived at the Kerouac School, but they were beginning to fall away, especially when I considered the miserable condition that Billy was in. Now, I wondered, what gave them the confidence, if not the right, to stand up there and talk to us? They were still at it, after all these years, trying to explain the world: first to each other, then to the world, and now to us. And so I did it. I asked Allen how he got famous.

Allen put down his papers and looked at me. Always the teacher, he launched into a tale he must have told countless times, but one that he still loved telling.

It was an irony, I learned, that Allen Ginsberg became America's most notorious poet while he was out of the country, in the mid-1950s, visiting Burroughs in Tangier, traveling with Peter on very little money. That's when he got the word that Lawrence Ferlinghetti and the manager of the City Lights Bookstore, Shigeyoshi Murao, were arrested for selling *Howl and Other Poems* to a pair of undercover cops in plainclothes.

Allen told me that he had been ecstatic about the publication of *Howl* and he made a list of people to send copies to.

"Do you still have the list?" I asked.

"It was all in my head," he answered listlessly, blowing his nose. "The law is a dangerous thing," he continued. "I was using the U.S. mail to 'promote obscenity,' " he said, raising his finger in the air. Allen had sent copies to T. S. Eliot and W. H. Auden; Ezra Pound even got one at St. Elizabeth's Hospital, special delivery. So did Charlie Chaplin and his then-wife Oona, in Switzerland. Even Marlon Brando.

"The ACLU saw an opportunity to make a strong case for the first amendment," Allen explained. "They thought they could strike a blow for free speech."

All of a sudden, it turned out, Ferlinghetti had retained a team of topnotch lawyers. The obscenity trial began in the summer of 1957. Allen said he didn't think he had a chance; after all, the trial judge was well known as a Sunday school Bible teacher. I wondered if Allen feared that they would never let him back into America. He stayed away from the trial. "Peter and I traveled around Europe," he said, "sleeping on park benches."

Peter came upstairs and plunged both hands in the bucket, squeezing out the sponge. He took the sponge and mopped Allen's brow while Allen continued with his story. Peter was completely absorbed with his work of giving Allen a sponge bath, as if I weren't even in the room. I noticed that Peter's usual pink complexion, seen most often on the mountain men who came down into the city after bathing in mountain streams, took on a bilious hue in Allen's sickroom.

"We went by train with our knapsacks, making our way through Europe. We weren't about to give that up to come home for an obscenity trial, not with all the culture of Europe laid out in front of us." Peter wrung out his sponge and started over.

"We were meeting people like Mary McCarthy and Peggy Guggenheim. I read 'Howl' to Caresse Crosby in Alan Ansen's living room in Venice," he said, referring to the widow of Harry Crosby, the famous expatriate and founder of Black Sun Press who had committed suicide in a hotel on Central Park South.

"We visited Dostoyevksy's house. We visited Shelley's grave—"

"Remember when you kissed Shelley's grave and took a clover from it?" Peter interrupted. "And when we went to the Vatican, Allen got mad because there were fig leaves on all the statues!" Peter shouted in that loud voice of his, as if everyone in the room were hard of hearing.

C

O

O

L

Allen explained how a coterie of literary experts were called to testify in support of "Howl." He had the rare privilege of having his poem called great and important as part of the court record (most of the poets I knew would have died for that, and would probably die from the lack of it). It started to sound to me like the arrest and trial were the best thing that could have happened to Allen and the Beats. It made them famous.

"What was the verdict?" I asked Allen.

Both men turned toward me. "Not guilty!" they shouted, as Peter squeezed the sponge over my head.

It occurred to me that if the *Howl* obscenity trial had occurred today instead of in 1957, Allen wouldn't have missed it for the world.

Around the same time as the *Howl* trial, *On the Road* was published. But Jack Kerouac would never recover from that joyful event. Unlike Allen, fame didn't sit well on Kerouac; ultimately, he'd have almost no time to get used to it.

Allen once said that "everything in life is timing," and that was certainly true of the publication of *On the Road*. Had the novel been published six years earlier, when it was first written, it might have gone unnoticed, but the obscenity trial for *Howl* had put a spotlight on the Beats. Still, no one could have predicted the kind of success *On the Road* had in the fall of 1957—certainly not Jack. "It just exploded—it was the big one. No one knew where it would lead, or that it would lead to Jack just wanting to be left alone," Allen explained. "The story—and it's true—is a legend now, about how he got off the bus at the Greyhound station in New York, walked along Broadway till he got to Sixty-sixth Street, and bought a copy of the *New York Times*. There he saw a review of *On the Road*. I'm sure it had to have blown his mind. I'm sure he thought, 'What will become of me?' At the same time, it must have been so exciting. The reviewer compared it to *The Sun Also Rises*, the way Hemingway's novel gave voice to the Lost Generation. Jack said he felt paralyzed reading the review. The phone didn't stop ringing for years."

Allen explained how the novel was on the best-seller list for eleven weeks; how Warner Bros. bought the film rights for $110,000, how Marlon Brando wanted to play Dean Moriarty (Neal Cassady); how Jack was overwhelmed with offers to write for *Playboy* and *Esquire*, to read at the Village Vanguard, to appear on *The Steve Allen Show*. Kerouac's dark, handsome face became the face of the Beat generation; men everywhere wanted to fight him or to *be* him, and women wanted to fuck him. It was too much, and Kerouac responded by going on a five-week bender. It didn't help that all his buddies were away, leaving him to face fame alone: Peter and Allen in Europe, Burroughs in Tangier, Neal Cassady somewhere in California.

Burroughs later wrote about his old friend that "Kerouac opened a million coffee bars and sold a million Levis . . . [but] Kerouac and I are not real at all. The only real thing about a writer is what he's written, and not his life. We will all die and the stars will go out one after another . . ."

Then it was Bill's turn. Talk about the criminal boredom of men. Burroughs tried working as a private detective, a bartender, a bug exterminator, and, when all that failed, a criminal. *Naked Lunch* had begun as a series of sketches acted out by Jack and Allen. They used daggers brought back from Morocco and assumed different identities. After City Lights declined to publish *Naked Lunch*, Allen launched a campaign to get it published in the little magazines and periodicals where he had some pull. A few of the sketches thus made it into print, one in the final issue of the *Black Mountain Review* in 1957; the following year, *The Chicago Review* published nine pages (a columnist writing in the *Chicago Daily News* described the nine pages as "one of the foulest collections of printed filth I've seen publicly circulated"). University of Chicago officials then refused to publish any more of the novel, which caused the staff of the *Review* to resign and start up their own publication, called *Big Table*. Ginsberg, Orlovsky, and Gregory Corso appeared at a benefit

C

O

O

L

reading to raise money for the new publication so that it could pub-lish the suppressed pages of *Naked Lunch*. The first issue came out in March of 1959, with ten episodes from the novel, and it was imme-diately seized by the post office of Chicago as obscene material.

However, a year later, a Chicago judge absolved the novel of its obscenity charge, saying that it was "not akin to lustful thoughts." The judge, incidentally, was Julius J. Hoffman, who ten years later would preside over the trial of the Chicago Seven (Abbie Hoffman, Jerry Rubin, Tom Hayden, et al.), charged with inciting to riot at the Democratic Party Convention of 1968 in Chicago. At that trial, Allen Ginsberg infuriated Judge Hoffman with his testimony and by chanting on behalf of his friends.

The publisher of the Paris-based Olympia Press (who had pub-lished Henry Miller) had originally turned down *Naked Lunch*, but he changed his mind as a result of the publicity and offered Burroughs a contract for $800, and gave Burroughs ten days to hand in a publishable manuscript. He did.

Burroughs later said that the pressure of having to pull the man-uscript together in ten days was just what he needed, but when the galleys came back to him in no particular order, Burroughs decided to stick with that. It was as if he had thrown the manuscript up into the air, gathered the pages together, and agreed to have it published that way.

When it finally came out from Olympia Press, in 1959, it didn't get one review. Burroughs had to make up his own review, with an invented critic: " 'The book grabs you by the throat,' says L. Marland, distinguished critic, 'it leaps in bed with you and per-forms unmentionable acts . . . this book is a must for anyone who would understand the sick soul, sick unto death, of the atomic age.' "

In the early sixties, Barney Rosset, the pugilistic publisher of Grove Press and the *Evergreen Review*, was fighting fourteen censor-ship trials over Henry Miller's *Tropic of Cancer*. Once those trials were settled, Rosset was able to republish *Naked Lunch*, in 1962. Writers like Mary McCarthy, Norman Mailer, and Henry Miller championed the novel, and it was soon accorded a place in the literary pantheon as a kind of grotesque masterpiece. The book—a phantasmagoria of cannibalism, homosexual violence, graphic hangings, and ejaculations—was banned one more time, in Boston, and it reached the Massachusetts Superior Court, where a majority of the justices ruled that *Naked Lunch* was not obscene. It was the last literary work to be suppressed by the U.S. government or any government office.

As Allen would later tell us in class, describing the effect of *Naked Lunch* on the world of the 1960s, "the word had been liberated." For Allen, it was more important than D-Day.

As for me, I never could read *Naked Lunch*. I didn't like reading about ejaculations. It wasn't that I was a prude, but I preferred Flaubert's *A Sentimental Education*; that was the dirty secret I carried around with me at the Kerouac School. I preferred Flaubert to flagellation. And you know what? So did Bill Burroughs.

I would soon discover that the book Burroughs slept with under his pillow at night was Stephen Crane's *The Red Badge of Courage*. Burroughs had a streak of gentility, of elegance even, belied by his scorched-earth prose. It was as if Burroughs's novels simply turned the body inside out, so that the cancer was made visible. But he read Jack London, Stephen Crane, and Booth Tarkington for pleasure.

6. Ginsberg Saves His Beard

Within a few weeks Allen had regrown his beard. He kept it more closely cropped, but he was beginning to look like a member of the Russian mafia.

Rinpoche was coming over. He lived in a beautiful Georgian-style mansion that his followers called the Wedding Cake House.

A gray Mercedes pulled up outside Allen and Peter's apartment.

C

O

O

L

The Vadjra guards were the first to leave the car. They were the young security officers who protected Rinpoche wherever he went. Dressed in identical-looking black suits and carrying walkie-talkies, the Vadjra guards were students of Rinpoche's who were given some training in martial arts and meditation to aid in their awareness of all potential situations.

They opened the door for Rinpoche and he moved slowly out of the backseat of the car. They accompanied him into the apartment. Peter had cleaned house like a demon. He even cleaned the sidewalk in front of the house with a toothbrush. Allen had taken a bath and a shower, and he was wearing his best suit and the pin he was given upon his induction into the Academy of American Arts and Sciences. It was like inspection at military school. Allen made sure my shoes were polished and that I had worn my seersucker suit. Peter was wearing sandals, but with socks. He was making tea.

Rinpoche was coming for one of his poetry lessons, which Allen gave him from time to time. They wrote three-line poems together: Ground. Path. Fruition. One idea embodied in each line. Allen's latest City Lights book was dedicated "to Chogyam Trungpa, Rinpoche Poet": "Guru Death your words are true / Teacher Death I do thank you / for inspiring me to sing this Blues."

Rinpoche was a practitioner of what he called "crazy wisdom." Allen loved that phrase. It seemed to mean that Rinpoche could do whatever he wanted, and his students would study it and try to learn a lesson from it.

"I still think you're too attached to your beard," Trungpa told Allen as soon as he arrived. "I think you should go upstairs and cut it off again."

Allen looked unhappy. "But I don't want to cut it off." He stamped his feet like a little boy. "I just grew it baaaaaack." He even said "whaaaaa," imitating a baby crying. But he went upstairs anyway to shave it off.

I was left on the couch in my seersucker suit. Peter was sitting with Rinpoche, and the Vadjra guards were situated throughout the house, as if the president were upstairs taking a leak. Peter tried making small talk with the leader of the Kagyu lineage of Tibetan Buddhism.

"I haven't been with a woman in thirty years," Peter said. "That's a long time not to taste pussy, don't you think, Rinpoche?"

"Too long," Rinpoche said.

I couldn't tell if Peter was a genius or a complete idiot. When I saw the movie *Being There* with Peter Sellers, I thought that Jerzy Kosinski must have known Peter Orlovsky. Peter's honesty was painful to watch, like someone trying to walk after a stroke.

I suddenly remembered that *Head of the Poet Peter Orlovsky* was the name of Robert LaVigne's painting that Allen had seen before meeting Peter in Foster's Cafeteria in San Francisco so many years ago. LaVigne had painted Peter's giant head on a canvas four feet by six feet. Peter, from a Russian family, looked a lot like Sergei Essenin, the poet who married Isadora Duncan and who had once prowled the halls of the Plaza Hotel, naked, wielding a pistol. Essenin was one of Allen's heroes; he kept a tape recording of Essenin declaring his poetry to a Russian throng in the 1920s. Whenever Allen played it, he cried. Essenin slit his wrists in a hotel room and wrote his last poem in his own blood. Allen once recited that poem to me, his eyes filling up with tears: "In this life, there's nothing new in dying, / But nor, of course, is living any newer." He said the poem is called "Goodbye, My Friend, Goodbye." I thought at the time that you would really have to be a serious poet—if not a great one—to give a title to a poem after you had slit your wrists.

Allen would play the tape on an old reel-to-reel, looking over at Peter sitting up straight in his chair, hands splayed out on his thighs, like he was posing for another portrait or had become a piece of Russian sculpture. Allen would gaze at Peter's beautiful Russian head and hair as if Essenin himself were in the room with him.

Allen and Peter had an unusual relationship. They had taken a

C

O

O

L

vow, a kind of marriage vow, but Allen seemed to have hundreds of lovers, young men from the streets of Boulder and Naropa students, and Peter wanted to have a family. "But," Allen later told me, "I'd have to support Peter, his wife, and a baby. I'm too old for that. At the same time," Allen said, "Peter can't live on his own, he doesn't know how."

I don't think anyone in the Orlovsky family was ready to live on his own. Allen showed me a photograph he had taken of all the Orlovskys seated together on a bed. Allen was a wonderful photographer; his Leica, which he kept in an old-fashioned brown leather case, was never far from his hand or eye. When Peter visited his family some years earlier, Allen took their picture.

It was a terrifying sight, like a picture out of Dostoyevsky's *Notes from Underground*. Peter's mother, Katherine Orlovsky, sits on the rumpled bed in a housecoat, barefoot, completely deaf from a botched mastoid operation, the nerves of her face severely damaged, looking like Charles Laughton. Peter's brother Lafcadio, in slippered feet, sits next to shirtless Peter, Lafcadio's hand touching him tenderly around the neck. Katherine holds Lafcadio's hand, and Lafcadio's half sister, Marie, stares sullenly at the camera, barefoot in a polyester dress. Marie had once lived with Allen and Peter for a time on the Lower East Side. She had to quit natal nursing school because she started hearing voices. "The voices traded in filthy gossip," Allen said. "She would roar things at people from the window of the apartment." The Orlovskys all lived together on a lonely road somewhere on Long Island, cashing their various disability checks, spending a small fortune in taxicab fare to do their errands and to go to the supermarket, which they did all together, never wanting to be separated. I remember Peter looking over our shoulders at the picture, beaming with pride at his family. He told me that another brother, Julius, lived in a group home with patients from the state hospital at Binghamton. "It's run by a nice woman and her husband," Peter said. "Mr. and Mrs. Finch. Like the bird, only they have a large family, not of birds, of patients, and my brother is one of them."

Now, sitting in Allen's living room across from Rinpoche, Peter struck me more and more like John Clare, the nineteenth-century English poet who loved nature and a girl named Mary, slept outdoors, and always ran away from the madhouse to return to his rural English village. Clare suffered from a delusion that he was Lord Byron. His poems are full of misspellings, like Peter's, he spent time in the madhouse, like Peter, and he loved nature, like Peter. And, like Peter, he "kept his spirit with the free." Peter was luckier than John Clare, though—Peter had Allen. Clare spent the last twenty years of his life in the asylum, and he continued to write about nature and his village, Helpston, as if he still lived there. Like John Clare, Peter too was reckless with his poems. "It would be hard," Allen said, "to rescue Peter's poems from all the places they might be—guitar cases, the backseat of cars, old notebooks. It's time to preserve Peter's poems," Allen said with great tenderness, as if to say, "I've preserved Peter all these years, why not his poems?"

Did Allen know that Peter liked talking to me about his affection for "girls," as he called them? Peter often said he wanted to get married. He said he had always wanted to, but that he took a vow with Allen and could never leave him. Peter said that in the beginning he was simply too shy to tell Allen that he liked girls and wanted to have a family of his own. He was getting over his shyness now, he told me.

A lull fell over the conversation. Then Peter asked whether or not Rinpoche was going to come to the first Naropa dance, and if he was going to bless the first Naropa class. He then pointed to me.

"That's Sam Kashner," Peter said. "He's our first Naropa poetry student. Allen says he writes good poetry but no one can understand it. I like to write simple poems. Poems about compost heaps, and trying to remember what pussy tastes like. Sam doesn't write poetry about that."

Rinpoche nodded and smiled.

G
I
N
S
B
E
R
G

Saves His Beard

C

O

O

L

Allen was taking forever shaving off his beard. It was a shock to see him so obedient. They had known each other for about five years, Allen and Trungpa. Trungpa liked to tell the story of Allen "stealing" his taxicab in front of town hall; Allen had just wanted to get his father, who was sick, off the street and back into bed.

At last, Allen emerged clean-shaven, like the first day I saw him several weeks earlier. I noticed he had cut himself pretty badly on one side of his face. It made me mad at Trungpa. Rinpoche, I think, loved Allen, but I would later conclude that he wanted some of Allen's fame and some of the same devotion that people felt for Ginsberg. Trungpa might be enlightened, but I came to believe that he also harbored some old-fashioned, Western-style jealousy. He was pushing Allen to improvise most of his poems and to let go of his ego. He came up with a phrase he liked to use on Allen and on his friends: "Ginsberg resentment." He said that all American hippies had it. He warned Allen to prepare himself for death.

I came to Naropa because I wanted to meet the writer who, in the 1950s, told off America, who said sarcastically that his mental health depended on *Time* magazine. I fell in love with "Ginsberg resentment"—the aggression and anger in Allen's poetry was a beacon to my aggrieved teenage life. I carried those City Lights books to school in my pants pocket. My heart was in my pocket, right next to *Howl and Other Poems.*

But it was Allen Ginsberg made gentle—pacified by Rinpoche, sent on retreats where he had to sit and meditate all day and couldn't write—that I found waiting for me at Naropa. The CIA-mafia-FBI paranoia of the Chicago Seven Trial now seemed to be a kind of dream. Had I made it up in junior high school just to express my own weird angers, to feel better about my life?

After the Vadjra guards had cleared the room and helped Rinpoche out of his chair and down the stairs, Allen kicked off his shoes and loosened his tie. I went upstairs to bring down some of the work we had put away for Rinpoche's visit. I went into the bathroom to tidy up—it was one of my jobs.

A cigar box peered out at me from a stack of towels. I lifted up the striped towels and reached for the box. I opened it. It was full of what looked like curly iron filings, like that game where you dragged the filings with a magnet along the face of a man to give him a beard. That was it. These were the hairs from Allen Ginsberg's famous beard. The beard that his ego was too attached to, according to Rinpoche. I put the box back between the beach towels.

When I came back downstairs Allen looked at me, as if he knew I had found the box. "No one will recognize me without the beard," he complained. "I'll be the most famous, unknown poet in America. No one will come to the Jack Kerouac School if they don't believe I'm here."

"I believe you're here," Peter said.

"Me, too," I said. "But I still like 'Ginsberg resentment.' That's why I came here." Allen smiled. I think it was good for his ego to hear that.

If Burroughs, Ginsberg, Kerouac, Corso, and Cassady were the core group of the Beats, added to that were two muses, Orlovsky and Herbert Huncke. Some people thought that it was Herbert Huncke who had first introduced the word "beat," or the idea of it, anyway. Huncke was a writer, but first and foremost he was a thief and a junkie. His character appears in Kerouac's first novel, *The Town and the City,* as well as *On the Road;* there are glimpses of him in Burroughs's early dime novel, *Junky,* which he published under the *nom de needle* William Lee (a book that Allen always loved for its "just the facts, ma'am"–style of storytelling; he called it a "dry classic"). Ginsberg wrote about Huncke, too, who walks on the snowbank docks with his shoes full of blood in the middle of "Howl." Kerouac got a lot of stories from Huncke and thought he was a great, natural storyteller.

Later, when I had the occasion to meet him through Allen, I thought Huncke was scary. He appeared in Allen's apartment one

C

O

O

L

night, hunched over the kitchen table, and with his death's head he looked like Yorick holding out his own skull and talking to it. He kept talking about how the law is a dangerous thing, how he hated honest work, how honest work is for suckers. What he really was, though, was a sucker for crime. He seemed to love the idea that he was a criminal, or that people thought of him as one. Whenever Allen spoke of him, it was with veneration, the way women in a small Irish town talk about the parish priest. Huncke said this, Huncke once did that. He seemed like the kind of person who could have murdered someone once, somewhere. Huncke seemed to believe that more people would go into crime as a profession if it weren't for the risks involved. The *idea* of Herbert Huncke might have been exciting, but Huncke himself scared me.

I don't think Huncke really liked Allen, and Allen's veneration for Herbert made me wonder about his judgment. Whenever Allen left the room, Huncke seemed to attack his old friend, although Ginsberg had often given him money and had looked after him. Huncke complained that "life's been hard for all of Allen's friends, but not for Allen." He said that Allen had been living off his friends, not with money but by *living off their lives*. He said, "Allen's a big talker, but he's really timid, really careful. That's why he's a big deal now, and here we are standing with our hands out—it's a nice little gimmick."

I wasn't enjoying this conversation with Huncke. I wanted to leave, but I couldn't leave in the middle of Huncke's coughing fit. He coughed up a whole cemetery right there in Allen's apartment. He coughed himself into a blur of a human being. He couldn't seem to stop himself; he seemed to be sputtering about the window, how it needed to be closed so he could stop coughing. But closing the window didn't help. He was still choking, his hands held up to his face like an old gardenia wilting in the night. I remember thinking it didn't seem worth it—to live so desperately just to come up with the word "beat" and be remembered for it.

7. A Shady Character

By the time the summer session was nearing a close and I was gearing up for the fall semester to begin (and bring with it more poetry students?), I was becoming a shady character.

I was working late in Allen's apartment one night, looking over a section on Whitman, "old courage teacher," for a lecture Allen was preparing for Naropa. Whitman in his old age had become a fascinating topic for Ginsberg. Whitman had given Allen the courage to grow old, to write about death, the body falling apart, a soft cock. Ginsberg admired the old Blake, the ancient Pound. They sanctified old age by writing about it, by choosing it as a subject. He loved the fact that Whitman wasn't trying to top himself, that he had kept current. Allen tried to do that, too; he was trying hard to like punk music. He called it "crybaby music," until he met the Clash. They invited him to play on one of their upcoming albums and Ginsberg happily accepted.

Allen was rewriting his journals from the sixties. At first I thought it would be hard for someone like Allen to grow old. After all, he worshiped beauty and youth. He told me my ass looked good in my dungarees. I always put up a kind of wall when questions of sex came up between us. I was too shy, too much in awe to give Allen a straight answer about whether or not I was queer. I would say things like, "How should I know? But that's the way it is." Or, "I never thought about it before."

It was dark when I left Ginsberg's apartment. Suddenly, I heard Johnnie Ray's 1952 song "Cry" playing on an eight-track tape, as Billy pulled up in front of the apartment complex in his car. It could've been something Neal Cassady had driven from his girlfriend's apartment in the Bronx to the Golden Gate Bridge in one of those automotive rants, with Cassady driving for forty-eight hours straight.

I loved reading about Neal's capacity for driving, Allen's descriptions of Neal in a muscle shirt, driving with his elbows so that he could light up endless joints and cigarettes. I used to read about Neal's driving when I sat in the backseat of the car during driver's ed at John F. Kennedy High School in Bellmore, Long Island. I never finished it. They took Neal's book, *The First Third*, away from me. He wrote about stealing cars and driving them around. They asked me to leave driver's ed. They said I was a threat to myself and the other students. But my driving teacher, Mr. Baitinger, said I shouldn't feel too bad. He said Jack Kerouac never liked to drive and he became a great writer. My poetic license hadn't been revoked.

"Hey, Sam," Billy shouted. "Get in the car."

Billy was in the front seat but he wasn't driving; one of the freckled Westies with a gold front tooth was behind the wheel. Jubal was in the back, with Peter and Burroughs. In the dark, Burroughs wore a kind of kerchief on his head, like the ones Jacqueline Kennedy liked to wear walking around Manhattan. It was even tied under his chin. He looked like a Daumier drawing that could've been called "The Toothache." Jubal sat beside him in the one thing Jubal ever wore, an expensive-looking suit, without a tie. In fact, Jubal wasn't wearing anything under his jacket. I saw some chest hair spilling out like moss. Burroughs's cane was laid out across his lap. I thought of Kerouac's description of a much younger Burroughs in Texas, sitting on the front porch with a shotgun on his knees, watching the sun go down into the bloody earth.

"Ah, Peter. It's you!" I said gratefully as I climbed in and sat between Billy and the driver. I was comforted to see Orlovsky in the car, the only one sensibly dressed for the cold air of the mountains, even in early fall. He looked like a Sherpa. I didn't quite know where we were going, but I felt sure it would be an adventure. And I thought that looking after Billy was still somehow part of my job.

We made the slow, perilous climb up the hill, which turned into a slow, perilous climb up the mountain, until you couldn't quite see the town of Boulder anymore, just lights twinkling in the distance that looked remote as stars. We parked on a cliff, not strictly speaking, but it was the edge of something. Everyone piled out of the car. Peter looked down and yelled into the abyss, "Has anybody seen my dinosaur? My dinosaur is missing, please hellllp!" It was very dark. It seemed like the place where someone might be killed. Burroughs took off his tie. Suddenly it crossed my mind that maybe I could be strangled up there.

Burroughs's concentration was intense. The high beams from the car flooded the place with light as if it were a movie set. I watched Burroughs, his skin drawn tight over his cheekbones and his mouth full of large teeth. He was nearly bald on his pate and his hands had brown spots. I couldn't tell if they were liver spots or freckles. He had a sharp nose that made him look like a bird of prey. And he had thin lips, which he moistened while he studied the situation. He had a remarkable memory, especially for obscure facts and for studies no one had ever heard of. His memory was important tonight.

"I can see it from here. I wonder if we've given it enough cover. We'll need our own trucks. Probably should have done this four miles farther up. The growth there is better. I'd say it could mean the difference between eight and ten thousand dollars. It's just a guess, without having a table of freight rates at hand."

"You're right about it, except for one thing," Jubal said.

"Where am I wrong?" Burroughs asked.

"You weren't here, so you don't know that most of this has been moved. I moved it. So you owe me an apology. You'll have to be more careful in the future." Jubal began yelling. "Don't go off half-cocked. That doesn't mean there won't be a next time. You better sit in the car, Bill."

Jubal called himself the "chief engineer" of the project. He was the engine running the whole thing. Jubal was treating Burroughs like a little boy, punishing him for not knowing the full story about the pot they had planted up in the mountain. I couldn't believe it when Burroughs went back to sit in the car.

The others began harvesting the pot while I went back to sit in the car with Burroughs. I put the tape back on. Johnnie Ray again. I put in another tape. I couldn't really see in the dark. It was *Sgt. Pepper's Lonely Hearts Club Band,* and I suddenly realized that William Burroughs was on the cover of that album. His head begins to eclipse Marilyn Monroe's. Edgar Allan Poe rises above Burroughs like a chimney.

Burroughs asked me to put the overhead light on in the car. He laid some blueprints out on the backseat. He reminded me of Walter Huston in *The Treasure of the Sierra Madre.* One thing was certain; he was not the kind of prospector who put on hobnailed boots and danced a jig when he found his treasure. But he seemed to want to come out of that tradition. He was one of those scions who, though they are born rich, want to go backwards and make nothing of himself.

On the other hand, Burroughs wrote and talked like a man who seemed to know everything. I could still barely bring myself to speak to him. I thought of him as the George Washington of the Beat Generation, the man who refused to be a king—King of the Beats—but who was still revered.

Jubal came over to the car and asked for the blueprints.

"Show the son of a bitch whatever he's entitled to see, but keep him away from me," Burroughs said.

Jubal took out a gun. It had a long nozzle and he pointed it through the window, not at Bill, and not quite at me, but it was definitely in the car with us. It looked like the sort of gun a U.S. marshal would've carried in the Old West. I thought I might pass out. I tremblingly gave Jubal his plans. Billy, Peter, and the Westies driver seemed to be doing all the work. Peter was singing an old Negro spiritual. The car lights began to flicker and dim. The battery was running low.

"We must return to the mother ship," Bill said, to no one in particular.

I could've sworn I heard a helicopter in the mountains. I waited for the others to return to the car. The trunk was soon weighed down with bales of pot.

"How many are there?" asked the author of *Naked Lunch*.

"It'll be a miracle if we can get down the mountain," I said nervously. I could just see my parents reading about it in the *Daily News*: "Merrick Boy in Pot Bust."

"We should've used mules," Burroughs remarked.

We made the long, slow trip down the mountain. The car moved like it was carrying the Lincoln Monument. I couldn't wait to be in my bed in my safe little apartment, but the boys wanted to go to Tom's Tavern to celebrate.

"That's part of the fun of working for a big company," Billy said, and everyone laughed.

Back in Boulder, in front of Allen's apartment complex, Jubal straightened his suit when he got out of the car and shook my hand. "Let's just say we understand each other a little better now," Jubal said. "You're smarter than I gave you credit for. William seems to like you. Maybe we'll have you over for a company dinner."

I walked back to my apartment. I was afraid to fall asleep. I didn't want to dream about Jack Kerouac, or Jack London, or Neal Cassady. I still had that poem to finish for Allen, the one about giving Neal a blow job. Are all poets crazy? Am I crazy, too? I remembered a line from Allen's commonplace book that I had copied out: "Thou gavest the tears of pity away / In exchange for the tears of sorrow."

8. William Burroughs Was Crying

Some nights Allen didn't get much sleep. He would see his mother, Naomi, who had spent years in a mental hospital for schizophrenia, in a dream. I would be working late, Allen would come down. "I saw her again," he said. "She was taking me for an egg cream at the Gem Spa on the corner of Eighth Street and Second Avenue. She told me

C

O

O

L

that she loved me and that I was smarter than Eugene [Allen's brother]. Then we walked along the beach at Belmar, and there was a big couch at the edge of the water and she patted it, as if to say, come and sit next to me, I'm your mother. Then she said, I want to tell you a secret, Allen. Every man over forty-five should watch his weight. Then she got up and walked into the ocean. I wanted to follow her," Allen said, "but she said I shouldn't try. She said, try to remember me. She said it without turning around."

"You *have* remembered her. You've done even more than that." Thinking about Allen's poem "Kaddish," I said, "You've made her immortal."

I couldn't believe I'd said something that stupid, that sounded just like flattery, the kind of thing I could already tell Allen was so used to. I had promised myself I'd never say anything like that to him, or to any of them, even if I meant it, which in this case I did. His answer surprised me.

"It's the only poem of mine my father ever really liked. It made him cry. It was the only time."

Occasionally Allen would send me, like a go-between, to Burroughs's apartment. Sometimes it was just to deliver a simple message like, Dinner at eight. Or, Did I leave my red tie, the one that was a present from Henry Miller, in your bathroom? More often than not, I think he was sending me to check on his friend.

One afternoon, a sweltering one, Burroughs had the air-conditioning turned off; he was sitting alone in the middle of the room, all the shades drawn. He was wearing his uniform: a black suit and dark, heavy Florsheims. He was talking about Jack.

"We all came up out of the swamp," Burroughs explained. "But Jack, ahhh! Jack was different. That beautiful boy. I feel more passionate about him now than I ever did. His own restlessness was a thing of beauty. I was crazy about him. Sit down. Sit down," Burroughs said. "Needle was the boy. Needle was the boy. Didn't he live in Needles as a boy?" Was Burroughs asking me about where Jack Kerouac lived?

"All those women! Probably Chinese girls and heaven knows what else," he continued. Tears were gathering in the corners of his eyes. "Jack was seducing me, when I was a boy. I didn't even know it. Seducing me without even holding my hand. I felt him doing it. You need a writer to take you like that when you're so shy."

William Burroughs was crying. The private was becoming public. He was looking away from me now, gazing thoughtfully at the brass posts at the foot of the bed. *"The Call of the Wild,"* he said. He was looking away from me now, gazing thoughtfully at the brass posts at the foot of the bed. "The call of the wild. No philosophy. A great writer. Should have run for president. I first read him sitting in a tree. I hope he's in heaven now. Or at least not besieged by maiden aunts in San Francisco. Poor Jack London with his rotted teeth. I should have followed him. Tried to map out my life like that. Like a seaman on the *Essex*. To wear a raccoon coat and a high silk hat to keep the Trib dry when on land."

So William Burroughs wasn't weeping for Jack Kerouac but for that other Jack—the one who had left home but didn't return to his mother: Jack London. His life going off like a rocket. That was the life Burroughs had really wanted for himself. I saw the bottle of J&B nearly empty beside him.

"That's good to hear," I said helplessly. "Hang in there."

9. Fortunato's Son

If you have a choice between two things and can't decide between them, Greogory Corso once said, take both.

I was afraid to meet him. Corso was a much scarier person to me even than William Burroughs, who was often depicted as a kind of carnival barker in one of Dante's circles. But unlike Burroughs, Corso really had been in prison. At sixteen he was busted for

C

O

O

L

robbing a Household Finance office. He was the youngest inmate at Dannemora. He was like a commedia dell'arte performer sent to jail. He survived prison by being funny. And by reading. Corso, who had stopped going to school in the sixth grade, was the best read of all my teachers at Naropa, with the possible exception of Allen. He was proud of how much he had read in prison. He spent three years behind bars reading the dictionary—1905 edition. He loved classical literature. He loved the Greeks. He loved Shelley. But he wasn't a snob. He read Mickey Spillane's Mike Hammer detective fiction at the same time he was reading *The Frogs* by Aristophanes.

Not long after my trip to the mountains, Allen told me that my new job at Naropa would be Gregory. He said that New Directions had given him money for a book, but that Gregory was doing everything but getting down to writing. He had a new girlfriend that he'd met at a party Jubal had given in Burroughs's apartment. I knew her slightly. She had a very dramatic profile. A big nose and strong chin. She had the straightest hair I had ever seen. It was like she was peering out of a waterfall. She was very skinny and wore tight, mod-looking striped pants. She always had on red lipstick. Her name was Doris, but Gregory renamed her Calliope.

I knew that Gregory would be hard to handle, much harder than Billy Burroughs. Allen told me almost casually that Gregory would probably try to ask me for money, that he would try to score heroin even while he was teaching. Allen said to let him know if that happened. I didn't want to be a snitch, but Allen said I had to get Gregory to sit down and write his poems, or at least dictate them to me.

Gregory was always testing people to see if they cared for him. He came into Ginzy's apartment—that's what he called Allen, "Ginzy"—wearing a white shirt with two pockets on the front and epaulets on the shoulder. He wore reading glasses around his neck on a chain. He wore khaki pants and loafers without socks. He was dressed like a movie director, or some colonial administrator in the Bahamas. He had long curly hair that was turning gray. He wasn't wearing his dentures when I met him, so it made him look much older than he was—his lower lip looked like it was riding up on his face.

Once upon a time, Gregory was known for his looks. Anne Waldman used to see him as a young kid wearing a torn black sweater and the hand-me-down pants from an old zoot suit on the streets of Greenwich Village, and she would just stare at him. But Gregory reminded me of Charles Schulz's cartoon character Pigpen, the one who always arrived in a cloud of dust. That was Gregory Corso.

Gregory arrived in Boulder at the beginning of the fall semester. He came dancing into Allen's apartment, his glasses bouncing off his chest, his New York street-kid accent cutting through the late summer air like an electric fan—his words all running together. Like a knife thrower in the circus, Gregory just hurled his words at you, coming perilously close: "Hey,ginzy,ineedmoneywillpayyoubackifnotyoucanafford it—you're a famous poet now and besides you're a Jew. Jews always have money, right, Ginzy?"

Who the hell is this? I thought.

"Don't look so scared," Gregory said to me. And then, to Allen: "Where'd you find him? He looks so ghetto." Gregory spun around to talk to me. "Do you have any money? Come on, your parents must've sent you here with plenty of money, give me your Diner's Club card."

How did he know? My parents *did* give me their Diner's Club card—for emergencies. Don't despair, I told myself. If you believe you're a poet, then you're saved.

Allen turned to Corso and told him that I was to look after him, get him to write, that I would become Gregory's baby-sitter.

"I don't need a baby-sitter!" Gregory said. "I need money. I now have a title for my book. It's a brilliant title—why bother to write any poems? The title is the most important thing. *Les Miserables*— all you need to know about Victor Hugo is in that title." The torrent continued.

C

O

O

L

"Ask Allen how we met," Gregory continued, jumping from one subject to another in a stream of consciousness. "Get this, I'll tell you, it's fucking beautiful how we met." Then he turned to Allen, and in a slightly wheedling voice, said, "Max needs milk and food. We have to have these things, Ginzy."

Max was Gregory's baby. He was in Boulder with his very young mother, Lisa. I wondered if they knew about Calliope. Gregory's life all of a sudden seemed like a whirlpool I was getting sucked into. His voice began to sound like swirling water. It was like being in a boat with Ulysses, the Aeolean winds blowing me farther and farther away from my old life of suburban comfort and ease. Had I thrown myself out of paradise? Here was someone who had slept in the subway and on the roof of Allen's apartment in New York, who stole lunches from kids in the playground, who wound up in juvenile court at an age when I had gone to Astronaut Camp in Towson, Maryland, who broke out of a Christian Brothers home and lived on the street until he was arrested in Florida for robbery.

And yet, I would soon discover, we both loved the same things. When he started talking about Shelley, about Dante, about "unapprehended combinations of thought," about having sympathy and love for all things, it was as if the wing of some angel passed over him and he wasn't scary, mad Gregory anymore. Poetry saved Gregory Corso's life. It pulled him back from the brink. The same way it made men mad, it gave Corso what sanity and clarity he knew. It was the only time he seemed to float easily, calmly through his own life. Otherwise, it was a maelstrom.

I could tell that he liked to shock me. He liked to call Allen and me, and all Jews, "christkillers," and "matzah-christas." But I didn't take it too seriously.

He and Allen explained how they had met. They traded the story back and forth, handling the details like some demented version of The Newlywed Game played out in a Bowery flophouse.

Allen first met Gregory in 1950 in a lesbian bar. The poète maudit,

Allen called him. "I loved his looks, and he had poems with him," Allen remembered. "He was a beauty. So were his poems. Many incredible lines, like Shelley by way of Genet, *Our Lady of the Flowers* and *The Thief's Journal*." ("The Stone World came to me, and said Flesh Gives you an hour's life.") Allen remembered great swatches of Gregory's poetry, as if he had written the lines himself.

Allen confided that Gregory would have to warm up to me at first, that he didn't make friends too easily. It was prison to blame for Gregory's not making too many friends. "He'll like the fact that you're a poet," Allen said. Hearing Ginsberg almost casually refer to me as a poet, as if to say it's no big deal, I know you're one and that's all there is to it, was like graduation day in a moment. I could go home tomorrow. It would be all right.

I knew Gregory's poetry—his great "Marriage" poem, which was in all the anthologies, his elegy for Kerouac, which begins with the Indians in the forests of New England, and which broke my heart reading it on a Greyhound bus coming into the Port Authority from my college in upstate New York. I remember I had the flu, and so was coming home to be sick in my own bed and spit into my Spider-Man trash can and read *Playboy* under an enormous blanket. This was right before leaving Hamilton College and enrolling in the Jack Kerouac School. I read Gregory's poem called "Bomb." I read it during an air-raid drill in high school, my desk melting in my imagination like Dalí watches, while Gregory's words exploded all around me.

I wasn't prepared for the story of how Allen and Gregory met. At first, I thought they were only trying to shock me, to scare me, it was all a test to see how much I could take, to see me red with Keats-like embarrassment. But then it dawned on me that perhaps this was just the Beats confessional, as always: trying to stake out some intimate new ground by killing all small talk. *You have to talk about your life,* they seemed to be saying. What else is there to talk about?

In a lesbian bar on the Lower East Side of Manhattan, Gregory

C

O

O

L

and Allen traded life stories. Gregory told Allen about a secret thing he did at night that had become a kind of religious ritual. He lived in an apartment on West Twelfth Street, and from his window Gregory could see another apartment. It seemed to belong to a young woman. Gregory would watch her taking a bath, then she would step out of the bath and into the bedroom where her boyfriend would be waiting for her. Gregory liked to watch them making love. Nearly every time he watched them he would begin to rub himself. He would masturbate to their lovemaking. One day, Gregory told himself, he was going to go over there and introduce himself to the girl. He wanted to quickly tell her the story of his watching her.

Allen said that during the conversation he began to realize that Corso lived directly across from Allen's girlfriend's apartment at the time, and that the couple Gregory was watching and jerking off to was Allen and his girlfriend. The following day, Ginsberg made Gregory's erotic wish-dream come true by inviting him over and introducing him to the girl.

Allen turned back to me and began explaining my new duties vis-à-vis Gregory. First off, he warned me about the bed.

"Gregory will ask you to keep it dry for him," he said. I didn't understand at first, but Allen explained that Gregory was a chronic bed wetter.

"I wet the bed," Gregory chimed in, completely unselfconscious and unapologetic. "I've done it forever," he explained. "My parents beat me for it. They made fun of me."

Allen explained that Gregory's parents had sent him to a foster home just a few months after he was born. It was Gregory's bad luck that the agency didn't believe in children developing a close attachment to their foster parents. By the age of ten, Gregory had been to three sets of so-called parents. "I was twelve years old," Gregory said, "and I stole a neighbor boy's radio. I got sent to prison for it. Four months in Youth House. I couldn't read yet. I was beat up. I was too pretty, too silly."

Allen, with a strange half-smile on his face, said that Gregory was so desperate to get out of Youth House that he put his hand through a window, just so he could go to Bellevue. Allen said that he didn't know Gregory then, of course, but that at one time Allen, Gregory, and his mother were all in Bellevue, at the same time that Peter was an ambulance driver there.

"So, I wet the bed," Gregory said, sucking his thumb. "I wet the bed because it reminds me of Michelina, my mother, and Fortunato, my father, may they rest in Heaven."

During all this Allen managed to peel off a hundred-dollar bill. It sat on the glass table in the middle of the apartment. Gregory palmed it before rolling out the door, his cloud of words and chaos and heart leaving with him.

Something told me that Max's milk money was going to feed Gregory's habit. If you believe you're a poet, then you're saved, I thought to myself.

10. Antler Wants a Drink of Water

Antler was standing in the doorway of Allen's apartment. Antler was another poet. He had long blond hair and a long beard. He wore sandals and his dungarees were flecked with paint. He looked like a Nordic version of Allen. Allen loved his poetry. Antler wrote a long poem, which he read at Naropa one evening, called "Last Words." It was about famous people and their last words. Everyone loved listening to Antler read his poems. Thanks to Allen, Lawrence Ferlinghetti at City Lights Books was going to publish Antler's first book of poems; it was going to be called *Last Words*.

I hated Antler. I was jealous of all the attention he got from Allen. I hated his poems about nature, about fishing and living outside; he even wrote a poem about shitting in the woods. I liked

C

O

O

L

writing poems about taking the subway, the Long Island Rail Road even. I liked going to record stores and bookstores. I even wanted to start going to the ballet because of Edwin Denby.

Edwin Denby was always an old man, at least he seemed like that to me. All the poets at Naropa loved him; they missed him when they had to leave Manhattan and spend the year in Boulder. Anne Waldman loved him most of all. She wrote down his dinner conversation and always talked about him. He was a poet who seemed to write only sonnets. But they were very beautiful. Anne said Edwin was the greatest dance critic of the twentieth century. He knew Balanchine and he knew Orson Welles. He was shy, very shy, and very modest. Anne and Allen thought Edwin Denby was practically enlightened. He had a very trim white beard and was extremely slender; even in his seventies he looked like he could've been a dancer himself. He had white hair. At the Jack Kerouac School, certain people, like Edwin Denby, Frank O'Hara, and of course Kerouac himself, became people you thought you knew, or should know. They formed a kind of holy trinity. We studied them like a catechism. Bob Dylan was a part of that, too.

Anne Waldman told Allen that he should introduce Antler at his poetry reading. It was the first one of the year. I asked Antler if he got nervous before a reading. Antler didn't answer. A young man with dark hair and a pencil-thin mustache, very skinny, his wrists jutting out of a white shirt that was way too small for him, seemed to appear out of nowhere; in fact, he was standing behind Allen's refrigerator. He was eating an apple.

"Antler doesn't speak today, he has a complete day of silence," the skinny young man said.

"Is it always the same day?" I asked.

"No," he said, taking a bite of his apple. "Antler tells me what day is going to be his day of silence."

"What's your name?" I asked. He said his name was Jeff. He and Antler had come from the woods of Michigan to visit Allen and to prepare for the publication of Antler's first book. I wanted to be doing that instead of typing Allen's poems and working on his ancient journals, my eyes watering from trying to read someone else's handwriting from the 1950s. In that way, I wanted to be Antler, only living in hotels, not in sleeping bags or in the Cumberland woods.

"Michigan, that's where the University of Michigan is," I said, already aware of what an idiot I must've sounded like, but I was working up to my point. "They have the Hopwood Prize there, don't they? Frank O'Hara won that, I think," I said to Jeff.

"I wouldn't know," Jeff said. "I don't know a lot about Frank O'Hara." I felt relieved about that. I told myself that Frank O'Hara would've hated Antler, too. Because Antler was rejecting what was really important in life—buying records and lots of books that looked great piled up on your night table. And watching movies like *Double Indemnity*, and watching Fred Astaire dancing—"Peach Melba of the feet," Frank O'Hara had called Astaire.

"Antler doesn't believe in the movies," Jeff told me, as if he had read my mind.

"What happens if Antler decides what his day of silence will be *during* his day of silence?" I asked.

"That would never happen," Jeff said. "It's only once a week."

Antler looked at Jeff and looked at the sink where Peter was running the tap. "Antler wants a drink of water," Jeff said. I went to get it. I handed Antler his glass of tap water—he held it up to the light like he was working for the health department. "Antler thanks you, Sam." I made a little bow. I wanted Antler to go fuck himself, but I knew how much everyone loved Antler and his *Last Words*.

William Burroughs came through the door looking like a Sunday preacher, or at least like Robert Mitchum playing a Sunday preacher in *Night of the Hunter*. Burroughs, god bless him, didn't love Antler. In fact, Bill didn't care for poetry all that much. Anne Waldman introduced Bill to Antler. The two men shook hands.

"Antler," Bill turned Antler's name around in that cement-mixer voice of his. "Ant-ler. Ant-ler." He said it like he was trying to recall something. "I killed a moose once, got up very close to it

C

O

O

L

and shot it with sodium pentothal, injected it. Killed it immediately. I got the truth out of the moose, too. Used the . . .”

Bill either couldn't think of the word or wouldn't use it out of politeness. "What'd you use the antlers for, Bill?" I asked, saying his name for the first time.

"Used it for a coatrack, could hold fifty coats and a lot of hats," he said. "The wood was shiny and thick as a beam. A thing of beauty."

Allen offered Antler his apartment for the next few days. I couldn't believe I'd have to work around these two all weekend. Blissfully, Jeff refused on behalf of Antler.

"Antler wants to camp out in the mountains, Allen," Jeff said. Big surprise, I thought to myself.

11. Fast Talking Woman

The next day I had my first conference with Allen; we were supposed to go over some of my poems. I spent a lot of time in front of the mirror before going over to Allen's because I noticed that the better looking you were, the more Allen liked your poems. For example, there was a guy named Bobby Meyers. I thought his poems stunk. Allen raved about what a genius Bobby was. At parties, Allen would introduce him as the next Ezra Pound. It always burned me up. Bobby was cute, with a lot of dark, curly hair and a cherubic face. He looked like one of the Romantic poets, even if he couldn't write, but for Allen, that was enough. Allen put my work aside and took out *Rivers and Mountains* by John Ashbery. He turned to a longish poem called "The Skaters."

"Now tell me," Allen asked, almost pleading at his desk. "What does this mean? I can't understand it. I want to know what it means, what is happening in this poem. Why does he have to be so mysterious about everything? Is it too much Manhattan psychiatry?"

Kerouac once told Frank O'Hara that he was ruining American poetry, Allen said, but Frank answered back, "That's more than you ever did for it." Allen laughed to himself. I wanted to explain "The Skaters" to Allen, but I had a hard time explaining it to myself. I only knew that I loved it.

I dodged Allen's bullet. I said a lot of people keep asking what Ashbery's poems are about, and he probably wants to know the same thing. "I think it's about skating, about falling through the ice of your own conscious mind." I was getting good at appropriating little phrases I had picked up from my teachers' interest in Buddhism. It seemed like a salve that covered all sorts of ailments. I also think that it may have really been what the poem was about. I wasn't sure.

"I hate feeling stupid, I hate not getting the idea," Allen said. Anne later said she thought Allen really wanted to be the smartest man in America. I asked her about Allen's poem "Ego Confession." She said that they were sitting next to each other somewhere in San Francisco when Allen started to write it, but that he was embarrassed or for some reason didn't want her to see him writing his poem, so he cupped his hand around the piece of paper like a schoolboy guarding answers on a test.

I returned to Ashbery's poem. " 'The apothecary biscuits dwindled.' I like lines like that," I told Allen. "I can't even explain why. It's just pleasing to the ear."

"But shouldn't it be about something?" Allen asked, really upset that he couldn't get a handle on Ashbery's poem, which was like a greased pole he kept trying to climb, only to come sliding back down again. I wondered what was wrong with not knowing something. I was certainly getting used to it here.

The phone rang. It was Anne Waldman. I could hear her voice coming from the phone pressed against Allen's cheek. Allen had to hold the phone a little away from his head, because sometimes Anne's voice gave Allen a headache. She loved deep-dish gossip. She said everything with a lot of power and authority. She never spoke in parentheses. Everything was given equal weight. She

F
A
S
T

C

O

O

L

never seemed to sit still. I wondered how she ever meditated. I once saw a woman in the park in Boulder reading under a big straw hat, the kind you'd see in an Impressionist painting. She was being perfectly still, she was wearing a yellow summer dress, and her long legs were crossed. She wore espadrilles. I moved closer to her. I was going to get to talk to Anne Waldman in a calm way with no one else around.

"Anne," I said, "am I disturbing you?" The woman looked up from under her straw hat. It wasn't Anne. It couldn't have been. I should've known better. Anne would never have been that still for that long.

Anne was beautiful. I think everyone was in love with her in some fashion. There were even rumors that she had just been having an affair with Bob Dylan during the Rolling Thunder Revue. This made her even more unapproachable. She wore polka dot scarves tied around her neck and a red protection cord that Rinpoche had put around her throat. She wore peasant blouses that she had brought back from Czechoslovakia with beads and rings on her fingers that she had picked up in exotic places or that her lovers had given to her. She had come to the Jack Kerouac School as a leg- endary heartbreaker—books by the younger teachers of Naropa were dedicated to her. The poet Lewis Warsh lived with Anne, and they were married briefly. Then Lewis went away and Anne fell in love with Michael Brownstein, a young novelist and poet who had been to Paris on a Fulbright. When Lewis came home, Michael was there, living in Anne's apartment, living literally in Lewis's place.

Anne billed herself at poetry readings as Fast Talking Woman. She made long list poems and recited them in a rapid, breathy style, taking over the stage in her long boots. During her readings, people got swept up in the excitement and applauded her like a rock star. Anne wanted to be a rock star, a rock star of poetry. She was a real-life bohemian. She may have had lovers but she was married to poetry.

She loved Allen. She was the only woman Allen seemed to *see*. He recognized her in a way he didn't recognize any other woman, except those from his past. (Later, I would wonder if Allen, deep down, was still angry at his mother for going crazy.) He gave Anne his undivided attention. She, in turn, tolerated his temper tantrums, his bursts of ego, his euphoric ideas about the Jack Kerouac School, and his melancholy despair about Peter drifting away from him.

Like Koko the Clown, who arose from Max Fleischer's bottle of ink in those Betty Boop cartoons, Anne Waldman had emerged from the Lower East Side the daughter of a poetry-loving mother and a father Anne described as "a hack writer." I always hated that phrase, especially when she said it. I thought it was so unfair to her father. She seemed embarrassed by him. He wrote for a magazine called *Why?* I once tried to find it in the library but it was too obscure. He wrote articles about how to give up smoking and the dangers of drugs.

Anne had grown up the opposite of a feral child. They didn't eat with their hands, they ate quoting Epicurus. Her mother was a translator. Anne went to Bennington, where she fell in love with poetry and, more important, with poets, while still a young woman. She seemed to know everyone. She was the doyenne of the St. Mark's Poetry Project in the Bowery. All the poets were in love with her. The picture on the back of one of her early books of poetry shows a very young and beautiful woman, part Pre-Raphaelite, part French film star. She looked like a cross between Bardot and Monica Vitti. She had that scraped-away face that looked as if she might have been a beauty in utero, and so nature stopped doing anything else with her. She scared me. I never saw anyone that confident before. She seemed to soak up not just all the air in the room but all the attention from the men, even though Allen, Peter, and Bill were all queer.

I met Anne's mother once. She was like Esperanza Wilde, Oscar's mother. Anne's mother had lived in Greece. She even married a Greek poet. She helped to revive the ancient Greek festival in Delphi. She was crazy about poetry. Anne said that poetry was the food of her mother's life. She said that some of that must have rubbed off on her. She got chills the first time she heard "The Idea

F
A
S
T

of Order at Key West." And she fell in love with "The River Merchant's Wife: A Letter," Ezra Pound's poem written in the style of a poem by Rihaku. "At fifteen I stopped scowling." Anne was fifteen when she first heard it. She grew up on MacDougal Street in the Village; she practically lived at the Eighth Street Bookstore— the same store that I had rushed to as a teenager as soon as I climbed out of Penn Station and got into a cab heading down Seventh Avenue. She devoured Donald Allen's famous poetry anthology, which was now required reading at the Kerouac School. She used to see Bob Dylan walking around the Village, or sitting in front of Café Reggio sipping espresso, and Gregory Corso, who "was so gorgeous," she said, "like Rimbaud."

I met her for the first time at a dinner, held in Allen's apartment, for all the poetry apprentices. She smiled and held out a long limp hand for me to shake. "So this is our apprentice," she said. "Naropa's first certificate student."

"Not exactly," Peter said, and unable to lie if his life depended on it. "He's our *only* student." No wonder I had been alone at the first apprentice dinner. No wonder there was no party for us to get together and talk through our homesickness. I was alone. I *was* the Jack Kerouac School of Disembodied Poetics. Here on the lower east side of the Rockies, alone with Allen Ginsberg, William Burroughs, Gregory Corso (wherever he was hiding), and Anne Waldman, the core faculty of the Jack Kerouac School. Allen was driving this whole thing. I was their experiment, their first matriculating student. Would I end up their "Ode to Failure"?

It was clear to me now that they had all come together to this quiet town to get away from their fame, to slip out of their legends for a while, but at the same time they had to trade on it in order to bankroll their getaway. Yet here they were, and here, like it or not, was I. I had beaten a path to the door of the Beats; like Allen with his meditation teacher, I was learning that gurus can be hell on earth.

As I got to know her better, I noticed that Anne was surrounded by talk. She was always on the telephone; she kept the radio on; the telephone in her apartment was hot from constantly holding it to her ear. She said my education at Naropa was going to be like Yeats's poem "The Cap and Bells."

"Do you know it?" she asked. I didn't. I felt like Mamie Van Doren when in some terrible movie she's asked if she knows anything about astrophysics, and she answers, "I know some very handsome men like it." I told Anne that a lot of interesting people I know and respect really love that poem. Anne said that, in the poem, the jester sends his soul dressed in blue to the young queen, but she shuts her window against him. Then he sends his heart wearing something red but she dismisses it with a wave of her hand, or maybe her fan. He finally dies, but he leaves his cap and bells, his jester's uniform, and that's what possesses her.

Anne said that she was going to encourage me to be who I am. She said that what should possess people was to be as authentic as possible. Anne was going to give me an assignment. She said I had to read a poem that was as great as "The Waste Land," and even more provocative. It was "The Skaters" by John Ashbery. She said it changed her life. I wanted to tell her that Allen didn't understand it. He had asked *me* what it meant!

"Ashbery's constantly playing with illusion and reality," Anne said. "There's such subtlety and duplicity in the poem." She said the poem was like a great meal, great food for one's head. She described it as a four-part symphony. She told me I had to bring back a paper on "The Skaters." And I was going to ask Allen for help!

Anne had an entourage, well, at least a couple of women who followed her everywhere—her "sirens," Bonnie and Nanette. They were like ladies-in-waiting to Queen Anne. Anne's poetry, especially the poems about Sappho, made me wonder if they were all sleeping together (at least it was exciting to think about). They both wrote poetry and I'd see them all together in a restaurant having dinner. Whenever they waved to me or motioned for me to come inside and talk to them, I felt as if I had entered a harem. I blushed and felt terribly shy around these poetwomen.

FAST

C

O

O

L

"Don't be so scared," Nanette said to me one night at Pelican Pete's, a vast fish restaurant with an enormous lobster tank that fascinated Burroughs and his son. They would peer into the lobster tank, mesmerized by the bands that held the lobster claws together, "so they don't start slashing at each other," Burroughs said one night, in his Midwestern drawl. Billy liked to drop a little plastic paratrooper into the tank when no one was looking; he liked it when all the lobsters went crazy climbing over the little submerged man; he called it his science-fiction movie. After seeing that, I always ordered the filet of sole. Ginsberg also refused the lobster, but on religious grounds. "A Buddhist can't eat lobster," he said, just as the waiter brought two huge, live lobsters to our table. "As a Buddhist, you can't condemn a living creature to its death."

The three women, as usual, were dining together, and they called me over. "You look so haunted!" Bonnie said. "You could win a Franz Kafka look-alike contest." They all laughed.

Oh, great, I thought. I remind them of Kafka or, worse yet, one of his stories. It could have been worse, I suppose. Bonnie could have compared me to Gregor Samsa, Kafka's hero who went to bed a man and woke up a cockroach. I hated seeing Anne laughing, not really laughing but grinning at what was a thoughtless and stupid remark. I wondered why Anne, who had her life changed and her heart touched by poetry, would want to be around anyone who could say something like that. Being toyed with by Anne and her maidens put me back in junior high school again, being teased by the sexiest girls in school in Merrick, on the south shore of Long Island, where we lived up the street from Amy Fisher. I think I even baby-sat for her once.

At school, my friends were the geeks, the misfits, the guys who didn't date. That's probably why, for my bar mitzvah, I wanted to take my friends to the Playboy Club. Those clubs still existed in the late sixties. We must have passed the one on East Fifty-seventh Street in our car a hundred times, leaving the city for the Fifty-ninth Street Bridge, heading home to Long Island. I would catch very fleeting glimpses of it through the backseat window of our car—the darkened windows, the gold key that meant "members only."

My father decided it was a good idea. We showed up at the door and asked to come in. We found out it was against all the rules to have minors as guests, but because it was my bar mitzvah and my father was with us, the manager let us in.

When we arrived, the women were just getting into their bunny costumes. My friends and I were all in our temple suits; we had come into the city after services. I still had my yarmulke in my pocket when the mother bunny had me sit on her lap. They fussed over us like glamorous moms, giving us ice cream and complimentary copies of the May issue. For some reason, my father spent the whole time on the pay phone. When he finally joined us at our table, he took out a pencil and sketched a caricature of one of the bunnies on a napkin. That was one of my father's few hobbies, drawing caricatures of people in restaurants. She turned her profile to him and sat with her head thrown back like a real artist's model. I kept thinking, "Today I am a man. Tomorrow—who knows?"

One of the bunnies asked me what I was planning to become after I went to college.

"A poet," I said.

She smiled and started to recite "Trees" by Joyce Kilmer. "She's my favorite poet," the bunny said.

Even at thirteen I knew Joyce Kilmer was a man, and not a very good poet. But I didn't say anything. When she recited the word "bosom" at the beginning of the poem, her own bosom rose up to greet me, and suddenly Joyce Kilmer's "Trees" became the greatest poem in the English language ever written by a man with a woman's name, recited by a woman dressed as a rabbit, while my father sketched like Toulouse-Lautrec on a cocktail napkin and the weekend traffic rumbled toward the bridge.

Bonnie and Nanette were still laughing. To cover my embarrassment, I made a joke about Anne Frank—a joke I was ashamed of

F
A
S
T

Talking Woman

C

O

O

L

making—about how Anne Frank should've gotten out of the house more. I thought about how my grandmother back on Central Park West, with her thick Yiddish accent, would have been so hurt by what I had just said. But I said it to keep my tears in check. I knew I was being too sensitive. Maybe I did have a haunted look about me. I was uncertain of myself, and maybe Rinpoche was right after all, in the one conversation I had had with him so far, sitting next to Peter Orlovsky in Allen's living room. He said the real reason I had come to the Jack Kerouac School was to be *released* from my heroes—to find out the truth about them and be free of them, to be able to live my own life.

Allen said that Rinpoche loved the title of a magazine created by Ed Sanders that came out of the Lower East Side in the 1950s and early '60s—*Fuck You: A Magazine of the Arts*. By then, that first Beat scene had begun to break apart. Frank O'Hara's death didn't help things. Like his great poem, his "Account of Talking to the Sun on Fire Island," Frank was a kind of sun. He brought the uptown and downtown scenes together, and with his death, as Anne explained it, things drifted, until Anne, home from college, began working at St. Mark's Church, holding readings and putting out a magazine called *The World*.

Anne liked having Bonnie and Nanette following her. She liked to read her long list poems, and she wanted to be the center of attention. If someone else entered the room, she would get a look on her face as if she had just missed a train, or expected to win the Irish sweepstakes but had all the wrong numbers.

She wrote poems with everything going on around her. She said all her heroes could do it—Frank O'Hara and Ted, meaning Ted Berrigan, who was coming soon to the Jack Kerouac School, as soon as there were some students to teach. Anne said Ted was one of her greatest teachers and mentors, but she warned me that he liked to lie on the couch all day balancing an ashtray on his huge stomach, and living on Pepsi, candy bars, and amphetamines. They said he had grown up in Tulsa with Dick Gallup, whom Anne had brought to Naropa from New York, where he was married with two young kids and driving a cab.

One evening Anne stopped by Allen's apartment because Allen was in despair. She entered the room the way Isadora Duncan entered a room. Or at least, the way she imagined Isadora Duncan entered a room, all scarves and drama, long fingers moving in the air when she spoke, like she was signing for the benefit of the deaf.

I was there doing some typing for Allen, but Allen was in a funk because he said he now hated the name "Jack Kerouac School of Disembodied Poetics." He thought no one would ever come because of the word "disembodied." He had his white shirt unbuttoned and he looked pretty fit, a little hair coming up from his belly. He wore khaki trousers and was barefoot, and his beard was growing back from that punishing day when Rinpoche had made him shave it all off. He looked nice. He had his head in his hands. Allen was miserable. He loved to smoke cigarettes, but Peter wouldn't allow it in the house, so he had to go sneaking around to other people's apartments to smoke. Or else, if he was working, he'd smoke in the house but exhale into the air-conditioning vents. He was behind in his prostrations, he hadn't done enough, he said—too busy. Rinpoche told him to make the time. So his guru was sore at him. And now he didn't like the name of the school he helped found.

At first Allen thought the name was a good joke because Kerouac was dead, but now he thought it made the place sound silly, and not real. (After all, it still wasn't accredited.) He wanted it to be great, part of the only Buddhist college in America. He wanted it to be a feast and a wedding—a wedding of East and West, and a feast of poets and musicians and dancers and psychologists and meditators all working, Allen said, on their suffering.

Anne tried to cheer him up, but he wasn't having any. Wearily,

F
A
S
T

Talking Woman

C

O

O

L

he got up and took out his harmonium and sang a little song he'd made from something Rinpoche had said in his lecture the night before at the Sacred Heart auditorium: "Born in this world / You've got to suffer / everything changes / you got no soul."

Anne later confided in me that for Allen, meditating was really hard. "Trungpa doesn't approve of pot or psychedelics," Anne said. "He thinks they're too trippy, they create uncertainty, he believes in things being grounded, he just doesn't approve of Allen's smoking grass and taking acid. I think Allen's going through withdrawal."

Anne told Allen that it was too late to change the name of the school because the catalogue for the summer had already gone to the printers. And then she said that Bob Dylan's Rolling Thunder Revue was coming to Denver in a few days, right after Naropa's first official gathering. She said that five tickets would be waiting for them at the box office.

I tried to figure out who was going—Allen, of course, which meant Peter was going; Anne; and who else? It was getting late. "Don't be grasping," Rinpoche said to us the other night, "be non-ambitious, it's the only way to achieve sanity." What I wanted to know, Mr. Rinpoche, was how do you achieve a ticket for Bob Dylan and what was left of the Rolling Thunder Revue? Or would I—born in this world—just have to suffer?

12. The Wyrde Sister

The next day, I walked along Pearl Street with Allen. He was wearing a white shirt and his khaki pants and he carried a shoulder bag, which made him look like a postman in a Greek fishing village. I noticed people recognizing him. Teenagers on skateboards and older hippie couples acknowledged Allen and I even thought they gave *me* some sort of respect, out of respect for him. Perhaps, I thought, a few of them will think that I'm one of Allen's lovers. I was kind of surprised that the idea, at least what I thought other people were thinking, didn't bother me at all. I kind of didn't mind them thinking that. I was getting very mixed up, very fast. I enjoyed the reflected glory. The only problem was, I was too shy to talk. We walked along for a long time in silence.

A crazy woman with a Scottish accent seemed to be holding court across from a record store on the mall. I just knew this was going to be bad, that something was going to happen between Allen and this woman. I thought about the woman who shot Andy Warhol. I thought that, despite meditation and becoming famous for chanting *Om* in Lincoln Park during the 1968 Chicago Democratic Party Convention and thereby helping to avoid a riot, there was an aura of violence or at least potential violence around my Beat teachers. Gregory and Burroughs, even Billy Jr., seemed to wear the threat of violence like a cape—they unfurled it when it suited them, took it off at more respectable gatherings, made grand gestures with it, although I never thought they made very believable criminals (except for Gregory). Maybe that's why they loved Jean Genet so much (Allen had escorted Burroughs and Genet to that same Chicago convention). And I once heard Burroughs tell Billy that he wanted to be buried or cremated with something by Genet (or was it Gide?) in his coffin.

The Scots woman, who looked like one of the Wyrde sisters, approached us, wiping her mouth on the bottom of a red plaid shirt. She didn't have many teeth, her red hair was still shiny, even beautiful, and it occurred to me that she probably wasn't very old. Like a lot of people living on the street in Boulder or in the mountains, she had beautiful skin. She began shouting at us.

"You two Jews, you Bolsheviks, you Greenstein, Allen Greenstein, and your boy, your little boy, you bug me, you buggerer! You bunghole! You jewbeatle!" She was pointing at us. I felt like Peter Lorre in *M*. There was nowhere to go. The tunnels of Berlin were too far away. There just was nowhere to hide from this crazy woman. I wondered

C

O

O

L

what Allen was going to do. He had dealt with crazy people all his life, starting with his mother.

Allen spoke to her. He didn't humor her, in fact, he argued with her! "I'm not a Bolshevik," he said calmly. "My mother was a Bolshevik. I'm not even a communist. I'm a Buddhist. I meditate. I don't give people a hard time." Allen then explained to her what the hours of mediation practice were and where she could get meditation instruction.

We moved away from the woman, who seemed much calmer after talking to Allen. She stopped insulting us. She didn't shoot us. Allen had the good but stern manners of an ambulance driver. He seemed to know how to handle lunatics.

On the way back to Naropa, Allen explained how he tried to deal with anti-Semitic remarks. He said that he even got Ezra Pound to "take it back," to admit that it was a dumb, suburban prejudice. Allen knew that I liked Bob Dylan, so he told me that he had played *Bringing It All Back Home* for Ezra Pound, played the record for him at St. Elizabeth's Hospital. Allen said he'd had to deal with it in Jack Kerouac, too. Even at the end, during their long-distance talks over the telephone late at night, Jack would provoke Allen with a lot of what Allen called "dumb-ass jive about Jews."

"He was trying to get me into a fight, to draw me in to a fistfight with him over the phone," Allen said. "It was just a test, to see how strong my ego was, after years of meditating."

"What did you say to him," I asked. "Did you take the bait?"

"I told him 'your mother's cunt is full of shit and you like to eat it.'" Allen started giggling. "I completely bought into it, I fell for Jack's trap. He sprung it, and I fell for it, I put my big foot in the rope."

Allen said that I should ask Gregory about Jack, that I should read Gregory's long poem about Kerouac, that it was the only thing about Jack worth reading. It was called "Elegiac Feelings American." He said Gregory didn't like to talk about Kerouac's funeral but that I might be able to get him to talk about it a little.

Gregory was haunted by Kerouac's funeral, Allen said. And Gregory was having trouble finishing his new book because his love life was so complicated, and because he was still buying drugs. Allen told me that I would be on the express elevator to heaven if I could bring Gregory back down to earth and get him to finish his book.

I didn't really want to spend my time at Naropa following Gregory around, like he was Ray Milland in *The Lost Weekend*— watching him hock his typewriter and doing God knows what to me because I was keeping him from his drugs. But I loved his poems, and he was completely uninhibited in a way that I wanted to be; he seemed to have no superego, no censor. Poetry and life. They were both real to Gregory.

The Naropa dance was hours away. The dance would feature a band led by Charlie Haden, who *was* the music department at Naropa, at least for a while. Haden was a jazz legend, though I didn't know enough about jazz to appreciate it at the time. He had played with Ornette Coleman and Art Pepper. He had used heroin and had been to Synanon. He was a small, compactly built guy with a sweet and boyish face; he wore glasses. He played the stand-up bass. I got to know him a little bit. He once offered to play the bass while I read some of my poems. We were going to do it at a local nightclub in Boulder, called the Blue Note. But the night of the performance, the Go-Gos came to town, and the local impres-sario told us that the Go-Gos had offered to play there at the last minute, so our services were no longer needed. After that, Charlie Haden always winked at me. "What would Beethoven do?" Charlie said, after we were fired.

"Write a symphony?" I asked.

"No, go for a long drive."

But neither one of us had a car, so Charlie hired a cab to take us to Stapleton Airport. We sat on the roof of the cab and watched the planes take off and land. I realized that any one of those planes

THE
WYRDE

Sister

C

O

O

L

could take me back to Kennedy Airport, which was only thirty minutes from my house. The airport was making me homesick.

On the way back, Charlie hummed an entire aria from *Madama Butterfly*. Charlie said that he lived to be sober now. I had told him about my other job, the one Allen wanted me to take, to get Gregory to finish his book. I told him how I thought that Gregory was buying heroin with the money Allen was giving him. Charlie said that Gregory reminded him of himself—how many winters and summers he had spent getting high, how in all that time he finally came to realize that he had never really cared about anyone, any one person, whether or not they lived or died. He said that even getting in bed with his wife didn't make him feel the way heroin did. He said that he had to kick in order to see that playing music was the only real excitement he'd ever had.

"What can be bad about something that makes you feel that good?" I asked Charlie, who was cleaning his delicate tortoiseshell eyeglasses with a locomotive engineer's red handkerchief.

"How do you stay alive," Charlie said, "long enough to know any of those other things, the other things that can bring you joy? What price would you put on that? It's not really an equal relationship. Heroin takes all your money, all your time, and it leaves you broke. I don't approve of Bill Burroughs, and all that horseshit about how you can practically smell it going into your veins. I hope he doesn't teach you that. He should stick to books."

Charlie then told me that, in his opinion, Burroughs was not a real junkie: "He's a dilettante junkie. He wouldn't forget to take his antibiotics. On the other hand," he confided, "Gregory's the real thing. Be careful, he might do something crazy. He's going to make you read *Gilgamesh*. He believes everything he's ever read is true, especially if it's great. He's a real poet, he feels he can only speak the truth, whatever it is. But be careful of him."

Charlie was starting to scare me. Gregory already scared me. If only I could share these fears, these uncertainties with some of the other poetry students at the Jack Kerouac School, but where were they?

And was I going to be included in the Rolling Thunder Revue night of extravaganza, which was right around the corner?

13. Last Gasp &/Or Gasm Sock Hop

I had managed to survive the summer session at Naropa and the fall term was just around the corner. On August 11, there were at least five hundred people in the shrine room the night of the Naropa sock hop, to inaugurate the Jack Kerouac School. Allen, Burroughs, and Anne had held a conclave to come up with the perfect name for the event: they emerged with "Last Gasp &/Or Gasm Inaugural Night." It was printed on posters and people from town were invited to come—they needed more bodies in the room.

Large red banners featuring the karmic wheel hung from the rafters. Charlie's combo stood on a makeshift stage. "Don't get up, gentleman, I'm just passing through," Burroughs told Allen and me as we sat on the edge of the small stage waiting for Rinpoche to arrive so the festivities could begin. That night, the Jack Kerouac School would finally come to life as a full partner of the Naropa Institute. The core faculty would be presented to the rest of the school: Allen, Bill, Gregory, Anne, and the young poets she had brought from New York: Ted Berrigan, Michael Brownstein, Larry Fagin, and Dick Gallup, who formed what Allen called the Second Generation New York School.

All the teachers and students stood at attention and bowed from the waist as Rinpoche entered the room. He was dressed like a colonial governor, in khaki pants and a rich, cream-colored silk shirt with epaulets. As usual, he was holding a fan, which he furled and unfurled in the overheated shrine room.

"Ladies and gentlemen"—his voice a hoarse whisper into the microphone held by one of the Vadjra guards—"welcome to

L

A

S

T

C

O

O

L

Naropa. I hope you will partake of each other's wisdom, of the golden sun of dharma. Welcome to the Jack Kerouac School of Poetics." I noticed he'd forgotten "Disembodied"; I wondered if he did it on purpose. (Peter said Rinpoche was enlightened and didn't fear death.) "I will turn the festivities over to Allen."

Allen was handed the microphone and he introduced Anne Waldman, who looked very sexy; she had so many bracelets going up her arm that she looked like that Man Ray photograph of Nancy Cunard, the shipping heiress who loved poets and lived in the 1920s and who took black lovers. I used to study her photograph. I fell in love with her picture. But Anne, like Nancy Cunard's photograph, was unapproachable. She seemed to inhabit a world I knew only from the outside, the glass between us thick and impenetrable.

Allen introduced the other teachers. William Burroughs stepped from the darkness into a spotlight, leaning with both hands on his cane as if he were going to break into "Putting on the Ritz." The younger poets, Allen's "second generation," made the first-generation Beat poets look like chaperones. It reminded me of the sock hop scene in *Bye Bye Birdie.*

"I want you all to meet the first graduating class of the Jack Kerouac School of Disembodied Poetics," Allen announced. All of a sudden, the spotlight Burroughs had been standing in seemed to swallow me up, blinding me. I felt the heat of it on my face. I stepped back to look at my fellow poets, the other students, Allen's army of apprentices. I saw nothing. No one. The room was strangely quiet. Charlie Haden's bass played a kind of funereal chord. I was alone. I was it. Naropa had dozens of students of dance, music, meditation, calligraphy, religion, but the Jack Kerouac School of Disembodied Poetics had no student body except for mine, the one that stood trembling in the glare of the spotlight.

Anne thought of rescuing me from my embarrassment, but she only made it worse. "Who would like to dance with the Jack Kerouac School's first student?" she asked. For a moment I felt I was in junior high, terrified of being picked last for the team. And then another thought crossed my mind: if I was the only poetics student at the Jack Kerouac School of Disembodied Poetics, how could this institution survive? Would we all go bankrupt, and would I be sent packing back to Merrick? Would Ginsberg, Burroughs, Waldman, Corso & Co. have to fold up their tents and return to the steaming streets of the Lower East Side? I had a feeling they were as desperate to remain in the austere, beautiful foothills of the Rockies as was I.

Mercifully, Barbara Dilley, who headed the dance department at Naropa, crossed the room, snapping her fingers to Charlie's bass beat, high-stepping over to me. She pulled me out of the spotlight and spun me around the dance floor, ending my embarrassment and my end-of-Naropa fantasy. I felt as if I might crack in two from relief and joy. All the other dancers, students, and wallflowers fell in around us. The shrine room suddenly filled up with music, with talk, with real life. Barbara flung me back into the crowd. A woman whose father was the richest man in Boulder, owner of the biggest department store in town, kicked off her shoes and kissed me on the mouth. She was wearing a dress with zebra stripes on it. I lost her when she leaned her head against Charlie's bass so the sound could enter her head even faster. Then the Naropa secretary, a woman named Monica whose husband was not a student of Rinpoche's and who disapproved of Buddhists, came up to tell me something.

"Call your mother. She said to call when you get a chance."

Call my mother? I couldn't believe it. I guess I should've gotten my phone installed already instead of just relying on Naropa's office phone. Well, she can't ruin my reputation, or so I thought, because I don't have one yet. "Just give her time," the bluebird of unhappiness whispered in my ear, the one that I seemed to carry on my shoulder. How do you stay alive when you're dancing with Beat poets and your mother calls?

A band of Naropa musicians, Charlie's students really, had nudged their teacher off the stage and took over, playing loud. The shrine room floor, always polished and shiny as a mirror, squeaked with all the dancing and general jumping around. Rinpoche had

L
A
S
T

C

O

O

L

long gone but Allen and Peter stayed behind. Allen wasn't a big dancer, not at all, but he liked watching the kids move, and he always found someone to go home with.

I headed for Monica's office to make that call back to Long Island, to reassure my parents that they hadn't made the wrong decision to let me go to Naropa. They didn't quite know what to do—my parents had never really had the chance to go to college. My mother had dropped out of Stern College for Women in New York to go to work during the Second World War after her brothers were drafted, and my father had been working, supporting his brother since the two were orphaned at a pretty young age.

My parents had never tried to stop me from writing poetry; they never really censored my reading, except maybe once, when on a trip to my grandmother's in the Catskills I bought a Signet paperback copy of *Goldfinger,* and my father, after thumbing through the book, decided it "wasn't for me." I was twelve years old at the time. It was the movie tie-in version of the book, with the woman's body painted gold, wrapped around the front and back covers. Later, at my grandmother's, I saw my father reading the book at the kitchen table; he stayed up half the night finishing it.

My parents secretly liked the fact that I wrote poetry and admired writers more than baseball players. They thought that would mean I would do well in school, but I don't think they counted on my wanting to *be* a poet. Allen Ginsberg was something of a controversial figure in our house. His beard and hippie countenance, his radical politics, some of the obscenity in his poems must've troubled my parents, but when I called home from my first semester at Hamilton College, miserable, homesick, and unable to convince any of my teachers to let me do an independent study on Neal Cassady and his influence on the Beats ("a guy who stole for a living?" my adviser at Hamilton said; "he's just a petty criminal"), I just knew I had to go to Naropa. And my parents, they didn't stop me. They probably had their hearts in their mouths, but they let me go.

I left the dance to find the telephone. My parents were a bit like

Allen's, I thought, as I made my way to the office to call my mother. A quiet, sensitive father, the soul of an artist under his suit jacket and tie; a lively, outspoken mother, a kind of bully of almighty kindness: They drove me crazy but I loved them for their indulgences, now becoming too many to mention.

Outside the shrine room, in the foyer, I ran into Gregory and Calliope, who were sharing a cigarette. Gregory was holding a cat and he waved me over, a conspiratorial look on his face. He had a plan.

"You're not used to money yet, kid, so you don't know the first thing about life. Sit down." I kept standing.

"Five hundred big ones," he continued, warming to his theme. "That's what you're worth to me. I'll write you a poem for five hundred big ones."

I wanted to like Corso. I loved his poems. I loved the fact that he took pity on strays and gathered them up in his arms, that, as allergic as I was, his apartment was full of cats. Gregory wrote about missing his cats: "My water-colored hands are catless now / I am catless near death almost." He seemed calmer with a cat cradled in his arms. But I saw how he sometimes lashed out, and he wouldn't give up this rant about the five hundred dollars. He certainly didn't try caressing it out of me.

"Look, I'll sell Calliope to you," he said. "She likes screwing poets. I've made a careful study of this. How much would you pay for her?" Gregory asked me. "Now you might think she'd go to bed with you anytime, but she won't," Gregory explained. "I made a little study of you, too. I know that Ginzy's set it up so that you can watch me. I'm a great poet, I don't need some kid looking out for me. All you care about is my writing, am I right? Of course I'm right."

I had to say something. If only because I didn't want Calliope to think I was a wimp, being bullied by Gregory. She did look great, she was sexy, and I didn't want to feel humiliated.

"Why does any of this worry you?" I asked Gregory.

"Worries *you*," he repeated.

C

O

O

L

"Worries me?"

"I don't give a shit about you. I don't ask *you* a lot of questions," Gregory said, moving his jaw up and down like he was gumming a piece of turkey at a mission dinner. "I need five hundred dollars; now what would you require of me for five hundred big ones?" At the word "require," he made a flamboyant gesture and spun every syllable out, like he was a French nobleman with a handkerchief in his sleeve. Very theatrical.

So I blurted out, "Tell me about Frank O'Hara. Tell me about Kerouac's funeral, Allen said you might tell me. I'll give you five hundred dollars for that!" I couldn't believe what I'd just said. My curiosity was the only thing I could trade with Gregory. I wasn't about to let him sell Calliope to me, as much as I secretly and idiotically hoped she would like the idea.

"You do think things out, don't you?" Gregory asked. "Sit down. You might as well hear this from me. Jack's funeral was a traffic accident."

I could hear Charlie Haden's deep bass thrumming from the shrine room, and I felt a pang of guilt for not calling my mother back, but I really wanted to hear this.

"There were too many people," he continued, stroking the cat. "I'd been to a funeral parlor before. I once saw a child's funeral. The tiniest coffin I ever saw. Mrs. Lombardi's son—he was one month old. It was in Rizzo's funeral parlor. I saw it in its coffin. I wrote a poem about it, about its small purplish wrinkled head."

Corso stopped, took a deep drag off the cigarette Calliope was holding, and scrutinized me. Then he asked for the five hundred dollars.

I didn't have it. How was I going to get five hundred dollars? This man spent three years in prison! But Calliope saved me. (Women I didn't know seemed to rescue me just in the nick of time.)

"Gregory, that's not enough. You're cheating him," Calliope said, putting out her cigarette in the tiny glass bowl filled with rice and a stick of incense on a small shrine table in the lobby. She must've thought it was a sand-filled ashtray like the ones in front of hotel elevators.

"Ten black Cadillacs hauled Mrs. Lombardi's month-old son away," Gregory continued, ignoring Calliope, "to the cemetery. They had a high mass for it."

I thought it curious that Gregory would tell me that story. He didn't know what an impression his poem "Italian Extravaganza" had made on me. It was just a couple of lines, but I never forgot it. It was obvious now that neither did Gregory. Abandoned, orphaned by mixed-up kid parents, the little coffin was sort of Gregory's childhood—his was over too soon, too.

"I'll tell you about the other thing, after you give me the *mohney*," as he called it, drawing the syllables out. "My life isn't free, it isn't open to the public, you know."

I had my father's Diner's Club card; my mother made him give it to me for emergencies. This was definitely an emergency.

"Okay, come with me," I told Gregory and his girlfriend.

The three of us went down the long skinny staircase, leaving Naropa to go outside onto the crowded weekend mall at night. I took them to one of the drive-through banks where I cashed the checks my parents sent me to keep life and limb together while I received my sentimental education from the Beats. Gregory and Calliope played on the grass like a couple of young lovers, though Gregory was old enough to be Calliope's father, maybe even her grandfather.

"Don't give him your money until he tells you," Calliope said.

"Okay, okay," said Gregory. "This is the perfect place." And right there on the grassy patch next to the drive-in bank Corso acted out Jack's funeral, even his thoughts while viewing the casket and talking to Jack's wife.

Gregory Corso could've been a great actor. Al Pacino would make a great Corso. Corso would've made a great Al Pacino. It's no accident that Gregory came into the picture as a writer at the Poets

L
A
S
T

Theatre in Cambridge, Massachusetts. That's where he met Frank O'Hara and the other poets. He was a kind of protégé of Bunny Lang, the eccentric doyenne of the Poets Theatre, the sun around which all the poets and artists seemed to revolve. O'Hara had written about the three of them—Bunny and Gregory and Frank, in costume, bowing to one another and to the audience. He said they looked like jinxes. Gregory, though older now, still looked like the jinx O'Hara had remembered him to be.

He loved Thomas Chatterton, read him in prison. I, too, was obsessed with Chatterton, the seventeen-year-old poet genius who pretended to have found the long-lost, Old English manuscripts of a poet named Thomas Rowley, but in fact had written them all himself on old church parchment. Unable to support himself in London, he bought poison with the last few coins he had and died in a garret. I was in love with Chatterton's story. Gregory had brought Chatterton into even more romantic glory by reading him in a prison cell.

Gregory was only twenty-six when Bunny Lang discovered him living on the streets of New York, completely destitute. She asked the members of the Poets Theatre to take up a collection to pay Gregory to take care of the theater. He wanted to sweep up after everyone had left, to look for wallets and loose change. Gregory always seemed to be able to get people to take care of him. Bunny Lang arranged for him to live in a room kept by a young novelist at Harvard. Gregory made him construct a tent made out of dyed sheets and hang the sheets on metal poles for Gregory to live under at Eliot House. He continued to wear mostly black, though recently Calliope tried to get him to wear brighter clothing.

I was afraid to show him my poems, and dreaded the idea of giving a poetry reading at which Gregory might be present. I knew he talked back to the screen, as it were, shouting down other poets, confronting them about being phonies. "You're not a poet!" he had once yelled at Archibald MacLeish when he ran into him at Eliot House.

In Gregory's apartment, I saw a copy of an old play I'm sure he had written for the Poets Theatre called *In This Hung-up Age*. Beauty is a character in the play; she's a pill-popping saxophone player. Poetman is her opposite. I didn't want to turn into poetman, "a little magazine type with social complaints." I knew that Frank O'Hara loved Gregory's poetry, and that made Gregory even more of a legend to me.

O'Hara had the kind of sophisticated life I wanted to have in New York. At least I thought he did. His friends were all in love with him. Men and women. He didn't even seem ambitious for his poems, which were great anyway and seemed so tossed off, though of course they weren't. When he died after being hit by a dune buggy on Fire Island, an accident that sounds almost as lightheartedly strange as his own poems, he was barely forty years old. He died in 1966.

Ten years later, Gregory, O'Hara's friend, was standing on the grass waiting for me to give him some money. It sounds silly now, but at the time it was as if I had a physical connection with Frank O'Hara through his friend Gregory, and that's why I wanted to give Gregory the money. It was like buying a kind of membership that was going to get me into a world, not just a club. It was a world I thought I could live in forever. Like *Invasion of the Body Snatchers*, though I didn't fight sleep, I wanted them to come and get me. I wanted to speak their language, to sound like them, to dress like them, to be as open to the world and to experience the world as they did. I wanted their hipness and confidence to cover me like a blanket—I would awake calm, and hopelessly hip and new. But as someone once said, whistling in the dark hardly ever becomes music, and Gregory wanted his money right now!

"The funeral," I said, five one-hundred-dollar bills fanning out in my hand.

Gregory took the money and stuffed it in his pants pocket. Then he sat down on the grass and began to tell his tale.

"I saw Jack in the funeral parlor, everyone was there," he said. "I

L
A
S
T

wanted to take him up out of the coffin and throw him against the wall or something. It was a Buddhist or a Zen idea I had. I thought Jack would like it if I just took him and flung him across the room, like when John Barrymore died and all his buddies, Errol Flynn and W. C. Fields, they took him out of the funeral home and brought him back to Errol Flynn's house and they played poker and drank with him in a chair. A real Irish wake. I mean, it's just a body."

Gregory stopped and put his reading glasses on as if he could see his thoughts better.

"I would've been arrested, probably sent back to prison—or worse, the funny farm." Gregory peered at me over his reading glasses. "I know you're scared of me, but I'm not dangerous," Gregory continued, putting his hand on my cheek.

"I thought at the time you should end this medieval agony, the hypocrisy of the funeral! People in mourning for something that no longer exists. That was it. That's the last shot," Gregory said. "The last shot: I had to do something for my friend, my dear friend, but it only occurred to me when he was dead in his box."

Suddenly the brick, drive-through bank looked like a crypt. A sliver of moonlight hung in Gregory's hair. He stopped talking, got up, and he and Calliope disappeared into the night.

14. Rolling Thunder

"Make sure you get the money," William Burroughs snarled to Allen. "When a man asks for money you can't back down, you'll lose your self-respect." Ginsberg had come into Bill's apartment the day after the Naropa dance to tell him that he and Anne were setting out for Denver to attend the Bob Dylan concert that night. A huge storm was expected and the clouds were already passing over us. The sky looked like an iron vault.

I was setting up the mah-jongg table, wondering if anyone had found an extra ticket for me. I was too shy to ask. Bill and his son were going to be playing mah-jongg. I couldn't imagine the two Burroughses playing a game my mother and her girlfriends were playing on Long Island.

"Ask him about the money," Burroughs said again. Allen had written a letter to Bob Dylan asking him for $200,000 for Naropa.

"He's never going to give it to us, Bill. He doesn't even read letters like that," Allen said.

"Then get someone to read it to him," Burroughs snapped.

Allen was put on notice: ask for the money or have Burroughs walk away in disgust. I never wanted to see that happen. Burroughs seemed to live in a constant state of contempt, although I'm sure it was just the way that he talked and the fact that he looked like someone who had never completely gotten over trying to kick his heroin habit. He had the driest-looking skin I'd ever seen. Even his sweat looked dry. It also looked like I wasn't going to get to go hear Dylan under a thunderous Denver sky. The number of people and the number of tickets—the math just didn't look like it was going to come out in my favor.

Gregory could care less. He dropped by Burroughs's apartment holding his baby, Max, who had Corso's wild, dark, curling hair. Max ran around without clothes most of the time. He liked to run upstairs and poop in all the empty rooms. He seemed like one of those children brought back to civilization after years of being raised by wolves in the forests of India. Anne waltzed in, dressed like an Arabian princess for her rendezvous with Dylan. There was something definitely going on there, I thought. How great to be there. At least Antler wasn't invited either. Anne was actually wearing a sari—it was going to become completely see-through in the rain. I was even sorrier that I wasn't going. But Anne astonished me by asking if I wanted to come along.

My heart almost fell out of my chest. I could've kissed her toe rings, her cardinal-red lips. I couldn't believe that Anne, who seemed to all but ignore me, had come to my rescue.

But Allen cut me down from the heavens.

"No," he said. "I think he should stay with Gregory. He's got to start getting him to sit down to work, and I think he's taking the money I'm giving him and buying drugs again. I don't want the Kerouac School to start out with an overdose of a major poet."

I didn't know Allen well enough to beg him to let me come to the concert. I tried to make it look like it didn't matter to me, that looking after Gregory and scraping Max's poop off the rug was what I really wanted to be doing that night. In fact, I did want to help Gregory finish the book, but one night out of my sight wouldn't matter, and it was Bob Dylan in Denver! Maybe Allen would go backstage, maybe . . . I couldn't even begin to finish the thought. I thought of something Allen had told me, how in Big Sur, a poet had taken Dylan to see Henry Miller, who was pretty old even then. When the old novelist asked whoever had brought Dylan, "Would your poet friend like a drink?" Miller's third-person hospitality got under Dylan's skin. "Even my best friends didn't put me down that badly," Dylan later said. That's what I wanted to tell Allen.

After all, the long connection between Dylan and Ginsberg was one of the magnets that had first pulled me to the Jack Kerouac School. I harbored the secret thought that perhaps Allen's influence would prevail and that Dylan's first teaching job would wind up at Naropa: "The Milarepa Chair in Advanced Poetics—Dylan, Bob, instructor." In fact, Dylan wasn't even about to answer Allen's fund-raising request, at least Allen didn't think so, and now Burroughs was putting all this pressure on him to collect.

Allen did hope that Dylan would show up at Naropa. Allen wanted the movie Dylan was making during his Rolling Thunder tour to have its premiere at the Jack Kerouac School. Allen called it a "dharma movie"—it would later be released under the title *Renaldo and Clara*. Allen had already brought the director out to Boulder.

Allen explained to Burroughs that even after all this time, he didn't think he knew Dylan at all. He wasn't sure that Dylan

had a self, because of all the changes he'd been through. During
the Rolling Thunder Revue, Allen had asked Dylan if he was
enjoying himself, if he was experiencing any pleasurable moments
on the tour.

"Pleasure. Pleasure?" Dylan said. "What's that? I never touch
the stuff."

Allen left Burroughs's apartment and went back to his place to
get ready for the concert, with me following behind. I could tell
that Allen was nervous about seeing Dylan again. He said he never
really felt secure in that relationship. He said that he had gone
through a painful stage of being in love with Bob Dylan. "He was
skinny and had a big nose like you," Allen said to me while getting
dressed for the concert.

I had always hated my looks, but Allen comparing me to Bob
Dylan made everything all right, even Allen's making me stay
home and picking this of all days and all nights to nail my feet to
the floor as Gregory's keeper.

The two men liked to tease each other. Allen said that Dylan
brought out a sarcastic streak in him that he didn't know he had.
Allen teased Dylan a lot about religion, about God. "I used to
believe in God," Allen once told him. "Well, I used to believe in
God, too," Dylan had said. "You write better poems if you believe
in God, Ginsberg." He didn't want to have to ask Dylan for money.

Sometimes they went for years without talking. Allen said he
was too shy to call Dylan. He wrote him letters that Dylan ignored.
Then one day Dylan called him, answering Allen's letter on the
telephone. Allen had written to Dylan telling him how much he
loved his song "Idiot Wind," calling it "a national rhyme." Allen
sang a phrase to me while pulling on his socks, a blue and a black
one. "Idiot Wind / blowing like a circle around my skull / from the
Grand Coulee Dam to the Capitol." Allen said that was Dylan's
favorite line in the song, too. Allen said it appealed to the Buddhist
in him. The craziness on the left and the right. Allen said that
Dylan was a great poet—the Walt Whitman of the American pop
song—and instead of dedicating his book of songs *First Blues* to

Rinpoche, he thought it really should have been dedicated to Bob Dylan. Allen said it was always heartbreaking and thrilling to see Dylan. He thought he and Bob Dylan should have been lovers.

I didn't know what to say. I could tell he'd be upset if Anne stayed in Denver and spent the night with Dylan. "I introduced them," Allen said.

Gregory just didn't share their adoration of Dylan. He couldn't care less. "Everyone thinks Bob Dylan is writing about *them*," Gregory once told me. "I don't give a shit if I'm *in* a Bob Dylan song—I just want some of the royalties! I told Dylan I'd write him a poem for one song's royalties. I'll write him a beautiful poem in exchange for the royalties of 'Just Like a Woman.' That song's about Ginzy anyway. The woman in the song is really Allen—not about his being a faggot, just about his unrequited love for Dylan. Now you don't feel so cheated about that five hundred dollars, right?"

Allen said he wanted to take me somewhere before driving to Denver for the concert. If he sensed that I was disappointed about not being invited to meet Dylan, he didn't show it. As we left the apartment, the threatening sky had opened up and the rain began to pour. As we headed back toward Naropa headquarters in the rain, Allen said he wanted to go to the shrine room, to sit. That meant he wanted to meditate. I could tell whenever Allen was nervous or anxious about something. He always thought meditating would help. Sometimes he meditated when he thought his ego was getting too big. He was under a lot of stress: Everyone seemed to want something from Allen, especially his students. Eventually there would be quite a few. Sometimes kids would show up for registration without any money, and Allen would ask why they had come to school without funds. "I had a dream that I should come see you," one said. "I read 'Howl' and it changed my life. I thought maybe you needed someone to come take care of you." Sometimes young gay men would show up hoping Allen would take care of them, or at least make it easier for them to come out to their parents. "Would you tell them?" they'd ask. Sometimes Allen gave them money to go back home. Sometimes he took them to bed, then told them to go back to school and get married.

I thought most of the time Allen took all that attention with a lot of humor. Rinpoche certainly helped Allen take a more humorous view of himself and of his fame. Before meeting Rinpoche, Allen wasn't known for his sense of humor. You could never tell him a joke. He would always ask you questions about it—why the person in the joke did a certain thing and not another. Peter had a better sense of humor, but then he'd had a much sadder life.

When we arrived at the Naropa building, I didn't want to go into the shrine room. I had avoided it ever since I arrived at the Jack Kerouac School. I think I'd absorbed some of my parents' worry that I would become a Buddhist. They knew that Allen chanted *om,* and that he was Jewish, but that he was also a Buddhist.

The shrine room frightened me. It shouldn't have. It was quite beautiful really, with hundreds of red meditation cushions, a yellow sun in the middle of each one. It was a large room made to look like a Tibetan monastery, with mandalas hanging on the walls, and dragons breathing fire on bright yellow cloth. Allen felt at home there. He said that synagogues made him feel anxious and inadequate.

I worried about what would happen if I went into the shrine room, took off my shoes, and sat on the meditation cushion. I thought of my mother and my grandmother, and I suddenly realized that today was Friday, and they'd be lighting candles for the Sabbath. My mother wasn't even all that religious. After lighting the candles we'd sometimes all go out to the Flagship Diner in Freeport for bacon cheeseburgers. We were those kind of Jews. (That was then; she keeps kosher now.) My mother hated "the black hats," as she called them, the ultra-Orthodox Jews who threw rocks at your car if you drove through their Borough Park neighborhoods on a Saturday.

Allen liked asking me about my Jewish parents. He said being Jewish was one of his mother's obsessions, so maybe that was why

ROLLING

C

O

O

L

he turned his back on it. Naomi had suffered so much, and had made him suffer: maybe that's why Judaism caused him so much pain. He said seeing Hebrew letters in a prayerbook recently made him weep.

"I never understood the Jews' fear of death," he once told me. He said that Buddhism made him think of death all the time. I told him I was a *kohen*, and that I wasn't allowed near a dead body. I said that if I were a religious Jew, I wouldn't even be allowed at a funeral, which was okay by me.

"What about your own funeral?" Allen asked.

We stepped out of our shoes and left them at the threshold. In the beautiful, empty shrine room, which smelled like old shoes, incense, and Johnson's floor wax, Allen put me down on a meditation cushion. He straightened my back, he lit some incense, he bowed toward the elevated area where Rinpoche often sat, which had framed portraits of all the lineage holders. Allen said he wanted to initiate me into sitting, so that I wouldn't be so afraid of it.

Before we began, though, we talked about the Dylan concert. He must have sensed how badly I wanted to go.

"You know, Sam, you'd be doing me a great favor by looking after Gregory," he said. He added that he was hoping the rain would lift, and that he would be released of his longing for Bob Dylan's approval. I thought of that old song by Rodgers and Hart, with the line, "unrequited love's a bore." I hoped Dylan loved Allen and appreciated him. Allen was like an Indian alone in the shrine room praying for rain, except he was praying for the rain to stop. He thought meditating would help remind him that he should just enjoy the concert and not worry so much.

"If you stay and watch Gregory," he told me, "I have a surprise for you. I've arranged for us to watch the movie Dylan and I made together." He said that Sam Shepard wrote the screenplay for *Renaldo and Clara* (in 1976, I didn't know who Sam Shepard was), but that he, Allen, had created many of his scenes with Dylan. We were going to watch it at Gregory's house after the concert, projecting it onto one of Corso's blank walls.

"Gregory doesn't feel the same way about Dylan as the rest of us," he explained. "Gregory distrusts people with a lot of money, especially artists with money." I supposed that was because Gregory never knew where he was going to sleep from one night to the next. For a long time, when he lived in Europe, Gregory's address was just the American Express office. Once he was arrested for sleeping in the Parthenon.

After I tried sitting for a while, and Allen prayed for the rain to stop and to be delivered from Dylan-longing, he dropped me off at Gregory's apartment, as if I really were the baby-sitter.

Allen said good-bye and kissed me on the lips. Gregory ran up and kissed Allen on the lips, too. Baby Max, his soggy diaper dripping, clung to my leg and sat on my shoe. He liked to hold on and have me jump up and down like a pogo stick. Max's mother was a dark, very young woman. She didn't say very much. Calliope was nowhere to be seen.

Apparently, Gregory felt like he had to keep earning my $500, so he decided to tell me what Kerouac's wife had said when he showed up at Jack's funeral. "This'll be it," Gregory said, "this will square us."

15. Gilgamesh in Boulder

"The first thing Stella said to me when I came to the funeral," Gregory, smoking furiously, began, "she said, 'Gregory, why didn't you come sooner? Jack wanted to see you. Why didn't you come when he was alive?'

"I told her, 'How do I know when people are gonna die?' I have no idea. I wrote out a poem and stuck it in Jack's jacket, but there was already a piece of paper in there. I didn't read it. I wanted to know who else thought of that, putting a poem in there. Maybe it wasn't a poem—maybe it was a cleaning bill."

G
I
L
G
A
M
E
S
H

in Boulder

C

O

O

L

Before Gregory could finish his story, Allen interrupted, telling Gregory about his plans to show a rough cut of *Renaldo and Clara* at Gregory's apartment after the concert, but Gregory wasn't interested. He didn't want to see *Renaldo and Clara*, he wanted to meet Calliope and get high. He turned to me and said he was thinking of a great way to get money, and that he would discuss it with me tomorrow. Allen left, in a hurry to make it to Denver in time for the concert. I was left alone with Gregory, Max, and Lisa, his sullen wife.

He handed me two poems he said were meant for his book. He said one of them was a love poem to Shelley, which he wrote after having a dream in which he and Shelley were married. He said he never has thoughts like that in real life, but he has them in his sleep. I wondered why that wasn't a part of real life.

Gregory then informed me that my first job was to read the epic of *Gilgamesh*; he said he couldn't work with anyone who didn't know it. Furthermore, we would discuss it. I was supposed to read it to Max and his mother. With that, Gregory headed for the door, no doubt on his way to find Calliope and score some dope with some of my money.

Lisa didn't try to stop her husband from leaving. She just took Max in her arms and went upstairs. Max started crying. Gregory sang something from *La Traviata* to Max from the bottom of the stairs, and then he was gone.

"Gregory left this book for you," Lisa told me from the top of the stairs. "You have to read to us till we fall asleep." I climbed the stairs, a little apprehensively, picked up the book, and sat on the edge of her bed. Max was being breast-fed by his young mother. I tried not to look.

Gilgamesh, I found out later, was a kind of bible for Gregory—he loved quoting from it. It was the first book he was going to teach at the Naropa Institute. He already told me that he wasn't interested in my poetry—not yet, anyway. I thumbed, or as Allen liked to say, *thrummed* through the book, which I thought was kind of skinny for an epic. Gregory later said it was a shame we couldn't read it in Sumerian. Or rather, that he couldn't.

I started reading aloud: "Of him who knew the most . . . who made the journey; heartbroken; reconciled . . ." Max stopped breast-feeding and sat up in bed, leaning against his mother, with his wild bird's-nest hair, and Lisa with her sad eyes like those of a gypsy fortune-teller in a storefront window in Atlantic City.

Gilgamesh was a hero of the twenty-seventh century before Christ. He was a god of the underworld. No wonder Gregory loved him, having first read him in his prison cell. Statues of Gilgamesh appear in ancient burial rites—he's a kind of god of the dead.

I glanced over at Max and his mother; both of them were fast asleep on the great rumpled bed. There was no withstanding the power of Gilgamesh, I thought, "neither the father's son, nor the wife." I slunk down and read in a corner of the bedroom. I started to understand why Gregory loved the story of Gilgamesh so much. It was close to his heart because it was so close to his art: it was the story of Gregory's life as Allen Ginsberg's friend.

Gilgamesh is a work of about a thousand lines. Gregory seemed to know each one by heart, I would later discover. In the story, there is a Wild Man who is created by the gods because he's the only one who can match Gilgamesh. They become best friends and travel together. Both Gilgamesh and the Wild Man go on a journey searching for fame, but Gilgamesh wants true immortality. He wants unending fame, unending life. The Wild Man is not interested in that kind of quest.

It suddenly dawned on me: Everyone keeps thinking that Allen is the Wild Man, but he's not—*he's* Gilgamesh. Hadn't Rinpoche told Allen that he was too in love with his fame and his notoriety? Isn't that why he had made him go upstairs and chop off his beard, which Allen had saved in a cigar box? Gregory was always teasing Allen about wanting to be a rock star, about using his enormous energies in the wrong way, to serve the wrong master, as Gregory liked to put it. "Ginzy could be a great poet," Gregory would confide in me, "but he's a terrible judge of his own poems." Once Gregory asked Allen to show him what he considered to be his greatest poems. Allen gave him poems like "Punk Rock Your My Big

G
I
L
G
A
M
E
S
H

C

O

O

L

Crybaby," "Blame the Thought, Cling to the Bummer." Gone were "Supermarket in California" and "Sunflower Sutra," and in their place was a dreadful poem for Anne Waldman called "Pussy Blues."

I knew that poem; Allen had asked me to help him finish it. Allen was attracted to Anne. He used to like to tease her about sleeping with him. He said he sometimes wondered what it would be like to be married to Anne and even to have a baby. I didn't think it was very mature to write a poem to Anne called "Pussy Blues." He said the last thing you want to think about when you get old is maturity. He said only young people think about that. I felt embarrassed; I told Allen the poem shouldn't come from me. He said it wouldn't.

The poem had evolved out of a session of making up spontaneous blues songs while sitting in the empty bandshell of a park in downtown Boulder. It was the Fourth of July, when the whole nation was celebrating its two hundredth birthday, and we were watching the fireworks going off in the mountains. Allen sang: "You said you got to go home and feed your pussycat / When I ask you to stay here tonight. Where's your pussy at? / Hey it's Fourth of July / Say it's your U.S. birthday / Yeah stay out all night National Holiday / Tiger on your fence / Don't let him get away." And that became "Pussy Blues."

Gregory knew that it was Gilgamesh who ventures into the forest to cut down the great cedar and thus win all the glory. "My fame," Gilgamesh announces, "will be secure to all my sons." Gregory, I would come to realize, knew that his vagabond life was not conducive to being famous, as famous as Allen. "I've read stories about Allen in the *International Herald Tribune*," Gregory would later tell me. "I read about Ginzy all the time and think, no dog would eat the kind of food he has to eat. Penguin dust!" he shouted, reciting his own line from "Marriage," meaning *inscrutable*, the marriage of opposites, the fantastic and the divine, the silly and the stunned. But sometimes he used it as an expletive.

Had Gregory given me the key to his relationship with Allen by leaving *Gilgamesh* behind for me to read, while his wife and child, their heads thrown back and their mouths open in sleep, looked like they were in the netherworld reclining on the couch of death?

And then I read it: the last line in *Gilgamesh* about the one who enters the underworld without leaving anyone to mourn for him (a scribe who wanted his pen to dispense justice in the world): "No dog would eat the food he has to eat." *Gilgamesh* expressed Gregory's fear that Allen, the world-famous bard, and not Gregory—reprobate and drifter—would wind up emptied out by fame, alone and abandoned by all the young men who would leave him and begin families of their own. Gregory was obsessed with being alone at the end—being "motherless" and even "catless"—but at the time he saw that as Allen's fate, not his own.

I went downstairs, tiptoeing so as not to waken the sleepers. I sat on the couch and waited for Gregory, "the Mad Honeymooner," as he called himself in his great poem "Marriage," to come home to his wife. He certainly was raising Max, his latest baby, the way he imagined himself raising a kid in "Marriage"—making a rattle out of broken Bach records, tacking pictures of *The Flagellation* by della Francesca along its crib, and sewing the Greek alphabet onto its bib. Gregory wanted to build for Max's playpen a roofless Parthenon; instead, they all dwelled in an apartment in Boulder with constant traffic of strangers, Gregory's hot, New York City accent filling the rooms.

But Gregory didn't come back that night. I walked home in the early-morning light, "all the universe married but me."

16. Kerouac's Grave

Anne Waldman hadn't come home after the Dylan concert. Allen must've felt squeezed, jealous from both sides. Dylan didn't ask him to stay, and everyone assumed something was going on between Anne and Bob Dylan. (Anne had a boyfriend, Reed Bye, but I don't think he knew. He was a local guy, a roofer, with an

C

O

O

L

almost angelic, feminine face. Anne liked beautiful men—men who looked lovelier than their girlfriends. Reed Bye was sweet-tempered and he had a gentle manner, even though he stomped on people's roofs and most days ate his lunch above the treeline. He was writing poetry in his spare time, and Anne was giving him books to read.)

When I saw Allen the next day, he didn't look like he'd had a good time at the concert. He asked what we thought of *Renaldo and Clara*, and I had to tell him that we didn't see it. Sotto voce, I told him that Gregory didn't seem too interested. Trying to sound as if I didn't really care, I asked him about the Dylan concert.

He said that the concert was held during a driving rain, and that Dylan sang "Idiot Wind" as a tribute to Allen. He sang "A Hard Rain's a Gonna Fall" while it was falling.

As a kind of consolation prize, Allen brought a few of us together that evening to watch scenes from *Renaldo and Clara*—Billy Burroughs, Barbara Dilley, some of the Vadjra guards. But watching the movie only made me sad. I saw Allen beaming during the scenes he and Dylan were in, but I thought they were making fun of him. He took Dylan so seriously, he loved his music, he thought of it as great poetry. In the movie all the musicians called each other "poet," as if that were the highest compliment you could make to someone. I, myself, was beginning to wonder. I did, however, like the fact that Dylan had brought his mother on the tour. Some people said that whenever Bob sang "It's Alright, Ma (I'm Only Bleeding)," Mrs. Zimmerman would stand up and say, "That's me!" I thought that was incredibly cute. Allen liked it, too. "The mysterious Bob Dylan had a chicken-soup, Yiddishe mama," Allen told me, "just like us."

Allen said the most touching and moving experience for him on the whole tour wasn't in the movie. It was a visit with Dylan to Kerouac's grave in Lowell, Massachusetts. I know Allen was a Buddhist, and most Buddhists are cremated, but Allen dug graves. I don't mean with a shovel; he liked visiting them. He went to Poe's grave in Baltimore. He went to Apollinaire's grave in Père

Lachaise in Paris. At Jack's grave he and Dylan stood and read a section from Kerouac's *Mexico City Blues*, which was the first thing by Kerouac that Bob Dylan had ever read, when he was still a young man in Minnesota.

According to Allen, the poems in *Mexico City Blues* are really Buddhist poems, in that they're about the ego as an invisible man that wreaks havoc. You try to catch the ego as it leaves footprints in the snow, but it's too fast and too tricky. You just have to sit still and be patient, and wear it out. That's what Allen said I should do.

Allen and Dylan sat down on Kerouac's grave, and Dylan played Allen's harmonium, then he played a slow blues tune on the guitar. Allen said he made up a song on the spot about Kerouac as a kind of Horatio figure, his skull peering over the horizon looking back at Allen and this musician in a white hat, the two men sitting on Kerouac's chest, bothering his heavenly rest. The graveyard was littered with fallen leaves, and Dylan picked up a leaf that had fallen directly onto Kerouac's grave and put it in his shirt pocket.

"Which one of the *Mexico City Blues* did Dylan read?" I asked Allen.

He didn't remember. All he remembered was that he had picked out a poem for Dylan to read, but that Dylan had turned the page back and forth and decided to read the one on the opposite side of the page. Then Allen remembered the one he'd picked out. He went to his bookshelf and opened *Mexico City Blues* to the poem he had chosen for Dylan and read the lines, "The wheel of the quivering meat conception / Turns in the void. . . . I wish I was free / of that slaving meat wheel / and safe in heaven, dead."

There was another poem Allen had especially wanted to hear Dylan read to Kerouac's soul in heaven, a kind of list poem that names all the sufferings of existence. It ends with Jack kissing his kitten on its stomach, which he likens to "the softness of our reward."

I was sitting with Allen on the floor of his apartment. The movie had ended and all the other students and Vadjra guards had left. The carpet was gray as the ground in Lowell in winter. It was like being at Kerouac's grave. It was like being on the Rolling Thunder Revue. For me, sad about being left out of the concert, it was enough.

17. Last Words

The country was cleaning up after its giant birthday party, presided over by Jimmy Carter. There were still crushed cans of Billy Beer in the streets. Allen was gearing up for the first reading of the Jack Kerouac School, and he wanted everything to come off perfectly.

Antler was going to read from his book *Last Words*; he and Jeff were still carrying "their baby," as they called the book, still in manuscript form. It wasn't going to be published for at least a year. It was as if Antler and Jeff had conceived this book during some demented literary honeymoon. I couldn't believe they talked about it like that. Did William Faulkner talk about *As I Lay Dying* as if it were a fetus? I doubt it. But Antler did. At least on the days when he talked.

Allen introduced him. The reading took place in the shrine room. The Naropa High Command were all there, turned out because of Allen's pull with the Buddhist establishment at Naropa. Rinpoche kept everyone waiting for two hours. When he finally showed, he was with Osel Tendzin, his Vadjra regent, the man who would take over the teachings if Rinpoche died or decided to return to Tibet. (Not very likely, I thought.) The Vadjra regent's real name was Thomas Rich, and he once sold cars in New Jersey before coming to Naropa. A lot of the Buddhist students said he was a great meditator and Rinpoche's greatest student. He and his wife had just had twin boys, but there was a lot of talk and speculation that Osel Tendzin was gay.

The Jack Kerouac School turned out in force: the teachers—Bill, Anne, Allen, of course—and the second-generation Beats—Michael Brownstein, Larry Fagin, Larry's wife, Susan Noel (whose name Peter Orlovsky could remember only as Susie Christmas). Peter was there with one of his "ugly girlfriends," a young woman who was really quite sweet looking, an exceedingly tall and skinny redhead named Denyse King. Also present were about two hundred Naropa students from the various meditative disciplines, from flower arranging to archery to Buddhist psychology.

The reading finally began. But before Antler could get through even half of *Last Words,* Gregory decided to live up to his reputation as Wild Man. With Max on his lap, he leaped into that void Allen was always talking about.

"What are you not saying that you're kind of hinting at?" Gregory yelled at Antler after he'd finished one of his poems. "I mean that was beautiful, but so what? Do you think you have some monopoly on the way people check out of this world? What do you know, you're just some fag who likes to piss in the river, so you like nature! Well, take a shit in the woods and call it poesy!" Antler turned white as Gregory's rant became a rave. "Tell me something about life, tell me something about Molotov cocktails! Why don't you two get married, climb into the most bull-dykey outfits you own, maybe even a suit with pants, drop a cigarette on the floor and say, 'Oh, shit.' "

"Shut up, Gregory, let him read!" Allen tried shouting Corso down. Even Rinpoche stopped fanning himself with his fan so he could listen. This was gonna be good. "You don't have to have everyone hate you. Do you want to make the worst possible impression?" Allen yelled at Corso.

At that moment, I hate to admit it, I fell in love with Gregory. I thought he was wonderful. I thought he might kill me at almost any moment and not lose any sleep over it, but I loved him anyway. And then Gregory turned on Rinpoche, who was sitting serenely at one end of the room, slowly fanning himself and smiling his half-smile.

"You had a serious thought," Gregory said to Rinpoche, "but

L
A
S
T

Words

you blew it. Write down all your thoughts for five years and then see if you have any left!" Gregory told the holder of the Kagyu lineage of Tibetan Buddhism. "Then go for a hike on the weekends, and maybe you wouldn't come up with a major philosophy but you'll need new shoes, and while you're being fitted for them, you know, while your foot's in that metal foot with the black heel on it, you just might hit on some philosophical beliefs that could form the basis of a cult, then *he* [pointing to Antler] could join you and, dig it, you could save us all this bad poetry!"

Gregory was on fire. Even Max was smiling. He knew his father was swinging like Tarzan from tree to tree, and he started to shriek with happiness and run in and out of the rows of students and teachers sitting on the floor. Max flung off his little pants, and Gregory let him run wild and naked in the shrine room.

"Actaeon, hey Actaeon!" Gregory yelled at Antler. "You look upon the divine with a mortal's eyes!" Gregory kept comparing Antler to Actaeon in the Roman myth—the hunter, a mortal who accidentally stumbles upon Diana bathing in a stream. To punish him for his trespass she flings a handful of water in his face, causing antlers to sprout from his head. Actaeon is not only turned into a stag but the hunter's own dogs chase him down and kill him. He, apparently, was not worthy of gazing on a Divine.

For Gregory, myths were real; he invoked them and called upon them like an ancient Roman poet. Antler looked *furioso*; even his beard looked like it was about to catch fire. He looked as if he couldn't go on. In fact, he couldn't. He handed his manuscript over to Jeff, who finished the reading.

At the end of the program, Allen announced that there was going to be a party at Jane and Batan Faigo's house. They were a couple who taught tai chi at Naropa. Jane was short and chubby with a beatific blond face; her husband was from the Philippines, skinny with long hair and a sad face that flashed a gold tooth when he laughed, which was almost anytime he heard Gregory open his mouth. Jane and Batan were Gregory's guardians at Naropa. I was only his keeper, Allen's spy in the house of love.

I passed Gregory on the way out of the shrine room. I don't know if he saw me trying not to smile when he went after Antler, but I think maybe he knew how pleased I was, how weirdly proud of him, even though he was impossibly rude. As I filed out of the room, Gregory winked at me. The Wild Man had let me in on the joke, just a little.

18. The Lineages

Allen was always creating lineages where none really existed. He had an elaborate system of codifying groups of writers, creating circles within circles, like Dante, with the original Beats at the top in a kind of *Paradiso*. Whenever he was working on his lineages, he reminded me of an obsessed Mormon climbing the branches of his family tree, or a mathematician working out Fermat's theorem on a cocktail napkin. The covers of phone books and stray pieces of paper beside Allen's bed were filled with crossed-out names and names reinstated from exile. The New York School, which was really—let's face it—Frank O'Hara and his friends Kenneth Koch and John Ashbery; the San Francisco Renaissance, which included Peter Orlovsky, Philip Whalen, Robert Duncan, and Michael McClure; the Black Mountain poets Ed Dorn, Robert Creeley, and Robert Duncan. Then there were the "mid-American poets"— Allen's "Wichita vortex poets"—comprising Dick Gallup, Ted Berrigan, and Ron Padgett, all of whom had known each other as teenagers in Tulsa.

Allen kept another category he called simply "Women": Diane di Prima (who had been married at one time to Leroi Jones), Alice Notley (Ted Berrigan's wife), and Bobbie Louise Hawkins (who had been married to Robert Creeley, the one-eyed poet who would come to the Jack Kerouac School and try to teach me how to drive).

C

O

O

L

It occurred to me that even the women Allen bothered to mention in his lineage were the wives and girlfriends of the men poets he knew.

Then there were other categories, like third world (Miguel Algarin and Miguel Piñero of the Nuyorican café), gay and political poets, the meditation practitioners, and the music poets. One thing nearly every category had in common was that Allen had put himself in each one. He had written out his own name in every category, with the exception of the women's section. Allen's name was never crossed out, even in the category of ecological poets. Allen, who threw a temper tantrum when the landlord of the apartment complex had asked us to recycle soda cans. "I can't separate plastic from aluminum," Allen had shrieked one afternoon. "I can't tell the difference, and besides, I have important work to do!"

Ginsberg was always fighting with his ego. After all, hadn't Allen written once in a poem that he wanted to be the most brilliant man in America? I think he *did* want that. He also wanted to be rid of his ego. But he craved attention. That's also why he had come to Naropa, not just to rest his weary, world-wandering bones but to have students and lovers, in order to feed the lineage. "Meat for the synagogue," he would say. "The best teaching is done in bed," Allen was always reminding me.

He wanted to make love to his students, seduce them, and be seduced by them, to whisper Shakespeare and Milton to young men who had already fallen for Allen through his poetry. For Allen, the great teacher was Socrates. Allen used Eros to teach Whitman. What better way to receive knowledge than laying your head on the teacher's belly, like playing a tape to learn a language in your sleep?

At first, Allen's sexual candor scared me. I wasn't a prude. I certainly didn't want to be one. After all, I didn't want to have to disappoint him. I wanted Allen to love me without taking me to bed. I was starting to think that was impossible.

"Would you like to join in the fun?" Allen asked one night before jumping into the hot tub with Peter, both of them already naked.

"I'm here to protect Burroughs," I said.

"What from?" Peter asked. "He hasn't needed anyone's protection so far."

"He sure does now," I said. I don't know why I said it. Maybe I was thinking about myself, or maybe because Burroughs always looked so sad to me. People always thought of him as the toughest *hombre* in literature, the man who saw everything and who sees everything in the future, all of it terrible. I never thought so. I thought Burroughs, Allen, even Corso (liar, poet, thief, and lifelong junkie) all shared a kind of crude tenderness, an almost habitual gentleness. It just wasn't universal. It was limited to their relations with the people they knew, the people they felt "normal" with. Burroughs, with his sad bony face, looked like someone who you would've thought was solely responsible for the atomic bomb. Allen Ginsberg had a heart as a big as a refrigerator.

Then there was Patrick Chandler, a musician who often accompanied Allen on his reading tours. He was a young, longhaired, skinny kid who had followed Allen to Naropa and who had a beautiful girlfriend with a name like a Dylan song—Ruthie. She looked like a gypsy. I hadn't been able to put two words together to talk to her. She never wore shoes, like Ava Gardner in *The Barefoot Contessa*. She and Patrick seemed very much in love. Yet Allen seemed to love Patrick.

One night I walked in on Allen without an appointment. I had screwed up my courage, and I was just going to do what the other poets did without thinking: drop in on Allen for a chat and a cup of tea. The apartment was quiet. I wandered over to the corner of the living room where Allen and Peter kept their meditation shrine. A trail of incense still burned from the shrine, with its red cloth, a *zafu* (the square, red-and-yellow cushion for sitting practice), and picture of Rinpoche in a tiny gold frame. A woman's cry came from upstairs.

I thought someone was in trouble.

There seemed always to be people I didn't know in Allen and Peter's apartment, people *they* didn't know, either. I ran upstairs.

T
H
E

C

O

O

L

Ruthie, Patrick, and Allen, naked as the truth, were rolling around on Allen's bed, with Allen being kissed and fondled by them both. I stood there, like Gregory Corso staring out of his Twelfth Street apartment so many years ago, on the Lower East Side. I was transfixed by the sight of Allen in bed with a woman, and Patrick in bed with Allen. I thought Patrick was straight, and I thought Allen was queer, but Eros had turned everything on its head.

The two of them were biting Allen's nipples like he was a gift from the Chinese—a giant panda in the National Zoo. What would I say to them the next time I saw them at the Naropa school? Did they know I had seen them all together? Maybe I was just being a hopeless square. My thinking was foggy, my mind not quite right, as I crept out of the threshold of Allen's bedroom. Peter was waiting to catch me at the foot of the stairs.

Peter could tell I was distraught. He sat me down and patiently explained to me how Patrick and Ruthie and Allen had been going to bed with each other for years. I asked Peter if Allen's affairs ever made him jealous. Peter said he wasn't jealous and that he liked to have sex with Ruthie and Patrick, too, but that lately he just wanted to have sex with girls. He said again that he would like to have a family.

"I like ugly girls," Peter said. "I prefer to make love to ugly girls, because they treat you nice and they don't leave you. The sex is better because they are so grateful."

I wondered if Peter worried about what people would think, especially girls, about his philosophy. Peter said that homely girls made the best mothers. He asked if I was still upset at seeing Allen with Patrick and his girlfriend, and then he laughed. (Peter's laugh sounded like he was clearing his throat; it was more like the imitation of a laugh.) I pretended to Peter that I wasn't scared, or confused, or bothered at all by what I had seen.

I had come to Naropa ready to learn about Blake, to listen to Allen talk about the four Zoas—Blake's four principles of human nature: reason, feeling, imagination, and, of course, the body. But I wasn't prepared for the final Zoa—to see Allen in bed with his guitarist and his guitarist's girlfriend. But why not? I hated my own prudery. I hid it from the Beats. I vowed to conquer my shyness if it killed me.

Later, much later, after I had been at the Jack Kerouac School for more than a year, I was introduced to Allen's psychiatrist, a handsome, middle-aged Italian woman. The two of us walked to the old cowboy hotel, the grand-looking Boulderado, and we sat on the veranda looking out at the foothills of the Rocky Mountains. She ordered a gin and tonic and I sipped a scotch and soda. I had never had scotch, but I ordered it because it was the only drink I knew because my uncles were scotch drinkers, so my mother always had J&B in the house for their visits.

I told her about what I had seen that night in Allen's bedroom, and about Peter's desire to be with a woman and to have children. In her thick Italian accent, she said that she thought the books would always get it wrong. She believed that Allen Ginsberg was essentially a straight man, but that he was in love with the idea of being Walt Whitman, in love with the idea of being the holder of a lineage. Without children, she explained, this is how Allen passed down the tradition of Whitman. She thought that Allen wasn't sexually incompatible with women and that he did have sexual involvements and crushes on women. Anne Waldman was his latest infatuation.

"For Allen," she said, "homosexuality is an incendiary device, a Molotov cocktail to throw into the windows of polite society. The real homosexual of the group," she added, "was Jack Kerouac."

Jack Kerouac? The he-man football hero from the hardscrabble shoe town of Lowell? Kerouac, with his ruggedly handsome, leading-man good looks, was the truly gay one among the Beats? Allen's psychiatrist said that Kerouac suffered from the fear that coming out as a gay man would crush his mother; he also thought that it was simply unmanly to be queer. No wonder Kerouac drank and looked so miserable in that photograph Allen had taken of him during Kerouac's last visit to Allen and Peter's apartment, five years before the end of his life.

Once when Allen was developing some of his photographs, I stood by his side in the small darkroom in the basement of the

T
H
E

Lineages

C

O

O

L

apartment complex. I watched as two of the many photographs that Allen had taken of Jack began to appear in their chemical baths. Side by side, in two separate trays, two images began to appear of Jack, just seven years apart. They looked like two different people, and in some sense they were. The earlier photograph, taken against Burroughs's garden wall in Tangier in 1957, just after *On the Road* was published, showed a cautious, handsome man wearing a newsboy's cap, a plaid lumberjack shirt open at the neck, with the glimpse of a T-shirt underneath. It must have been chilly in the garden of Burroughs's villa. Kerouac looks alert, smart, somewhat suspicious, but independent and ready for whatever the world will throw at him.

Right next to that image, under the red light of the darkroom, the second picture came into focus. This one was taken in Allen's East Fifth Street apartment on the Lower East Side in 1964. Kerouac sits in a chair next to his packed bags, holding his head in his right hand. He's wearing big, heavy dress shoes and a bulky checked sports coat that looks as if his mother had picked it out for him. But it's his face that haunts me—the face of a broken, heavy man waiting at a bus station who has made too many wrong decisions. He's scowling, lost in some sad, deep memory. Allen wrote, "The thing about this picture is how much Kerouac had begun to look like his late father, a kind of W. C. Fields shuddering with mortal horror."

I remember Peter telling me that he and Allen had given Jack a "blow job, as a going-away present" the last time they saw him, but Jack had just sat there without enjoyment, scowling and bored as the two men huddled together between his legs. It was simply too late for pleasure, too late for anything to make Kerouac happy.

Jack Kerouac never made it to the Jack Kerouac School. I was starting to think he would've hated it, but he might have at least liked the mountains of Boulder. Allen said once that Kerouac had wanted a quiet old age, a kind of hermitage in the woods where he could write his books. Because Kerouac was so important to Allen, he was the invisible dean of Naropa.

On the Road had brought me here, even though I didn't drive or even have a license. But I wanted to be Jack's passenger. I thought the trip was still on. For Kerouac, Neal Cassady's death in 1968 in San Miguel Allende, Mexico, never really happened. Everyone said that Jack kept expecting Neal to come back—or at least to call him. It was dawning on me that, in the same way, that's how Jack existed for Allen. He wasn't really dead. How could he be? Perhaps that's why the name of the school made so much sense to Allen, even though he always seemed to be a little embarrassed about it.

I didn't know then that Kerouac had moved in with his mother and had died in Florida, a place he loathed. I didn't know he hated hippies and was proud of our troops in Vietnam. To honor Kerouac, I thought, I should probably have joined the army! I learned later that Jack was put out when someone had suggested that *On the Road* had helped give birth to the hippies. Boulder was certainly full of them now, their ponchos filling the parks on weekends, like one enormous, scratchy Mexican blanket that just made me sneeze.

And it was Kerouac's books that had turned Ginsberg, Burroughs, Corso, Gary Snyder—and so many others—into myth. Kerouac had intended *On the Road* to be one long, shambling book of his life, with the same characters running through all of the books. It was the "maiden aunties" again—the editors and legal departments—who had made him change all the names from book to book. But it didn't matter; I knew them all. By coming to Boulder and entering the Jack Kerouac School, I wouldn't be taught just by Allen Ginsberg, but by Leon Levinsky of *The Town and the City*, Irwin Garden from *Vanity of Duluoz*, Alva Goldbook of *The Dharma Bums*, Carlo Marx from *On the Road*, and Adam Moorad from *The Subterraneans*. And it wasn't just William Burroughs crying over Jack London that I had witnessed, it was Old Bull Lee from *On the Road*, and Bull Hubbard from *Desolation Angels*. It wasn't merely Gregory Corso reciting *Gilgamesh*, but Yuri Gligoric in *The Subterraneans*, and Raphael Urso, one of the *Desolation Angels*. They were all here with me now, at the Jack Kerouac School— not disembodied, nor merely ashes, like Neal. The film of death no longer obscuring my eyes, I could see their genius flashing wildly before me and even hear sweet singing above what Allen liked to call "the ingrate world."

19. A Junkie's Gift

Billy Burroughs didn't look so good. I'd been at the Jack Kerouac School for only a couple of weeks before he started looking like a ghost. No one stopped him from drinking. Encouraged by the Westies (who liked it when he drank because he was funny and talkative) and treated invisibly by his father, Billy seemed to be disappearing even more deeply into alcoholism. He loved alcohol the way his father loved heroin.

Allen and Anne thought it best that Billy move into a rooming house run by students of Rinpoche's, people Allen described as sane and compassionate, who could keep an eye on Billy. Of course, the Buddhists in the house had no interest in him at all; they considered him an undesirable alien. He was too antisocial for them, too unsavory. They liked dressing up like Rinpoche and cultivating at least the appearance of wealth and success, whereas Billy wore his poverty like a badge of honor.

The smell of alcohol filled the third floor of the Naropa building where Billy lived. When he felt like eating, he ate candy bars, or food with curry—tuna fish, scrambled eggs—whatever it was it had to be doused in curry powder, the kind that made your eyes tear. Poor Billy always complained about his hemorrhoids. He said it was the one thing he had inherited from his father. "My father never had a completely functioning asshole," Billy said. "The toilet bowl was always full of blood."

Billy had written some wickedly funny books. Anne Waldman said his novel *Kentucky Ham* had become a classic. Billy loved satire. Sometimes he liked to read Jonathan Swift to me over his breakfast cereal (Lucky Charms was the only cereal he could eat because his teeth weren't very strong and the marshmallows were easy to chew.) I don't think Billy was even thirty years old when I met him.

Allen asked me to drop in on Billy from time to time and report back to him. He would then let Burroughs know how his son was doing. I never understood why Burroughs couldn't just walk over there himself, or call him up on the phone.

I liked Billy. I didn't like the fact that he seemed so unhappy all the time; with his aging Dennis the Menace face, he seemed to be on the verge of killing Mr. Wilson, or at least poisoning his dog. He liked taking me to a workingman's bar on the outskirts of Boulder, where women danced down a runway and took off their clothes. I had never been in such a place before. Billy almost never looked at the girls. He would order a double shot and lean his elbows on the counter. A lot of college students came to this bar, sat in booths, and idly drank their beers, staring at the sports on TV or covertly watching the girls at the edge of the runway. Billy seemed more comfortable here than with Allen's crowd or with his father's friends. I thought perhaps Billy felt the way I did about my parents' friends, about not wanting to socialize with them, thinking they were all stiffs who had terrible taste in everything—clothes, music, their politics beyond the pale. It was hard to believe anyone could think that about Allen Ginsberg and William Burroughs, but if you grew up around them, if your father's work was writing *Naked Lunch*, then maybe the Beats were just a bunch of old beatniks to Billy.

"You know what Lenny Bruce once said?" Billy asked me one night at his favorite bar. "There's nothing worse than an aging hipster." Billy then asked me if I liked his father, or if I thought his father was mean. I didn't know what to say. I wondered why these two men seemed so locked away from each other. I couldn't tell if it was William, as Anne liked to call him, who didn't know how to give as a father, or if it was Billy who simply refused his love. I couldn't imagine William Burroughs telling his son he loved him. I thought of love as a country that William Burroughs knew nothing about. I hoped I was wrong.

C

O

O

L

Billy was getting drunk again, which was the only way he could handle the great livid scar of his life. Suddenly, he grabbed me by the arm.

"How can I believe you like me?" he demanded. "How can I believe you like somebody you know nothing about? You don't know anything about me! You don't know where I've been. You don't know what life is like for me. If it wasn't for us barbarians, the world would have no art, no beauty."

Billy was working himself up into a rant. He said, "I don't care about art, and I don't like beauty." He was perspiring and breathing pretty hard by now, and I thought he might pass out. I was worried; I couldn't drive him home. He was trembling. I felt sorry for him. I thought about my own father, how sometimes in the car, on long trips up to the Catskills to visit my grandmother, I would dare myself to say, "I love you," just so I could figure out if he would answer me.

"No one is what he seems on the surface!" Billy shouted. "We all come from deep springs."

I thought about how he came from a very deep spring— William Burroughs seemed unfathomable to me—and how Billy's father was a kind of ghost haunting his son's life.

"My father offered to give me a kidney, if I needed it," Billy said bitterly. "He was excited about giving it to me. A junkie's kidney. What a gift."

20. "Who's Minerva?"

By my fourth month at Naropa—it was now September—I realized I had to stop calling my parents. It didn't help to be this lonesome and hear their voices.

One afternoon in Gregory's apartment, at work on what would become *Herald of the Autochthonic Spirit,* the book of poems

Gregory had taken money from a publisher to write, I would sneak upstairs and use his phone to call Long Island. A bit of larceny was creeping into my soul the longer I hung around Corso. Life around Gregory was like that musical I had tried out for in seventh grade, *"Oliver!,"* with Gregory Corso as the Artful Dodger teaching us our trade. In fact, Billy's and Gregory's Westies, the pale-faced gang of Irish amphetamine kids, often brought things they'd lifted back from Denver, their pockets filled with watches, spoons, gold chains; they'd dump them on the kitchen counter and Gregory would send me upstairs to work while he sifted through them.

The only people at Naropa I seemed to know at all were waiters, as I ate out for every meal, and the core faculty of the Jack Kerouac School. The other poetry students were just beginning to drift in. I supposed that the start of the fall term would bring the lemmings out to Boulder to sit at Allen's feet. They weren't even here yet and I was already jealous of sharing the Jack Kerouac School with any other students. On the other hand, I was starved for some co-respondents, some comradeship, someone to read my poems to, someone who wouldn't laugh at me, someone I could woo with the constellations of the stars—in short, a girlfriend.

Gregory caught me on the phone with my mother.

I had sneaked upstairs to make a long-distance call while he was supposedly working. My father always asked the same thing whenever I called: "Is the school accredited yet?"

"Well, not since the last time we spoke," I said, "which was Sunday. But they are preparing for a committee of people to walk through the school for a few days next month." It was true. Naropa would somehow have to get itself together and look like a real school for at least a week. It was going to be hard. Gregory would have to be on his best behavior. Burroughs would have to take the cure again, and not start talking about a Martian invasion of the Midwest. And Allen and Peter would have to live like two maiden

"WHO'S

Minerva?"

aunts in a parsonage. And I was going to be their model student, appearing in class every day with a bunch of extras we picked up on the street to act as students. I hoped it wouldn't come to that. But it was going to be close.

Gregory suddenly busted into the bedroom and caught me red-handed.

"Don't be such a pussy. Stop calling your parents every day!" Gregory shouted, and then he grabbed the phone out of my hand.

"What's your mother's name?" Gregory asked me, putting the phone to his curly-headed ear.

"Marion," I said, trembling with embarrassment.

"Minerva," Gregory shouted into the phone. "We have your son, it'll cost you ten thousand dollars to get him back. You can get it—you, who invented the bridle, you carry the thunderbolt in your pocketbook, get . . . what's your father's name?"

"Seymour," I practically whimpered into the carpet. "Seymour Kashner."

"Great name," Gregory said.

I perked up. I was always shy about my father's name, it was so old-fashioned and made him sound like a wimp, or an egghead, when in fact he was neither. An older father (he was thirty-five when I was born, his first child), he had even boxed for a while during the Depression. Gregory seemed to sanctify his name for me, even though he was coming in for the kill.

". . . get the king of Sidon to pay a king's ransom for this kid. The kid's excited about his new life, although he refuses everything: he refused our hashish . . ."

"Not true!" I sprang to my feet and tried to wedge myself between Gregory and the phone. "Not true!" What was I saying? I meant that what Gregory was saying wasn't true.

"And he refuses our opium, our *kif* . . ."

"No, no, don't listen to him," I yelled into the phone, sounding far crazier at that moment than Gregory himself.

"He even refuses our camel juice. Refuses camel juice, just imagine! And what's wrong with this kid, he refuses to get fucked!"

/ 127 /

Oh, no. He didn't say that, did he? I might as well be on drugs
after all. And to think that I had bragged about Gregory when my
mother asked about my "professors." My poor parents. And here I
was, the first in my family even to go to college. "All right, I'm
sorry," Gregory said into the phone. "He's shy. It's not your fault.
Maybe he's just having a hard time," Gregory told my mother,
"staying off the junk." Gregory was laughing now, very pleased
with himself. "Those first few weeks sans junk, Minerva, they're
very hard. He's holding up beautifully," Gregory reassured her.
"He'll be interested in girls after that," he said. "Good to talk to
you, too, Minerva. Did you build a little Parthenon for Shmuel
when he was a boy? Penguin dust!" Gregory spritzed into the
phone.

"Here," Gregory said, letting the phone drop into my lap, "she
wants to talk to you."

I thought I had lost the power of speech. I was going to be the
youngest patient at the Rusk Institute. Gregory Corso would be
written on my chart as the cause of my debilitating stroke.

"Who's Minerva?" my mother asked.

I waited for Gregory, a little too delighted with himself, to
leave. He went downstairs where I could hear him recounting the
phone call to a room full of people. (Oh, please don't let one of
them be Allen or Burroughs, I prayed silently.)

"Who's Minerva?" my mother asked again.

"She's a goddess," I said. "Zeus's daughter; she sprang from his
head."

"A goddess! What a sweet thing to say, he sounds very nice,"
my mother, Minerva, said. "It's cute how they want money for
you."

"What did you say to him?" I asked.

My father, who was on the other line in his downstairs office,
said he told Gregory it was like "The Ransom of Red Chief," the
O. Henry story where the boy is kidnapped, but he's such a terror
that the parents make demands of the kidnappers before they'll
even consider taking him back.

"W
H
O'
S

Minerva?"

C

O

O

L

"Oh," I said. I didn't know whether to be relieved or not, worried I might have to spend the rest of my life here.

"Are you eating?" Marion asked.

"Is he eating!" my father said. "Have you seen my Diner's Club bill for May and June?"

"Well, he has to eat," Marion said.

Suddenly, the two of them were having an argument over the telephone about me, without talking to me, over the two extensions in their house. Then I remembered why I had come to the Jack Kerouac School in the first place. And to think that Kerouac went home to live with his mother—after all those years on the road!

"Thank you for keeping us posted," my father, the king of Sidon, said. "And give Allen Ginsberg our love."

"We love you, you're our favorite poet," my mother said. How close embarrassment is to tears, I thought, and hung up the phone.

Downstairs, Gregory, baby Max, and some of his friends were all waiting for me—all sucking their thumbs. Max was the only one not making fun of me. I vowed never to call my parents from Gregory's again. Not ever.

21. Shopping with Corso

It was hard for Gregory to make friends. In prison, it had been really hard. He said poets make natural friends, "so how come we're not friends?" he asked me one day when we had decided to go shopping for new clothes. The air had turned crisper and there was that faint, exciting feeling that the season was about to change. We both wanted to be outdoors.

"Because of my job, because Allen wants me to chain you to this rock," I said, patting the chair and the desk where Gregory's poems were scattered like a bad still life among old donut bags and mugs of coffee and very rumpled Penguin paperbacks. They looked like English editions of poems: *Gilgamesh*, Chatterton, Rimbaud. (Anne was always comparing Gregory, when young, to Rimbaud. Allen did the same thing; he said we know what Rimbaud would have looked like if he'd kept writing poetry.)

Gregory didn't spend as much time with Allen and Burroughs and the other writers. He always drifted away. He liked to go off on his own. He said that it had taken him a while to become friends with Burroughs and Allen. He said that Kerouac once described him in a book as a "mooch"—"and that's just because I once asked him for a couple of bucks." Allen told me that if I wanted to know what Neal Cassady was like, I should get to know Gregory. He said they had a lot of things in common. They were both raised in a string of foster homes and they both became petty criminals, although Gregory wasn't a very effective street thief, Allen said, "but he tried." Like Neal, he had fallen in love with Stendhal and Dostoyevsky.

Gregory's clothes were a wonder to me. He always went to vintage clothing stores to buy his wardrobe. So on a brilliant azure day, just after classes had started, we left his apartment and headed to the VFW Thrift on Pearl Street.

We browsed around the tired bins of used clothing, in a vast room that smelled like my parents' basement after it had flooded. I managed to find a nice-looking Hathaway shirt and held it up for Gregory, but he just stuck out his tongue like he was throwing up. He then picked up a discarded postman's shirt with a U.S. Postal Service patch on the sleeve and tried it on over the shirt he was wearing. Eureka.

Next Gregory picked up a stovepipe hat that collapsed into a pancake; when you banged the rim it popped up again. Having exhausted his cash for the day, he asked me to buy the shirt and the stovepipe hat for him. Then he looked for the blue shorts that he said should've come with the postal worker's outfit. He found it

SHOPPING

buried beneath a monstrous ball of socks. Gregory asked me to buy that for him, too. I told him I would, but he must have noticed some hesitation on my part, because he immediately said that the whole ball game wasn't about money, it was about generosity.

"I want you to separate from your parents," he said, "and the best way to do that is for me to separate you from their money." He was really becoming Yuri Gligoric from *The Subterraneans*, making up the laws of the world as he went along.

After buying Gregory his clothes, he walked out of the store with a pretty little dress he had found for Calliope, rolled up inside one of the legs of the postal clerk's shorts. The dress was only $4.75 but I guess Gregory wanted to stay in practice. Afterward, I took him to lunch.

We waited on line at a health food store called Workingman's Dead. It was run by fans of the Grateful Dead, and the album *Workingman's Dead* was always playing on the record player. I had brought William Burroughs here the day before. Burroughs had stood on line for about a minute, looking over the sandwiches being prepared for customers holding their plastic trays. Burroughs said he couldn't possibly eat any of the food.

"I hate sprouts," he snarled. "They put them on everything they serve. Eating sprouts is like going down on a robot." We had to depart the premises "lest our health be seriously compromised," he insisted. "This food cannot possibly be good for anyone who has experienced a real meal. There is clearly a conflict of interest here between politics and taste. And, besides," Burroughs groused, his gravelly voice rising over the music, "it makes you shit, and hell already exists in my asshole." I figured that was a reference to the family hemorrhoids that Billy had mentioned. "We should scram, Salmonella Sam," Burroughs said. I held the door open for him.

Gregory, on the other hand, wasn't all that bothered by the food—beans and rice, tuna salad nestled on a vast aluminum tray, cooled off by an electric fan.

Gregory and I sat down with our trays. I looked over at his

Mexican plate special, which he was hungrily tearing into, hunched over his tray as if someone might snatch it away from him.

"How's your food, Gregory?" I asked.

" 'How's your food, Gregory?' " he repeated back to me, mimicking my concern. "How's yours?" he shouted. "Just let me eat."

I sat there not saying anything. I must've looked a little wounded. I still wasn't used to the idea that frankness was the fashion among the Beats. It was usually the preface for saying something rude.

I decided a frontal attack was best called for. "What do you really think of me? Down deep, I mean?" I asked Gregory. He looked up at me, rice sticking to his stubble of beard.

"People who aren't frank with each other have something to hide," Gregory said. "In limited quantities I'm very fond of you," he said. "In fact, you're one of my nearest and dearest friends here, and I don't make friends that easily."

I didn't believe him. I knew him to be a liar who also spoke the truth. Besides, he had already hurt my feelings.

Seeing my unhappiness, Gregory offered to tell me about "the pushcart incident." He thought that telling me a story—something I had already read about in *The Subterraneans*—would make everything better.

"Shmuel," he began, "I was in a bar named Fugazi's, back in New York, with Jack Kerouac. We left the bar and walked through Washington Square Park. That's when I saw this pushcart. 'Get in,' I told Jack, 'and I'll push you to Ginsberg's place.' "

So Kerouac and two girls they were with got in the pushcart, and Gregory pushed them through the park.

"They were looking up at the stars from this pushcart," Gregory reminisced, a strange light coming into his eyes. "I was pushing this thing so beautifully! Then I stopped in front of Allen's place. But that wasn't cool, because the landlord noticed the pushcart, and Allen's place is supposed to be safe, no den of thieves. The landlord didn't approve of the pushcart in front of the house, so he involves Ginzy, who had already thrown the apartment key

SHOPPING

with Corso

C

O

O

L

down to Jack." That was the only way to get into Allen's New York apartment—whoever was in had to throw the key out the window because there wasn't a working buzzer or intercom. "So Ginzy and Jack have a little fight about it, and then Jack throws the apartment key back at Allen. So now Allen is mad at us, mad at *me*.

" 'You've compromised the security of my home,' he yells at me from his third-floor window. Allen threw this hissy fit, and on top of that, he has this compassion for the poor shmuck who had his pushcart stolen!

" 'No, Allen,' I had to explain to him. 'No, you don't understand. You don't know the street. Have no worry for this poor bum. The many bums with their pushcarts, they dispose of them at the end of long bum days. The mafia really gobbles up the pushcarts for scrap.'

"We had a beautiful time in that pushcart," Gregory continued, lost in the memory of it, "and the pushcart had the best time that a pushcart ever had! These two friends, Jack and Allen, are fighting, and I'm thinking, 'Uh-oh, I fucked up again. I'm always doing something stupid and causing old friends' arguments.' I'm a pain in the ass, but in a nice way. It's in Kerouac's book, but all changed around."

After lunch I followed Gregory down the narrow stairwell and out into the blinding sunshine on Pearl Street. "I'll drive you home in a bicycle basket," he said, still trying to make up for having hurt my feelings.

Gregory ran across the street to where a lot of student bikes were parked. He picked one out, a girl's bicycle. "Get on," he said.

I held his new old clothes in a bag clutched to my chest while I climbed up on the handlebars; Gregory rode up the killer hill on this stolen girl's bike. I didn't think we were going to make it up the hill; I didn't think Gregory had the strength. The bike sputtered. We fell off the bike and spilled onto the grass.

"She'll look for it and find it here," Gregory said. "Maybe she'll come to us asking about it, and she will be beautiful and wonderful and become the mother of your bicycle children." And then he was off, leaving me to prop up the bike against a city hall statue of Lewis, without Clark, looking out over the horizon.

22. Beat Faculty Meeting

Anne came back from Denver two days later—in white face. She wore a turban and her face was frozen behind a mask of plaster. It was hard for her to speak. She told Allen on the way upstairs to meet Burroughs and Corso for a Kerouac School faculty meeting that Dylan had made up her face to look like his, and that all the women in the Rolling Thunder Revue took to wearing these commedia dell'arte masks, onstage and off.

I accompanied Allen to the faculty meeting. At first there was some debate as to whether or not I should be present when my teachers set school policy, being that I was a student and not just Allen's assistant. But Allen argued that my presence would save a lot of bother—notices wouldn't have to go out, I would be there when decisions were made, I'd be taking the minutes of the meeting. So I stayed.

At the beginning of the meeting, Peter announced that he had gone for thirty straight days without masturbating; he told the faculty that this was a record for him. Rinpoche had told him that it wasn't a good idea, although there was a perfectly reasonable Buddhist explanation for abstaining, Peter said, but he couldn't remember it.

Anne reclined on the couch in the faculty lounge and looked like Sarah Bernhardt under her turban and béchamel-colored facial mask. She wondered out loud where the other students were. "Where are my girls?" she moaned.

"They're coming," Allen said, and everyone laughed.

I scribbled a handful of notes in my terrible penmanship.

C

O

O

L

Someone was going to have to read this, I thought, so I tried to write everything out in capital letters. When Anne asked me to read something back, I couldn't make out my own handwriting. All of a sudden, Peter asked Anne if Bob Dylan had a clean asshole.

"Does he keep his asshole clean?" Peter asked, in that deep voice and the same grave tone he used for everything, even when asking me if I wanted chocolate syrup in my milk (the same drink with which he would greet me every time I saw him for a year, because I had asked for it the first time we met. And I always felt I had to drink it; eventually I found a way of feeding it to one of Gregory's cats).

Anne pretended to be a little put out with Peter. Anne loved the Beats more than anyone. She forgave them everything. She said they were a national treasure. I always agreed with her, even as I started to have questions about some of the things they did, even after some of the younger poets, like Michael Brownstein and Dick Gallup, rolled their eyes when Allen made some impossible demand or had a temper tantrum, like the time the poet Phil Whalen's plane was late coming in from San Francisco and no one would be there to meet him.

Whalen was one of Allen's gods. Like Burroughs, he was quiet and extremely well read. He could quote reams of Shakespeare and Cervantes, and he read Euclid and *Scientific American* for fun. Whalen was the great bear holding down the West Coast end of the Beat tablecloth. He, like Allen, had become entranced with Buddhism, but Whalen was an industrial-strength Buddhist; he would sit in a meditation posture for days. Once, a chiropractor had to pry Whalen out of the lotus position because he had lost all feeling in his legs and back.

I had always assumed Whalen was gay. Shortly after classes began, Allen had announced that Whalen would be at Naropa in a few days and that he had just gotten married. The only problem was that on his honeymoon, Allen said, Whalen announced to his wife that he had just become a Buddhist monk and that he was moving into a monastery.

Mrs. Whalen had already been on the phone to Allen, hysterical that her husband was about to shave his head and take on the maroon-colored robes of a Buddhist monk. "He even has a new name," she wailed to Allen. "I don't even know what it is! I couldn't reach him on the phone if I had to! What if there's an emergency?" It seemed to me, although I didn't say anything, that Mrs. Whalen already had an emergency on her hands.

I remember that Allen had told her to calm down, that he would discuss the situation with Trungpa. "Who knows, maybe Phil's orders will let you two live together at the zen center," Allen explained. Allen, who was often hysterical himself, was always in the position of smoothing ruffled feathers and talking his friends down from ledges, figurative and architectural. Allen's friends were always threatening to finish themselves off—they would quote Antonin Artaud about the artist suicided by society. They were always flying off the handle about it. Not Burroughs, though. Bill thought it was bad manners to complain about society. Stoicism was a vestige of his patrician upbringing.

"You don't complain," Burroughs said. "You don't fight city hall, you just approach it on all fours, lift your leg, and pee on it. And when in doubt, book passage on a transatlantic ocean liner."

I thought Bill's family had probably taught him that.

Allen and Gregory always consulted Burroughs; he was their father confessor and their therapist. He had the gravitas of a small-town undertaker. They brought their problems to him. Everyone seemed to, except for Billy Jr. He kept his troubles to himself. His father was never any help anyway.

At the faculty meeting, Anne refused to answer Peter's question.

"For the record," Anne said, "I never saw his asshole, Peter, and I wouldn't tell you if I had." Peter seemed satisfied with Anne's answer. I wasn't.

"Is asshole one word?" I piped up.

"No, not technically," Burroughs said, "it's hyphenated. Unless you want to break its hyphen."

Anne tried to laugh through her mask, but her white skin paint looked painful; it was starting to flake, tiny pieces falling to the floor. When she laughed, she reminded me of Mr. Sardonicus, the guy in the horror movie whose face is frozen into a hideous, death's-head grin.

C

O

O

L

I was dying to know if Anne had gone to bed with Bob Dylan. She had been gone for two whole days, but she said she was away writing a long poem about the tour and about Dylan as a kind of Provençal troubadour. Well, the troubadours were always climbing walls and vines and throwing themselves out of undeserved beds.

Anne went to the bathroom to try and take off her makeup. She said it had been on for days, but that no one wanted to insult Dylan by taking it off. She said that he kept his on for a long time.

Later, at Gregory's, I asked Calliope about Anne's visit to Denver to see Dylan.

"Oh, she's had flings with him before," Calliope said. "He's really a skinny little guy, but he's a fucking genius, a great poet, so who cares?"

I could've kissed her. I felt a lot better. I knew some people liked my poetry; I didn't hear a lot about my appearance. I didn't know how it stacked up. If a sexy woman like Calliope thought Dylan's poem-songs were a turn-on, then there was hope for me. So far, only Allen had commented on how well I looked in my blue jeans. I remembered being flattered by it. That was a compliment, wasn't it? I thought, whoever admires you, that's who you fall in love with. But I wished it had been Calliope.

Calliope told me that Anne accepted the fact that Dylan had a lot of women. "You just don't let yourself fall in love with him. You might never see him again. Anne was able to handle this, because she was practicing the idea of nonattachment."

When Anne came back from the bathroom after removing her white mask, she looked beautiful, but there were circles under her eyes. She looked like she'd been up for a long time. She looked sad to me.

"I had a wonderful time," she said. "Bob sang a song he dedicated to Arthur Rimbaud, and then he looked at me."

"What song was it?" Allen asked.

"I never heard it before," she said. "I remember the image of the street and the dogs on it barking, and night is falling."

"'One Too Many Mornings,'" I told Anne, and I wrote that down in the minutes.

She frowned. I knew the song title, and I wasn't even invited to the concert. I thought then that Anne and I were on some kind of collision course. She didn't like it when one of Allen's assistants showed her up—someone not under her wing. I was like an outlaw who retreats to the sanctuary of Allen Ginsberg, and Allen stands in front of the doors of the synagogue and says, "You can't come in here, he's under my protection." That's how it felt.

Allen beamed when I mentioned the song title.

"That's right. I love that song," Allen said. "Good, boychick," he said to me. "Rimbaud would've liked that song; he could've sung it sitting with one leg and strumming the guitar with a country dog chasing fireflies in Charleville at night."

Rimbaud's lost leg, his phantom limb, had kicked Anne under the table for me, kicked her in the shins, schoolboy-style, across time.

23. Heroin Doesn't Make You Immortal

It wasn't just Allen's idea that poets could be rock stars. After all, Allen thought that Dylan was really a poet masquerading as a rock musician. A "troubadour," he kept calling him. He and Anne said that a lot. "The troubadour just called," or, "The troubadour is coming to Denver, we should get spruced up and go," Anne had said. In fact, all the Beats at Naropa wanted to be rock stars. They were the ones who seemed to be inheriting the Beat gift for social dissonance and for outrageous behavior. They also seemed to be the ones who were getting all the press. Not to mention money and sex. During that summer, when the big rock tours were announced, Burroughs surprised everyone by sulking about it.

"The goddamn Rolling Stones," Burroughs said one afternoon in the backyard of one of Rinpoche's wealthy supporters, who had thrown a garden party for the Jack Kerouac School faculty, some of the other teachers at Naropa, and its only officially enrolled poetry student. "Mick Jagger pretends to be sinister," Buroughs explained, balancing a teacup and saucer on his bony knees, along with his cane. "I can't stand all that Aleister Crowley crap and the Stones in their wizard hats. The real evils are the Central Intelligence Agency, and childhood carcinoma. You could bring most of them"—meaning the Stones—"home to Mother." Everyone laughed.

"Even Keith Richards?" someone asked.

"Keith Richards made one mistake about heroin," Burroughs explained, ignoring the laughter among the Buddhists. "It doesn't make you immortal, it makes you improbable." It was the first time I had heard Burroughs say something about heroin that didn't sound like a travel brochure to some exotic island. But even Burroughs had appreciated the fact that Donald Fagen had called his group Steely Dan after the dildo in *Naked Lunch* and that Patti Smith had posed with him in New York, wearing a T-shirt with a silk-screened likeness of Rimbaud as a young, cravated schoolboy who had just finished writing some of the most powerful poems in the history of the world (or at least that's what I thought at the time).

Only Gregory, of all the Beats, didn't care about rock music or about wanting to be a rock star. He didn't care about sharing the stage with Bob Dylan or Patti Smith or Jim Carroll, who was another poet having success as a musician, writing songs like "People Who Died," a necrology of all the friends Carroll had lost to heroin. Carroll was addicted himself for a while—to the drug and to the danger of life. Corso loved opera, particularly the Italians, and especially Rossini. He loved Renata Tebaldi's voice. He said he heard her singing in heaven once.

But as little as Gregory cared for rock 'n' roll fame, that's how much Anne wanted it. She had seen Jim Carroll, with his long-legged skinniness and strawberry-blond hair, become something of a rock star. Jim was already a notorious presence on the Lower East Side, thanks to *The Basketball Diaries*, his story of being an inner-city basketball star and junkie. I picked up the book in what passed for the Naropa library, a small room that had mostly books Allen had donated or had sent from New York. I couldn't believe the sex in it. Jim was just a teenager but he claimed to have slept with women from every strata of New York society, from waitresses in Queens to Park Avenue matrons and even a few of his teachers. He also loved the movies like I did, and he wrote a whole book of poems about cutting school in favor of slouching down in the dark at the St. Mark's Theater, watching Montgomery Clift go to the electric chair in *A Place in the Sun*. Carroll, like Patti Smith and even Sam Shepard, had cut his teeth performing in the parish hall of the St. Mark's Church in the Bowery. So Anne watched this success and she wanted it. She wanted it bad.

Anne had an agent, well, a "manager," a woman named Linda who had married a man named Mickey Louie. She liked calling herself Linda Louie. It gave her, a Jewish woman from Teaneck, New Jersey, a kind of gangster chic. Linda Louie had curly black hair that was thinning. She seemed old to me at the time, though she was probably about thirty. She had a baby named Hadrian. "After the emperor," she explained. She liked me. She liked my poetry. She had very large breasts. I thought about them a lot.

Linda Louie said she had plans for Anne. She was going to make her a big star—a poetry star. Anne would give concertlike recitals, like they have in the Soviet Union. She'll fill soccer stadiums. She thought Anne should take some voice lessons and learn how to sing her poems. She and Allen could tour.

Because Linda Louie had a kid, she wasn't technically a part of Anne's entourage of sirens, like Calliope, Kitty, and Nanette. And because she often spoke to Anne in private meetings about Anne's future, the other women were excluded from these strategy meetings, and I think they resented her because she had Anne's undivided attention whenever she wanted it.

Allen hardly acknowledged Linda Louie at all. I had seen him

H
E
R
O
I
N

Doesn't Make You Immortal

treat most women somewhat invisibly, unless they were older, like his stepmother, his father Louis Ginsberg's wife, whom he genuinely loved and admired. Those women came closer to reminding Allen of his mother—they had "corsets and eyes." The younger women were ghosts to him.

Linda Louie's husband, Mickey, had long hair he kept in a ponytail, but he had a receding hairline that he often examined in restaurants, scrutinizing his reflection in a knife or a soup spoon. He was a short guy and very skinny. Linda told me Mickey might not look like much, but "ohhh, when it comes to lovin' me, he's got a huge sock." It occurred to me later that she had said cock. It was the first thing she had said to me, after I had been introduced to her husband. I could never quite regard him in the same way after that. But Mickey Louie's big "sock" didn't keep him from being the subject of other rumors. The most unkind was that the little boy Mickey was raising with Linda Louie wasn't really his.

Apparently, Linda Louie was able to devote herself to Anne's career because she had unlimited funds. The reason for it, people said, was her relationship with something of value: a connection to a lucrative pot and cocaine deal with Cubans living in Miami and quite a few who had stayed behind on the island. A small plane would deliver the pot to the Louies, and they would pay for it with money they carried in money belts, ferrying the pot by cross-country road trips or driving all night from Florida to New York and then over into Colorado. I wondered what my mother and father would've thought of this conversation I was having. I thought of Anne Waldman, who was relying on this couple to bring her fame.

Anne told Linda Louie that Allen had invited Diane di Prima to come from San Francisco to visit Naropa and give a poetry reading and perhaps stay to teach a class in the summer program when all the students would finally show up at the Jack Kerouac School. But Naropa didn't know how to pay her, and Anne asked if Linda Louie would help. She bailed out Naropa more than once that first year— a legacy of the Cuban revolution. I felt like Meyer Lansky just standing around with them trying to figure out how the Cuban connection could help bring di Prima and her impeccable beatnik credentials to Naropa for a couple of weeks.

Diane di Prima was one of the women poets Allen could *see*. She had a reputation as a very sexual Beat chick; she used words like *cock* and *cunt* and *fuck* in her work. She had Italian ancestors. She was born in New York and had dropped out of college—Swarthmore, I think—to become a writer, to try to become an artist. A few years before coming to Naropa she had written her beatnik memoirs. She had five kids, and one of her daughters with Leroi Jones was going to come to Naropa later in the year as a student. I took the news personally, as if she had told me I was soon going to have a friend.

Diane had written a poem that became very controversial, "Brass Furnace Going Out," about having an abortion as a young girl. She hated the fact that people opposed to abortion had appropriated the poem and were reading it at huge rallies.

There were a lot of sexy pictures of Diane around, and I had fantasies about meeting her. In one picture she was wearing a scarf and a dark sweater with a black skirt and white socks; you could see the calves of her legs. In another photograph, she was staring down into a book, looking thoughtful and horny. I couldn't wait to meet her.

24. Diane di Prima Loved Food

Once the fall semester was under way, Anne brought Diane di Prima into Allen's class, held in one of the Naropa schoolrooms above the New York Deli on Pearl Street—Boulder's main stem, which filled up with students and tourists most weekends.

She wasn't what I expected. Gone was the little sparrow on her book covers and in those famous photographs—Diane di Prima

C

O

O

L

didn't look like herself at all. I saw a woman who looked more like someone who'd stepped out of a Brueghel painting. She had long wild hair that hung stiffly down past her shoulders and looked like it had broken many a comb. She was short and built like a middleweight known for punching power, not speed, and she was wearing a tie-dyed hippie dress and a peasant blouse that had once been white but was unraveling at the sleeve. She was standing with a man even shorter than she was, who had long hair and a beard that was so long it seemed to pull down his young face, making him appear slightly hunched over. He made a lot of quick turns of his head and moved in speedy little gestures; he looked like a lawn gnome suddenly jarred awake after a hundred years. I think this was Diane's boyfriend, maybe her husband even.

I didn't know a lot about beauty. I didn't even think I cared that much about it. Some of the Beats looked as I imagined they would—they resembled the selves that had appeared in photographs and on album covers I had studied back on Long Island, or the few times I had seen them on television. I had watched Allen chanting over giggles on the *Merv Griffin Show*, talking about "the planet" before it became a fashionable phrase, a cliché even. Allen had made everyone else on the show look square. He made Arthur Treacher, Merv's sidekick, seem dead as the Greek language. They didn't get him, but I did. We did.

That afternoon at Naropa, Allen stopped talking to the few students in our class, which consisted of some kids who had wandered in off the mall and Naropa students from Dance or Buddhist Psychology who wanted to attend Allen's talks, plus a couple of hard-core meditators I recognized from Rinpoche's wildly popular weekend lectures. (Those lectures were held in the gymnasium of the local parochial school, Sacred Heart. I found them fascinating, though sometimes my attention would wander to the mural above the basketball hoops, depicting Jesus holding his flaming heart in his hands, offering it to the people in the grandstands. Once Rinpoche looked up at it and asked softly into the microphone, in his Tibetan-accented English, "What will they think of next?")

Allen introduced Diane as a poet from Hunter High School in New York and a lover of Leroi Jones. Diane looked a little upset.

"Allen, I love you," she said, "but you're always doing that." Diane was tough.

"What, what did I do now?" Allen wanted to know. "I'm glad to see you."

"I'm glad to see you, too, but you're always introducing me that way. You do that to all the girls. You need to know who they've slept with to figure out why they're important to you. It's annoying. It's like a tic or something, so cut it out."

I started scribbling something in my notebook. Anne introduced Diane a little more properly and said that she would be staying with us for a little while. She then announced that I was to meet them after class and show Diane around. Somehow this didn't seem as fraught with peril as baby-sitting Gregory or helping Burroughs move stiffly through a crowd of admirers. Except for Anne, the women who came through the Jack Kerouac School made me feel more comfortable, more able to be myself. I could finally talk to someone without feeling as if I were holding my breath underwater. But it's interesting to see how wrong you can be, and how often you can be wrong.

Diane di Prima loved food. I could see that. But she loved talking about it as well. She seemed to remember every meal she'd ever eaten. She even wrote a book about her food experiences. She asked me to tell her about all the restaurants in Boulder. She asked if I could cook, if I liked to cook at home. I didn't really. I liked going out to eat. I told her about the fish at Pelican Pete's, the pasta at Sage's, the exquisite dining at John's restaurant, which people seemed to go to for special occasions. I told her that Burroughs and Jubal seemed to go there all the time.

After her reading, Diane and I sat at an umbrella'd table in front of the New York Deli. We drank coffee and I told her I really liked the babka—they toasted it with a little butter on it. I offered some to Diane, adding that it was fun to share food.

D

I

A

N

E

di Prima Loved Food

"It's never fun to share food," she corrected me, before order-ing her own strawberry babka. When it arrived at the table, I thought Diane, too, looked a little babka-like. "The two babkas," I thought, one sitting in front of the other. One big, about to devour the other.

Diane said that the summer reminded her of being a young writer and of drinking iced coffee made out of powdered skim milk, and putting coffee ice cubes into the drink. She was still in high school when she and her girlfriends would wear something they had designed themselves, a kind of slip or half slip that was draped just above the breast and "tied with a sash just under your breasts or around your middle" or on your hips like a flapper. "They were very cool in the August New York city heat," she said.

"It was great then in New York," she continued, warming to her subject, "wearing these Isadora Duncan clothes and sleeping with girlfriends on mattresses on the floor, drinking iced coffee with the windows open. She later wrote about it in *Dinners and Nightmares*: "Sometimes a breeze would enter the room and the gathering of maidens would sigh and sit on their mattresses and make their plans about being great artists and having passionate love affairs, and then we'd fall asleep, like sirens on a rock."

Diane spent the afternoon talking about her life in New York. She spent the hour it took to eat our babka talking about how much she loved Oreos, and how one winter in New York that's all she did was eat Oreos, and that it used to be her favorite snack while read-ing Dante's *Divine Comedy*. "Oreos can make you fat," she said. "That's the only problem with food, Oreos especially. Even if you don't eat anything else and you think, shit, how can I get fat? I haven't had breakfast or lunch or anything like that, but I was kid-ding myself. Oreos make you fat!" She wrote about that, too.

She asked me if I was going to finish my babka. I said no. She moved our plates around so that her empty plate sat in front of me, and my unfinished babka sat in front of her. She finished it.

Diane said she was sleepy. It had been a long trip from San Francisco, and she wanted to see her apartment. But before leaving

the deli, Diane leaned over and said she was going to teach me how to write a play with a pair of dice.

"There are certain rules you have to know," she confided, but she felt sure that I would learn quickly. She said it was a good way to pass the time. She said that you make it up out of things close at hand—she used the radio and Elizabethan plays (a collection that she kept by her bed). She said she wrote this while waiting for one of her lovers to come to her apartment with a bottle of wine. He was going to teach her how to eat clams, to open them after they've been steamed and pick out the flesh with a tiny fork.

As we left the deli and headed for the apartment reserved for her visit, Diane said she would visit me at Allen's apartment soon. She heard that I'd be looking after the place once Allen and Peter had gone out to California for a reading. She'd teach me the playwriting technique then.

The thought of being alone with a woman in Allen's apartment reminded me of waiting for my first girlfriend to come over after my parents had left for my grandmother's bungalow in the Catskill Mountains. As soon as I was old enough to convince them I could stay home alone, I did. I would call up Rosalie and tell her that the coast was clear. The doorbell ringing a few minutes later would make my heart practically explode. Ten hours wooing her, as Gregory would say, then—the constellation of the stars.

25. Billy and Tangier

As the fall weather settled in, Billy Burroughs looked worse. A sad-looking guy, he looked even sadder as the weeks flew by. A skinny guy who used a rope to keep his pants up, he seemed skinnier than usual. I thought his skin looked gray—blue and gray, the color of ash. There was some kind of bump in his neck. Something was

B I L L Y

and Tangier

C

O

O

L

wrong. The only one who didn't seem to notice was his father. But Billy was used to his father not knowing what was wrong.

Billy liked his privacy, but when he got tired of that he wanted somebody to talk to. His friends, the Westies or whatever they were called, seemed to come to him only for alcohol and grass. They also liked his beatnik pedigree and hanging out with the son of the man who wrote *Naked Lunch*. I guess, in that way, they were a lot like me.

One day after my poetry class, Allen asked me to buy groceries for Billy because he didn't seem to have enough strength to walk through the aisles of the supermarket. You didn't have to be a brain surgeon to know that Billy needed a doctor.

His father finally agreed that we should visit the surgeon in Denver, the one they had made me call when I first arrived in Boulder. Trouble was, he was a psychic surgeon.

"He operates without cutting you open," Burroughs explained in Allen's apartment one afternoon. "They manipulate the body from the outside, they palpate and they remove without using the knife. It's been known to be successful in a number of cases." I told Allen that I thought Burroughs was dreaming, that Billy really looked sick. It was always a case of too little, too late where Burroughs and his son were concerned.

The next day, I carried a bag full of groceries up the steep walk to Billy's apartment, which you could pick out from the street because the window was decorated half in an orange karmic flag from Naropa with a mythical, fire-breathing dragon on it, and half with an old pirate flag bearing a skull and crossbones.

Billy's shopping list sounded like a condemned man's idea of a great last meal: steak and ice cream, ingredients for a malted, Hershey's chocolate syrup, and A1 meat sauce. He also needed lots of milk and cans of tuna for the cats that wandered in and out of his apartment, like the cats in Hemingway's house in Key West.

I later learned that Billy had come to Boulder because he needed to be somewhere safe. It was his father who had sent for him. He explained that Burroughs, whom he always called Bill, had done this before. When Billy had turned fourteen, Burroughs had decided he wanted his son back. At the time, Burroughs was living in Tangier and Billy was living in the lap of luxury with his grandparents, sleeping in a sleigh bed and having his clothes laid out by a servant. He hadn't seen his father in at least two or three years when he was summoned to Tangier.

Billy told me that Burroughs was living there with two men at the time. He said it was a strange feeling to see this strange man in a business suit waiting for him at the airport. Once they arrived at Burroughs's little villa, Bill Sr. had very little to say to his son. "He practically ignored me," Billy said. "I was just a fourteen-year-old squirt, very American, and very un-hip."

Billy had had to put up with a lot. The two Englishmen sharing the house with Burroughs kept coming into Billy's room to try and have sex with him. Billy said that after his first night in Tangier, he found one of the men, Ian, sitting on his bed. Ian took Billy's hand and tried to put it on his crotch. "I pulled my hand away from Ian's lap," Billy said. He told me this story while sitting up in bed smoking a joint.

After I brought the groceries into the apartment and put them away, some of Billy's so-called friends arrived. They took out their long clay pipes and turned the tiny apartment into a kind of opium den, throwing the pillows and cushions from the couch onto the floor. Billy recalled how, when he was in Tangier, Burroughs had made one of the Englishmen take Billy down to the Casbah to pick out a pipe.

Billy's apartment now looked like his description of the house in Tangier. It was a complete mess, with flickering lightbulbs and not an inch of unused floor space.

The long bowls came out and little vials of something that looked like tobacco were unscrewed and tenderly tapped out into the clay bowls. Billy asked me to share his pipe. He said that in Tangier he ate something called *majoun,* some kind of grass that you chew on and then swallow. Billy liked to say that it "will stone you into the middle of next week, possibly next month." I refused, the hypochondriac in me rising up. Marion would have been proud.

Curiously, though Billy's apartment was a mess, the little space where he wrote was a kind of pristine shrine. He said he had gotten that from his father. Burroughs had a sort of college or bunk bed in his bedroom in Boulder, which was very spare and clean. Billy said he only remembered a painting by Brion Gysin in his father's room in Tangier, a haunting painting of the moon, which turned the room into a kind of permanent nighttime. Burroughs also had an orgone box in his Boulder apartment, in which he would sit "like Eichmann in his glass booth," Billy said, and smoke *majoun* or pot—and after a few hours he would pounce on the Underwood and write.

Seeing Allen and Gregory was nothing new for Billy—he'd grown up with these men coming in and out of his life. He described how, in Tangier, the existentialist, expat hippies, who "looked as if they hadn't seen daylight for years and were dressed entirely in black—dark hair, black circles under their eyes," would hang around just to catch a glimpse of William Burroughs. They would watch him enter a club called the Casbah. Dressed in a suit, a long skinny tie, and a fedora, Burroughs would sit down with a glass of tea served to him on a tray. He sat motionless, in his right hand a cigarette burning down to his fingers, his lips parting to inhale the smoke. "Old Bill," Billy called him. "My dad." Then he'd laugh. He understood the absurdity of it. "I was still reading comic books and science fiction then," Billy said.

Billy admitted that his father's maternal instinct came out when he prepared a kind of chicken soup for his son, but even then he made it with so much pepper that Billy said it had tasted like whiskey.

In the middle of his disquisition on his father, Billy started nodding off, his words leaning over and falling against each other like drunken sailors on shore leave. I couldn't quite understand him.

"He didn't care what I did, or where I went," Billy mumbled, half asleep. And then, rousing slightly, he continued, describing a time when he went around stoned in Tangier, perching himself precariously on a cliff covered with trees growing sideways out of the rock. "I'd sit there smoking grass and waiting. I thought maybe Old Bill would come looking for me, and we'd have a heart-to-heart talk."

One night in Tangier, Billy explained, someone came into his room and told him that he was too young to know what he wanted, but what he really wanted was to go home. "Don't live in a house with a bunch of fags," one of the expat hippies told Billy.

"Does my father want me to stay?" Billy had asked him. When there was no answer, Billy repeated the question. As he recounted this tale, I saw beads of sweat on his brow, the clay pipe falling out of his hand. "Go to my father's room and ask him," Billy had told the hippie. "Ask him, does he or doesn't he want me to stay."

26. Burroughs and the Box

I thought I should tell Burroughs about how sick I thought Billy really was, how I didn't think that going to a psychic healer was going to help him. I was thinking a lot about the movie *Midnight Cowboy*, how Ratso Rizzo, the Dustin Hoffman character, died on the bus on the way to Florida. He had needed real medical attention, just like Billy. That movie really stuck with me. I saw it on a first date, when my girlfriend and I went into New York, a glamorous thing to do back then. I remembered how she and I had taken the Long Island Rail Road from the suburbs to be part of the audience for *Let's Make a Deal*, which was being broadcast from a Midtown television studio. I remembered how we were asked to leave the studio audience because we "looked too sad." Out of step with the adults and with most of America, we couldn't muster up the proper level of enthusiasm for the game show. On the way out,

C

O

O

L

my sixteen-year-old girlfriend muttered "capitalist pigs!" under her breath. So I took her to the Baronet Theater on Second Avenue, across from Bloomingdale's, where we saw *Midnight Cowboy* instead. That was closer to our mood and sensibility. Even better: sandwiched right between the Baronet and the Cornet theaters was Bookmasters, the great book and poster store where you could climb the shelves like Spider-Man and pick out the skinny little City Lights pocket poets. Series Number 14 was *Kaddish and Other Poems 1958–1960* by Allen Ginsberg, a dollar fifty. And then there was Series Number 8, *Gasoline/Vestal Lady* by Gregory Corso, a buck.

I left Billy asleep with the other Westies in his opium den and gently pulled the long clay pipe out of his hand. I didn't want to be responsible for Billy burning the place down. I'd never graduate Naropa that way.

I went over to Burroughs's apartment. I hated doing that. First, Jubal was often there and we'd never really hit it off. I hated the violent Westerns he was writing. He had read a few of them at one of the early readings, held in the basement of a private home where some of Rinpoche's elderly followers were living.

Finally, I decided it didn't matter what I thought of Jubal. I needed to speak with Bill about his son. When I arrived at Burroughs's apartment, Jubal was there, of course, guarding the gate.

"Jubal, is Bill around? I need to talk to him."

"He's in the box," Jubal said. "He may not be out for another two hours." A few weeks earlier, I would've assumed that Jubal was telling me that Burroughs was in the bathroom for a spell. But I now knew what he meant, that Burroughs was sitting in his orgone box, something that he had been doing for years, maybe twenty years or longer. One of my first jobs at Naropa that summer had been to help build the box from an orgone kit, so that it would be ready when Burroughs arrived. It was lined with metal and a kind of insulation on the outside made from bark of some sort. It looked like a tree house that had been turned into a bomb shelter. Building Burroughs's orgone box had not been easy.

It all started at the end of the 1940s, after Burroughs had read a book by Wilhelm Reich called *The Cancer Biopathy*. Burroughs flipped for Reich. Burroughs always thought of himself as a lay analyst. Gregory in fact told me once that Bill had given Kerouac the best psychological advice of his life when he'd said, "Jack, you're too attached to your mother, you've got to leave home and never come back."

"He did it," Gregory said, "and wrote a masterpiece, but then he moved back in with his mother and ruined it all." He should've listened to the Ol' Poisoner, as he called Burroughs.

Burroughs never thought much of most therapists, but he considered Reich a fucking genius. Reich built his first orgone box around 1940. Burroughs built his first orgone accumulator in the late 1940s; almost thirty years later we found ourselves standing around the orgone kit that Burroughs had sent on ahead of him to Boulder.

I asked Bill what the word "orgone" meant (it sounded to me like a cross between *ozone* and *orgasm*).

"You're on the right beam, my wee boy"—Burroughs occasionally liked to fall into *Treasure Island*–speak, as if I were the boy in the Robert Louis Stevenson story, and he Long John Silver, the pirate with the wooden leg and the parrot perched on his shoulder.

"It comes from 'orgasm' and 'organism,'" he explained; "it's a conflation of those two words. It is a cure the government doesn't want you to have. The bastards have too much money invested in the disease, so they aren't interested in the cure. The cure ruins their plans. The funny thing is, the cancer is on the body politic; it has taken over."

Burroughs told us that the FDA had investigated Reich and his orgone box "up the wazoo. It was the subject of more governmental investigation than the Hughes Spruce Goose, going back to

1946. They tried to bring down Reich, which they did. The orgone box is his cenotaph."

I knocked on the entry door of the box. At first, no answer. I thought about tipping it over, but Jubal was watching my every move. I knocked again and yelled.

"Mr. Burroughs, it's Sam. I want to talk to you about Billy. I think he's sick and needs a real doctor!"

Burroughs opened the hatch to the box and leaned over to shake my hand. Suddenly I felt like the little girl who wrote Lincoln a letter telling him to grow a beard. Burroughs emerged from the orgone box looking like our Civil War president, someone who has just seen a lot of death and suffering. I told Burroughs I was sorry to interrupt his session but that I was concerned about Billy's health, that he looked real bad.

"He doesn't seem to have any energy," I told Burroughs. "I know I'm something of a hypochondriac myself, and that sometime I can be a hypochondriac on behalf of others, but in this case I really think something's wrong."

"What do you think it is?" Burroughs asked me through the metal door of the orgone box.

"It could be something as simple as gallstones. He's very sensitive down around his waist, and his back hurts. I read somewhere that's a sign of gallstones. My cousin Sheldon had them when he was working in the diamond district; they had to carry him out of his booth on Forty-seventh Street, completely doubled over. He was gripping his diamond cutting tools so tightly they had to pry them out of his hand at the hospital."

Burroughs seemed genuinely interested in what had happened to my cousin.

"If I should need some jewels appraised, I will go to see him," Burroughs assured me. "They do come into my possession from time to time, gems and even the occasional necklace."

The point of my visit was unraveling.

"What I want to know, sir," I continued, "is if I can take him to the doctor here in Boulder."

"Whatever happened to our glorious frontier heritage of minding one's own business?" Burroughs growled, stepping out of the orgone box. "Billy should get in here now and this will help him. Bring him forward, laddie. Better yet, let him be for now. Orgones come in waves, and lately the waves have been at a very low ebb. We'll go to the surgeon tomorrow; he comes highly recommended. It's the sensible thing to do."

Okay. It looked as if we were going to the psychic surgeon after all. I wondered what Billy thought about all this, if he had any say in it.

"I hope the victim will be able to express his appreciation when it's all over," Billy said, in that sarcastic way he had of speaking, especially when speaking about his father and the other "unfortunate uncles," as he called them, that he had grown up with—Allen, Peter, Gregory, Herbert Huncke, and I guess Kerouac, the saddest uncle of them all.

We piled into the car, the same arthritic town car that had carried all of us up the face of the mountain and whose trunk we had burdened with pot. Peter was at the wheel. I thought of John Clare's poem "The Driving Boy"—although that was written about a boy at the plow—but that's how Peter Orlovsky drove, like he was sitting in a car tied to oxen waiting for them to move.

Bill and Billy, father and son, sat together in the backseat, and Allen and I sat beside them. I stared out the window to keep my mind off such august company. Gregory had left Max and Lisa and Calliope behind so that he could come along for the ride. Peter didn't seem to have control of the car. I thought we'd never get out of Boulder, at least not alive.

"I don't know what it is," Peter shouted at us over his shoulder. "The car seems possessed of some kind of spirit, it wants to be close to the flowers, it smells the flowers, Allen, the car smells the flowers!" We lurched closer to what in fact were flower beds and plants hanging out of windows on our way out of town.

B
U
R
R
O
U
G
H
S

and the Box

"Bill"—Gregory turned around in his seat, looking like a gargoyle perched atop Notre Dame, with his wild untamed hair, no teeth, and hawklike nose, or a gryphon with bifocals chained to its face—"Do you think insane people have visions worth hearing?"

"Ah." Burroughs thought for a moment, taking off his hat and looking inside as if the answer were written in the brim. "I don't think so. It's the insane who are so concerned with life, regular life, money and sex, food and its effect on their digestion. The insane are obsessed with the impression they make on others. The facts of life frighten the insane, and no man can detach himself, Gregory, from what he fears. As a consequence, the visions of the insane are unspeakably dreary."

"My whole family's insane, Bill," our driver cried out, "and they are very interesting to me. Don't you think my family is interesting, Allen?" Peter asked.

"Peter's brother Julius thought he was the baby Jesus," Allen said thoughtfully. "It made him very easy to be with—he was very mild."

Billy didn't say much. He asked how long the operation would take, if there would be any blood.

"I will get everything worked out," his father said, reassuring him. "This will be like bagging a jaguar, you'll bring the offending organism home in a sack."

Somehow none of this was very reassuring to Billy. Billy lit up a cigarette and took out of his knapsack a miniature bottle of Jack Daniel's that you can buy on airplanes. No one said anything. Gregory turned around as soon as Billy unscrewed the bottle and the smell of alcohol filled the car.

"Gimme some of that," Gregory demanded. "You have to feed the first baby-sitter you ever had," he told Billy. "Do you remember, Billy, when I took you out on the roof of that apartment building, with all the glass on the edge to keep out the burglars, and we threw the glass into the street and you said, 'Diamonds, we made diamonds'? And I took you to the planetarium and stole that cardboard mobile of the planets for you, and I liked it so much I stole it back?"

Billy smiled. Allen laughed.

"Writers, like elephants, have long, vicious memories," Burroughs said. "There are things I wish I could forget."

I, on the other hand, wanted to remember everything about being in the car with these men, though how strange we must have looked to the other motorists who glanced over suspiciously at us when the traffic slowed. They all looked like suburbanites going into the city to work or shop.

A family pulled up at a traffic light. A little boy in Oshkosh overalls smiled at us. His mother, who was at the wheel, pulled him away from the window. He looked like he would rather be with us. Burroughs looked the kid in the eye. "A timorous foe, a suspicious friend," he said. Gregory winked at the mother and stuck out his tongue, like he wanted to kiss her. She looked disgusted and drove off.

It takes about an hour to drive into Denver. I wondered what they were thinking as we approached the city. It must have a lot of meaning for them. The hobo jungles of Denver—Neal Cassady's Denver—were disappearing. There's an expensive Japanese restaurant where Jack and Neal once fell down drunk and laughing in the street, knocking their brains out trying to impress a girl who left them both for a college kid in maroon slacks who later became a country club golf pro.

The city meant something to Allen, too. Denver was in his poems as a place folded deep inside America where he had had his own satori—his flash of enlightenment, his glimpses of "ordinary mind," as he liked to put it. It was in Denver where he first saw himself as part of a lineage—a patrimony of poets—someone who should be committed to the welfare of the world by tending to his own sanity.

"In Denver," Allen said as we moved closer toward the skyline of the city, "I saw the inevitable beauty of doom, that Fate tells big lies. It's where I leaned against a brick building as if it were a Mayan temple and realized that we are phantoms, and that friendship fades."

I thought Allen was luckier than most. Even if friendship fades, he still had many of his friends. Gregory might be missing his teeth, but he was still here; Burroughs needed a cane but he looked pretty good for a guy who needed heroin to live. And Peter seemed strong as a horse. Allen was smiling, happy just to be with his friends in a car—not the famous Green Automobile that was Cassady's chariot but a town car (the Beats had status now) with a torn-up floor.

In one of Ginsberg's poems about Neal Cassady that Allen had handed over to me to finish when I first arrived at the Jack Kerouac School, he had written about how he could talk to Neal forever; that it was somehow more than conversation, it was a discoursing of spirits.

I didn't feel that, but I was grateful to be in their company, though I was no longer sure why. I couldn't enjoy it the way I would have with my own friends, but it was as if I had willed myself into their story, even though there really was no place for me as originally written.

As we approached the city limits, I could tell everyone's mind was wandering. Allen took out a piece of paper with directions on it. Peter made all the turns. Billy asked if we could stop at Duffy's, a bar he really liked in the city. Gregory said he had hemorrhoids and wondered if that could be taken care of while we were there. "There's blood in the toilet bowl every time I sit down," he complained, sounding like Burroughs. "It's like I'm menstruating. Can the surgeon do something for that, Ginzy? If it's expensive, can Sammy pay for it with that Diner's Club card of his?"

"Do psychic surgeons take Diner's Club?" Peter asked, suddenly interested.

"I'll write a check for everyone," Allen said. "Maybe he can help my Bell's palsy. Maybe you've found the fountain of life, Bill! *Phat, Phat, Phat, Svha . . .*" Allen chanted as Peter nudged the giant town car into a too small parking space in a drugstore parking lot in downtown Denver. The six of us climbed stiffly out of the car.

"I remember this drugstore—it has a soda fountain," Burroughs said. "I bought my first vial of paregoric there. Paregoric is rather yummy. No one admits it, though."

"It's like the *Wizard of Oz!*" Gregory said suddenly. "We're going to see the wizard! Come along, Dorothy." Gregory grabbed my hand and pulled me onto the curb.

A shingle swung from a rusty iron bar next to the drugstore, like a sign above an old tavern. *Dr. Shringwaym A. Surgeon.*

"This oughta learn you to stay away from them hoors," Bill said, as he escorted his son inside Dr. Shringwaym's office.

"Dig it," Gregory said, "there's danger here. The ball game with these places is that they take your money and give you chicken livers they hide up their sleeve. It's a magic ritual, Bill. These guys don't operate on you—they don't know how to open a letter!"

We entered the building.

There was a weird vibrating in the doctor's office, and for a second I thought it was an earthquake, but then I realized there was some construction going on outside. The doctor's assistant, a middle-aged woman, came out from behind a glass partition, explaining that they're building a new approach to the highway and told us not to be alarmed, that they were just dynamiting the road. She said it had ruined their business, that no one walks in off the street anymore.

The assistant walked over to Billy, probably because he looked the sickest, and escorted him into the doctor's office. Allen offered to go with him, but Billy said he'd rather go himself. If he was scared, he didn't show it; he shrugged and said this reminded him of a massage parlor in the Philippines he'd gone to once.

Dr. Shringwaym suddenly appeared. He was a giant. He had a dark face and wore wire-frame glasses and a green lab coat, with a black T-shirt underneath. As he strode into the waiting room, he looked like he had a sense of who the posse of friends waiting for Billy were, as if they were some kind of visiting royalty in disguise.

The doctor told Burroughs that he'd have his son back in about a half hour. Gregory asked to use the phone, then called Calliope, and they made some kind of arrangement. We sat in the waiting room, Allen reading a *U.S. News & World Report* and Burroughs resting on his cane, watching the goldfish in a bowl on the window sill. I just kept shuffling magazines, too nervous to make small talk with anyone. No one could tell what was going on in those other rooms. A few assistants shuffled in and out, wearing slippers and hair nets. I leaned over and told Allen that no good could come of

C

O

O

L

this. He agreed and gently told the receptionist that he'd like to see Billy Jr. All of a sudden we can hear Billy screaming.

The doctor came back and told Allen that Billy was not cooperating, and that without help he will not live.

It didn't occur to anyone to call the hospital.

Billy came out looking like death. His lips were white and he was shaking and bleeding from his nose. Dr. Shringwaym said he didn't have the chance to remove the growths, which are the cause of Billy's problem. Billy, still shaking, announced that he wanted to leave—he wanted to go to Duffy's and get "transported."

"I feel incredible evil in this place," Burroughs said as he rose from his chair.

"I would have Lionel Trilling operate on me before I'd let that Arab touch me," Gregory said.

We left, and Billy limped toward the car.

Wasn't it in Denver where Allen had had his vision, his cosmic flash in the pan, about how we're all phantoms talking to phantoms, a skull on a pillow? Is that why we were driving toward an Irish bar in the Denver darkness, some of the dust from the dynamited road in Gregory's hair and on Allen's beard?

I was glad to see those specks of dust. If we didn't exist, we wouldn't look like dusty, terra-cotta statues driving around in the dusk.

27. Gregory's Time Piece

The trip back was not easy. First, we got lost, and parts of Denver at night—even in that banner-filled year of America's two hundredth birthday—could be scary. Billy was aching and miserable. He wanted to get dropped off at Duffy's in downtown Denver. It was famous, Burroughs recalled, for a big multiple slaying years earlier. It wasn't a reassuring advertisement, not at night anyway. We couldn't find the place, and then Gregory noticed my watch.

My parents had given it to me before I left home to come to the Kerouac School. It looked like a more expensive watch than it really was. Marion, my mother, had selected it—she'd said it was a watch for a writer. The two hands were fashioned to look like writing implements—one a quill, another an old fountain pen. It was a little corny, but I loved the fact that it had come from them and that despite the fact that all my friends were in colleges like Stony Brook or Binghamton, my parents still blessed my going to the Kerouac School. I might as well have been going off to join the foreign legion. And what little they knew of Burroughs and Ginsberg was probably not going to help them feel they'd done the right thing by letting me go. I guess they'd just agreed to suspend their disbelief.

One of the first things Gregory had asked me about was my parents. "They let you come here?" he said. "To study with *unwashedbeatniksexcrazedcommiedopefiends?*" He laughed. "In fact," he told me, "we're just old men. Soon to poof into air. Look, I hardly have any teeth." He gave me a smile, mostly gums, with a few teeth left over that looked like the old, crooked tombstones he leaned his girlfriend against in his "Marriage" poem.

I discovered on the trip from Denver back to Boulder that Gregory thought it funny how respectable the Beats had become. He couldn't get over Allen's success; the acceptance by the academy of Allen's work was a source of wonder and irritation to Gregory. "A Guggenheim he got, the National Book Award! The *New York Times* gave Ginzy four hundred dollars for a poem he wrote about being mugged for sixty dollars!"

I also discovered, as the town car hummed and humped the six of us through the flat, back streets of Denver, that Gregory thought a lot about time, about what it had given him and what it had taken away.

"Sixteen years ago we were put down for being filthy beatniks," he shouted into my left ear, the two of us scrunched up in the backseat. "Now look at us. Allen's a member of the Academy of Arts and Sciences—he's even been pinned like a girl in school!

GREGORY'S

Time Piece

Peter's looking for a girlfriend so he and Allen can have a baby, Hermes willing. And Bill. Look at Bill! He got off heroin before me and he doesn't even smoke Camels! And I, Nunzio Gregorio Corso, I should be as famous as Bill and Allen and not neglected by fame."

Gregory made Peter stop the car in front of an old movie theater advertising a double feature of two Tarzan films: Johnny Weissmuller and Lex Barker, back-to-back, swinging from black and white into jungle color. Gregory suddenly sprang out of the car and dashed over to the box office, slapping down his money in front of a bored-looking woman behind the glass. We watched him disappear into the theater.

For the next two hours, the rest of us aimlessly drove around the streets of Denver, finally heading back to the movie theater. There was Gregory, standing out front, casually chatting up two girls, like John Dillinger emerging from the Biograph with his girl Frenchy and the lady in red, as if our entire trip to Denver was merely a parentheses for that moment.

It started to occur to me after we picked up Gregory, after having driven around in the dark waiting for Tarzan to leave Manhattan, that Gregory was always bolting. He just couldn't sit still. Upstairs in his apartment with Lisa and Max sitting out on the terrace, Gregory would often bolt from his desk, and he and his poems would simply disappear for hours.

Gregory climbed back into the town car and we sped off again. I decided to confront him directly about his habit of suddenly disappearing on everyone.

"Gregory, where do you go when you go out, when you don't let me help you finish the book?" (I wanted Allen to know that I was still trying to get him to sit down and finish his poems.)

"I go to the movies. I can't stand crowds, or to be cooped up."

These days, there would be a name for what I think ailed Gregory, his bolting like that. I think he was suffering from panic disorder.

"I think about death," Gregory continued in the backseat of the darkened car. "I'm not a Buddhist like Allen. Right, Allen?"

"You can take medication," Peter said from behind the wheel, his heavy gray ponytail, pretty as a girl's, lit up by the passing cars.

"If I feel like I'm gonna die, I have to excuse myself. I say, 'I gotta go!' And like you, Sammy, they always wanna know where. They sense something's wrong, they never know what to do. It's happening now. You're asking me, 'Are you okay? Can we get you something? Want to lie down?' Ginzy, tell him! Who wants to die amongst people?"

"That's the only way to die, Gregory," Peter says.

"Even when they can't do shit?" Gregory asks. "That's when I go to the movies, when I feel I'm going to die. So far it's worked. I used to wake up screaming from a dream of dying, and go out on the street to an all-night movie theater in Times Square, with a great overcoat over my pajamas, but even then we cannot escape getting older. The movies I saw when I was ten are old movies now, and all their stars are stars no more."

As we drove through the starless night, headed back to Boulder, Gregory went back to admiring my watch. "What do you want for it?" he finally asked.

I really didn't want to sell it to him, but it was hard to deny those guys anything. I struggled to keep the watch on my wrist, but I soon realized that Gregory was obsessed with wristwatches. He loved to wear them. He frequently put them into his poems.

In fact, Gregory was obsessed with time. I started to think that it was because of the time he had spent in prison—in Clinton and Dannemora—counting off the months, days, and hours until he was free to walk down MacDougal Street again, stopping at all the outdoor espresso cafés and pouring out a little sugar into the palm of his hand. No wonder Gregory was missing most of his teeth.

"Ginzy, give me fifty dollars for Sammy Davis's watch."

"Gregory," Allen said, "he needs his watch. Don't let him take it from you, Sam." Allen, who could stand up to Gregory, came to my rescue. He had no illusions about Gregory. He knew he was at heart still a street kid, still a hustler.

But I unfastened the watchband and gave Gregory my watch.

C

O

O

L

He looked at it like a kid at Christmas, kissed me, and put it on his wrist. His breath smelled like popcorn and alcohol. I looked away, embarrassed to see so much pleasure, so much pure joy in a man, a grizzled poetman old enough to be my father.

By that watch Gregory would miss every appointment we ever had.

Climbing back toward Boulder, away from Denver's haze, the night stars suddenly appeared. Gregory looked up at the sky, studying the constellations. "As long as I live," he said, "movie stars keep on dying."

Later, I would go back and look at *Gasoline*, Gregory's first City Lights book, the poems that had made Jack Kerouac compare his friend to Frank Sinatra—Caruso even—singing his Italian songs over the rooftops of Greenwich Village and Little Italy. Gregory, afraid of death?

And what about Bill, who seemed so frail? Allen had told me once that Burroughs had changed a great deal over the years, that he'd become grandfatherly, almost angelic. I didn't see it. He didn't even seem too interested in what was really wrong with his son. The Beats were lucky, I thought. They were still alive.

As if he could read my mind, Allen started talking about the longevity of his friends, men like Burroughs, Gregory, Peter, Gary Snyder, Phil Whalen, who were all still going strong since the 1940s and '50s, when he'd met most of them. It was the academic poets like John Berryman, Robert Lowell, Randall Jarrell, and Delmore Schwartz, Allen observed, who "wrecked themselves drinking."

"We were saved by marijuana," he continued, as Peter suddenly popped open the glove compartment where a baggy filled with pot and rolling papers magically appeared. "Randall Jarrell ran out into traffic and Sylvia Plath—they both committed suicide. The Old American Monster—alcohol—ruined the poets who thought of *us* as unsophisticated and ignorant."

"Beatniks!" Gregory shouted.

"We should have our own exercise tape," Burroughs mused. "It would make a fortune." (Had Burroughs anticipated the fitness-videotape craze of the eighties?)

"Alive, Kerouac was older than me," Corso chimed in, obsessing on time. "Now I'm a year older than Jack . . . and fifteen years older than Christ. I'm fifteen years older than God . . . and getting older."

"In the Catholic sense," Allen pointed out.

Gregory had always been the youngest of their group. The youngest everywhere! Even in prison, they said he was the youngest inmate at Dannemora and the youngest to leave. Like François Villon—the French poet-thief of the fifteenth century who was a kind of god to Gregory—he was the youngest "in the company of peers. Poets and convicts. The youngest for years."

Now Gregory was cooking; starting to rhyme in his conversation meant he was starting to write his poems in his head. Like recalling a vision, he recounted his poem-ideas and then would write them down, or, these days, call me up and recite the poems before even putting them down in his free-for-all handwriting, full of doodles and digressions, trying to maintain beauty in the ruin of his penmanship.

Now *I* was the youngest. At least tonight, in this black automobile climbing the steep hill back into town, past the University of Colorado at Boulder.

Didn't these straight college kids at the university know who was living down the street from them? Didn't they care? Maybe they didn't want to know. Maybe it was better that they didn't know. After all, it was idolatry that killed Kerouac. He ran from their love, as Gregory ran from Allen, Peter, and Burroughs. Gregory was always running away from them. He was the one who had spent most of his time living abroad, moonbathing in the Parthenon and sitting with his magic wand in a small apartment in Paris, living on grapes and casting spells that only he knew about. "The young must always run away," Gregory said when we left him at the bottom of the hill. I knew he wasn't going home but to Calliope. Was this also due to Gregory's fear of getting old?

GREGORY'S

C

O

O

L

"What's he running away from now?" I asked Allen after we dropped off Gregory.

"His shadow, seeing his shadow on the path." I knew just enough Buddhist jargon to know when to smile, though I didn't always get the joke.

"We should find a parking space," Peter told Allen.

"Like the Buddha said, 'Park the empty vehicle.' " He and Peter laughed. Burroughs was fast asleep with his eyes open. He awakened by closing his eyes.

"I just had the most extraordinary dream," Burroughs said. "Leonardo da Vinci and Lonny the Pimp accompany a woman dressed as a nurse. They appear at J. Edgar Hoover's office. 'We have come to give Mr. Hoover a high colonic, courtesy of Twentieth Century Fox studios.' Then they plant a time bomb up his ass, and leave."

While Bill had slept, Billy asked to be dropped off at a dark bar near the university. Peter pulled over. We all watched as Billy was swallowed up by the crowd at the door. I wondered why none of us stopped him.

"You're home," Peter said to me a few minutes later. Allen stepped out of the car. He kissed me good night, on the lips. It was a sweet kiss.

28. Saint Petersburg

One morning in the middle of the fall semester, Peter came over early to wash my face—he said I didn't do it right. He wore a white dress shirt and a pair of garish, green-checked Bermuda shorts and sandals. He said that I must not be washing my face properly because my skin had broken out around my forehead. I was embarrassed; that's not what I wanted to hear from Allen Ginsberg's longtime companion.

My parents almost never brought up the subject of bad skin, that splash of acne on my face, the gift of adolescence. It usually occurred just before some big, important event, and with the first student poetry reading coming up, that was perfect timing. Peter said he and Allen had realized on the farm they had at Cherry Valley, in upstate New York, that washing your face with ice-cold water kept your skin taut, and it seemed to cure pimples.

Peter had a beautiful complexion. I noticed how a lot of the mountain men—guys who lived by the rivers and streams up in the foothills of the Rockies and came back down the mountain to beg for money and to troll through the Dumpsters behind restaurants—had unusually good complexions. They also looked very rested. I would've thought living outdoors, with the constant hunt for food and shelter, would be exhausting.

Peter said he was going to make me exercise; he was going to make me strong. He said that I looked like "before."

"Before what, Peter?" I asked.

"Like the drawing of 'before,' " he said, insistent.

"Someone sitting before an artist, like a model?"

"No, like Charles Atlas bodybuilding—the drawing of Charles Atlas *before* he lifted weights." I was insulted and relieved at the same time. I hadn't mastered all of Peter's verbal tics. Allen and Bill spoke perfect "Peter." They knew what he was talking about at all times.

Peter said he was very strong. He showed me how he could crack a walnut with his thighs. We shared the walnut. I kept the broken shell. I thought it would be valuable someday.

After he taught me how to wash my face, Peter asked if I would type up his poems, which were going into his first book. He was very excited about it. He said that everyone thought he was ignorant, and that he just stayed with Allen because Allen was famous, but Peter said he had a lot of poems that he'd saved up through the

C

O

O

L

years. It's just that for a long time he took care of everyone, but now he wanted to take care of his poems, the poems he'd been saving. He once secretly showed his poems to Frank O'Hara, he said, and Frank told him they were wonderful and he should publish them. "Maybe one day Allen will accompany me to Sweden when I win the Nobel prize," Peter said, laughing. "Why don't they give out a Nobel Prize to the person with the cleanest asshole?"

I wondered about that myself, I told Peter.

Peter said he wanted to try out his book title on me—it was called "Clean Asshole Poems & Smiling Vegetable Songs." Then he read me one of his poems, one about Peter and lepers in India. In the poem, Peter tries to help people with leprosy: "week thin no legs no hands no / fingers, only stubs of joints / with the finger bones pokeing thru. / A bit like pigs feet in clean store jars." He proudly showed me the poem, with its many misspellings, in which he wrote about caring for a woman

> . . . rapped in pure dirt . . .
> still infested with active
> Leprocy growing by eating
> away the flesh . . .

> I gave some helpfull Indian soul
> to go get her a new fresh Clean
> sarrie a few ruppies . . .
> . . . on her Left behind
> I saw a 4 inch ring of open—
> saw infection full of magots
> cralling and happiley alive—

I was never too great a speller myself. But I thought it would be a mistake to change Peter's spelling. I remembered how John Clare's misspellings seemed to make the words even more alive. Peter helping this dying woman on the street in "Banaras" was so sad. Because of his Russian background, and because he cared for his brothers and sister, and because of his brief, former life as an ambulance driver, I started calling Peter "Saint Petersburg." He liked that.

In 1971, I found out, Peter had woken up from a sleep on Halloween night and written this poem. He was already thinking like a Buddhist about life, but before meeting Rinpoche I don't think he was thinking compassionately about his own life. I told Peter he was too hard on himself at the end of the poem, where he wrote: "I feel all the more Lazzey and Dumb and all the more domb & Lazzey Lazzey Bastard of a selfish Human Creap Sleep."

"But, Peter," I told him, "you are not selfish—you should be more so! And you were not sleeping a 'human creap sleep,' you were just tired! It's hard work caring for other people."

"I have to take care of Allen," he answered. "I said I would do it forever, even though sometimes Allen gets mad, but *that* he can work out with Rinpoche."

Peter then mentioned that he'd dropped by to ask if I would stay in their house when he and Allen go to California.

"Allen's going to give a poetry reading," Peter said. "Maybe I'll bring back an ugly girl and we can all live together."

"Maybe you'll get lucky," I said.

Peter had also come to my apartment to await the arrival of a friend. I expected a woman to show up, but a man arrived, whom Peter introduced as Long. He told me that Long lived deep in the woods and got his food from a creek. "If I could, I would live like that," Peter said, "but Allen wouldn't go for it, because now that he's a member of the Academy of Arts and Sciences he can't live in the country."

Long, or Mr. Long, as I called him, was short but powerfully built. He looked like a little machine, with strong arms and a thick neck. He reminded me of a generator, he even seemed to hum when he walked. Mr. Long showed me pictures of the place he and Peter were building in a very gloomy spot in the woods.

Peter said this would be the place that he would live in with Allen and the baby if they had one together, with Peter's undiscovered girlfriend.

"The sun never comes through the woods, so we have to cut down some trees," Peter said.

"You can't walk around without a club to kill the snakes, that's how bad it is," Long said.

Peter said some snakes are beautiful.

"They just can't be counted on to share your friendliness," Long said. "They're like some people I know."

Peter asked Long to take me up there and show me the property. I said, "That's all right, Peter, some other time."

Long seemed uninterested in Ginsberg, Burroughs, and Corso; the idea of the Beats didn't appeal to him at all. Every time their names came up he just acted as if he didn't hear you.

And then a noise like thunder came from the mountains. The sky got dark and Long took Peter away.

That night, Gregory and I went to John's, the most expensive restaurant in Boulder (paid for with Seymour's Diner's Club). We sat there drinking martinis like they were going out of style. I told Gregory about Peter's poems, and Gregory said loudly that Peter was "obsessed with assholes" because he didn't like having that kind of sex anymore with Allen. (The other people in the restaurant were looking at us by now.) In fact, Gregory didn't think Peter was at all queer, and that his true self was finally coming through: what Peter really wanted was to have a girlfriend and to have a baby.

Later, when I asked Allen about Peter's plan to have a baby with an ugly girl and the three of them living in Long's cabin, Allen said that Peter had always wanted a family; he wanted to fill up his house with boys and girls who would look like him and live on after him, because he grew up in a house that wasn't really a home. "Peter just had to content himself with a house full of ghosts," Allen said thoughtfully. "I just hope he doesn't regret the last twenty years, I hope he doesn't think he just got sidetracked."

29. Menstrual Pudding

I agreed to look after Allen and Peter's place when they were gone. I had the keys. It was like being given Neptune's scepter. I called my friend Jason back on Long Island to tell him I was sitting at Allen's desk, surrounded by his books and papers, and was drinking tea out of Allen Ginsberg's tea glass! I was seeing the things Allen saw when he woke up, like his tiny framed detail of Rimbaud, with his angelic face and nimbus cloud of hair, his wrist bent under his chin, part of a group portrait of Rimbaud and his lover poet Paul Verlaine and their friends in a café in Paris. I looked into the bearded face, also framed, of Allen's old courage-teacher, Walt Whitman, hanging near Allen's refrigerator in the kitchen. I didn't dare sit on the *zafu* in the shrine area, though I wanted to pick up the strange, ancient-looking objects that were lying on the orange cloth that draped the table. Cameos of Allen's Buddhist teachers, a portrait of Rinpoche, and a mandala hung above the shrine on the wall. There was even a tiny gong to call Allen and Peter back to their practice cushions. One of the objects on the table reminded me of the silver pointer that you use to point to the words in an opened Torah.

The bed was unmade. I was planning on sleeping in my own bed and coming to the apartment just to check on it, water the ferns that Peter had brought into the house, and get rid of the sour milk. Peter also left a note on the door for me to "Get the compost reddy!" I couldn't imagine what compost they would have in a student apartment complex. I should've asked someone before throwing the garbage down the chute, but I didn't.

M
E
N
S
T
R
U
A
L

Pudding

The phone rang. It was Diane di Prima. She was coming over to teach me how to write a play based entirely on chance, as she had promised me the night of her reading. A roll of the dice to make art. "That's all it is," Diane said. "Expect me late."

I was nervous about her impending visit. I still thought she was kind of scary. Reading about her sexual exploits made me even more afraid of her. I prepared Allen's place as if I were expecting Marilyn Monroe for dinner. I made Allen and Peter's bed, I even filled a pail with ice, made sure there were cigarettes around—Gitanes—even though I didn't know whether or not she smoked. I checked to see if the bath towels smelled bad. They didn't, so they could stay. I spent the rest of the day preparing for Diane's visit. At the appointed time, she appeared.

She had fierce black eyes that stared out at me in the doorway and coal black hair, and as if that weren't dramatic enough she wore eye shadow. When she looked at you, you forgot that she wasn't very tall, or very chic, or conventionally beautiful. She had arrived at Allen's apartment alone—no husband, no boyfriend, no lawn gnome (I didn't even know his name, so I couldn't ask about him). The apartment building was unusually quiet. It was like we were the only two people in the world. I didn't like it.

Diane said she wanted to cook and she seemed to know her way around Allen's kitchen. She took over. She said that when she was a teenager in New York, she used to make something called "menstrual pudding," just tomato sauce and potatoes, no meat and no spices, because she couldn't afford them then. You had to pretend there was meat and spices in the pot you were stirring. I asked how it got its name, and she explained that someone in the apartment she lived in at the time—"some cat named Jack"—called it that. Then she made spaghetti and garlic bread and poured us lots of red wine.

My head was swimming. I never drank that much wine before. It felt like there was a sun in my chest and it was burning through my shirt. Diane said she thought the wine might've gone off. I said I was going to lie down, maybe on the couch. She said I should get into bed. She opened the windows. There was a delicious breeze; I could hear the trees outside bending. She said good night. Then she asked if she could get into bed with me for a few minutes. I remembered one of Diane's laments, a tiny poem she had written and recited to us in Allen's class: "I have the upper hand but if I keep it I'll lose the circulation in one arm." I didn't have the upper hand. I was in some Elysian field with Diane di Prima. "I can show you baby enough love to break your heart forever." I could feel her breath on my eyes. I was lost. I had deserted my post. This was a woman who had used the word "cunt" in a lot of poems. We lay there for a few minutes with our arms around each other, talking about something, about nothing. Before I knew it she was going down on me and I didn't do anything to stop her.

I think I had had the fantasy of Diane di Prima as beatnik-sexfiend since the moment she came into Allen's classroom. I wondered if the lawn gnome would come and change me into something. There was something about being in Allen's house that seemed to encourage having sex. I fell asleep in Allen's bed, and woke up alone.

The next day, however, Diane returned with her boyfriend. She put her arm around me and told me she was going to give me her playwriting lesson, using the books and an old blues records in Allen's place. We went back into Allen's bedroom, alone, and looked through Allen's records, but nothing was said about the night before. Her boyfriend sat downstairs and waited for us to come down. I kept thinking he was going to say something. Did he even know? Did she get any pleasure from it? All I remembered was I'd passed out with her mouth around me, overcome by the wine.

Before she left I wanted her to send me her address, or a picture—I wanted to keep in touch. I was crazy. I didn't know how things were done. I had had only one girlfriend throughout high school. The Beats seemed to know something I would never know

MENSTRUAL

Pudding

about sex. They were like sexual Houdinis, slipping out of pad-locked trunks thrown into the river. They always managed to get out and get away.

30. Human Beings Need Meat

My parents called. They wanted to know how I was doing. They wanted to know how Allen was doing. My father asked if I'd grown a long beard yet. My mother wanted to be sure that I wasn't a complete vegetarian. She said human beings need meat. She told me that as soon as I had a dream about steak or liver, I should go out and get a steak dinner. She reminded me that it should be a good cut of meat and that I had my father's Diner's Club card if I couldn't pay for it.

"He still has my Diner's Club card, Marion?" my father asked her over the extension in his office. "No wonder I can't find it. What does he need with my credit card at Beatnik Camp?"

"Dad, it's not a beatnik camp, it's not a camp at all. I hate camp. It's a college, a school, the first Buddhist university in the Western world," I said, waving my nonexistent Naropa banner, and waving it high.

"Bub," my mother said to my father on the extension—she always calls him Bub, short for the Yiddish endearment bubbalah. "Your son is going to college with Allen Ginsberg." My parents often got into arguments like this while they were on the phone with me. I'd be completely quiet and they would continue to argue on the two telephones in their own house. Sometimes I'd hang up and call them back, and the line would be engaged—they were still arguing.

They wanted to know if I would be getting a report card. They wanted to know if they would have to sign it. I told them it didn't work that way. In fact, I was getting ready to go to William

Burroughs's lecture, held in the shrine room at Naropa, so I managed to get off the phone while they continued their conversation
without me.

Burroughs always had a big audience for his talks. He didn't teach
in the conventional way, walking down an aisle of desks asking
questions or writing on the blackboard. He conducted his classes
like a customs official behind a long table, and he was telling you
what you were allowed to bring into the country and what was pro-
hibited. Except he took more pleasure in what was contraband.
Burroughs took his teaching very seriously, though. He came prepared, unlike Gregory, who winged everything and riffed like a jazz
musician.

Burroughs had given me a printed sheet with certain reading
assignments. I expected titles of books to read, but what I got were
samizdat copies of obscure reports Bill said were prepared as top-
secret documents by the U.S. Air Force about flying saucers. Then
there was a book by Peter Bander called *Voices from the Tapes,* and
articles that had appeared in *Psychic News,* and something called
"References to Hitler Are Dangerous." The rest were books by
William Burroughs, such as *Exterminator!* That was something Bill
knew a thing or two about, as he had briefly been an exterminator.
The list included *The Last Words of Dutch Schultz* and of course
Naked Lunch. For today's class, Bill had given me *Your Tape Recorder:
A Tracking Station for Paranormal Voices from the Handbook of Psychic
Discoveries,* a book I had to order from the University of Colorado
bookstore. It took a long time to get it.

I sat with Billy Burroughs in the back of the class, which was
really just a row of seats in the shrine room that shimmered in the
heat. Bill sat behind a long table. He could've performed an
autopsy on it. He put down his hat and rested his cane at one end
of the table. He had an old-fashioned tape recorder in front of him.

"Certain tape recordings," Burroughs snarled, "made with no
apparent input have turned up unexplained voices. Actual recorded

voices, faint, and of unknown origin appear to have been recorded. The most complete source on this is *Breakthrough* by Konstantin Raudive. These voices seemed an appropriate topic to take up at the Kerouac School of Disembodied Poetics."

Burroughs began by talking about Brion Gysin, his partner in the cut-up, which had become Bill's modus operandi, the way he seemed to create most of his writing. He talked about how cut-ups put you in touch with what you know and what you do not know that you know. Burroughs and his partner Gysin had turned their attention to the tape recorder as a means for juxtaposition. "We went on to exploit the potentials of the tape recorder," Burroughs explained to the class. "Cut up, slow down, speed up, run backwards, inch the tape, play several tracks at once, cut back and forth between two recorders." Bill turned on the tape recorder to demonstrate what one of the tapes sounded like. "I have gotten words and voices from barking dogs," he explained.

I couldn't hear anything. Then, faintly, I heard what sounded like a dog barking from behind a door.

"No doubt," Bill said, "one could do much better with dolphins, which doesn't mean that dolphins have mastered the English language. Words," Bill continued, leaning into the microphone, which helped to carry his carnival barker's voice to the back of the shrine room, "will emerge from recordings of dripping faucets. In fact, almost any sound that is not too uniform will produce words. Every little breeze seems to whisper Louise." Burroughs was singing, and with his straw boater and cane he suddenly seemed like a midwestern Maurice Chevalier on junk.

"The very tree branches brushing against her window seemed to mutter murder murder murder murder. Well, the branches may have muttered just that, and you could hear it back with a tape recorder."

Someone raised a hand. Bill reluctantly acknowledged the guy with his arm hanging in the air.

"Mr. Burroughs," the young man said, "how can everything in the world, everything we see and hear, be available to us? It can't possibly be out there just for our use. I mean, isn't it only crazy people who think that the television is talking to them or that fire engines have some kind of personal meaning for them?"

Burroughs refused to look up at the man. He stared at the tape recorder. Then he stared at the desk. Then he told a little story.

"Some time ago, a young man came to see me and said he was going mad. Street signs, overheard conversations, radio broadcasts seemed to refer to him in some way. I told him, 'Of course they refer to you. You see them and you hear them.' "

I looked over at Billy Jr. He seemed to be shaking his head in agreement. I started to worry about accreditation. After all, I had just promised my parents that the Jack Kerouac School would get it.

Then Bill explained to us about Raudive's experiments with tape recordings, how they were carried out in a soundproof studio, how a new tape was turned on, blank but recording. Then, when the tape was played back, Raudive listened through very sensitive state-of-the-art headphones and to his surprise very recognizable voices and words were audible on the blank tape. Burroughs said that Raudive, in his research, has now recorded more than a hundred thousand phrases. He said the sound is rhythmic like poetry, like Anne's list poems or Buddhist monks chanting. He said many of the voices come from the dead—Hitler, Nietzsche, Goethe, Jesus Christ—"anybody who is anybody is there," many of them having undergone a marked deterioration of their mental and artistic faculties.

"Goethe isn't what he used to be," Bill explained. "Hitler had a bigger and better mouth when he was alive. What better way to contact someone than to cut and rearrange his actual words? Certainly an improvement on the usual scene where Shakespeare is announced, only to be followed by some excruciatingly bad poetry."

Then Bill read to us from his dream diaries, comparing Raudive's experiments with the utterances of schizophrenics and psychotics. He then read from a notebook: "The unconscious imitated by cheesecake.

H
U
M
A
N

Beings Need Meat

C

O

O

L

A tin of tomato soup in Arizona . . . Green is a man to fill is a boy. I can take the hut set anywhere. A book called *Advanced Outrage.* An astronaut named Plat. First American shot on Mars. Life is a flickering shadow with violence before and after it."

Burroughs's voice was the voice of American violence, I thought. It seemed to separate knowledge from feeling, which always brought cruelty. But it was simply a man's voice. He seemed like a man whose whole life had been a form of penance for what he called the stupid accident of his wife Joan's death. No wonder he spent all this time trying to contact the dead or convince us, himself, that the dead could speak to us on these blank tape recordings. Maybe it made him feel less guilty.

Burroughs pulled out a piece of paper and read from a list of phrases that he had been attracted to in Raudive's book: "Cheers here are the nondead. Here are the cunning ones. We are here because of you. We are all longing to go home. We see Tibet with the binoculars of the people. Take the grave with you . . ." Bill read quietly. "It snows horribly. Class dismissed."

31. A Spy in the House of Love

One day when I stopped by Allen's apartment to do some filing for him, Allen announced that he thought there might be a spy at Naropa. He didn't say who it was. Was he talking about me? I had no idea. There were few enough students here as it was. Could it be Burroughs, who seemed so in love with the idea of conspiracies, secret documents, government code words, *interzones,* like ones he'd put into *Naked Lunch*? Because the Beats had lived so long on the outskirts of society, I thought maybe it was starting to get to them. What would it be like to always have your mail waiting for you at the U.S. Consul's office or at American Express?

Hadn't Gregory called the only novel he'd ever [...] *Express*?

Allen called me up—I had to come ove[...] explained that the government had been listeni[...] phone for years. He felt that his mail was oft[...] told me about "Cointelpro," a government, m[...] discredit radicals or anyone deemed dangerous to the p[...] government of the United States—business interests, powerful families like the Rockefellers, the Hunts, Henry Luce, etc. Allen had a lot of names. He said that some of these people weren't even all that bad, he said that he once met Nelson Rockefeller and had liked him personally, that he loved art and wasn't stupid. Allen said it was the people who worked for Rockefeller, who "took care of business" for these powerful people—they were the dangerous ones.

I knew from Ginsberg's files that he had been gathering information on the government and its program of misinformation. He said they did it to Martin Luther King and to the Black Panthers. Allen told me all this while we were sitting around the kitchen table sipping Celestial Seasonings chamomile tea. Peter sat with us, listening, nodding his head. At the same time, he was admiring the Sleepytime Tea box, with its happy family of bears—Papa Bear sitting in his rocking chair wearing a nightcap in front of the fire, Mama Bear carrying Baby Bear off to bed.

"You've been staring at that box for a half hour," Allen told Peter. "What do you see in it?"

"I see the future," Peter said, "with you sitting in front of the fire and our babies coming to kiss you and their mother goodnight. Do you think you'd like to live in a cave with me, Allen?"

Allen laughed. It was a sweet laugh—a respite from his high seriousness—which I didn't see too often. His crooked mouth made it all the sweeter. Strange that it would come during this gentle-voiced tirade against the government, the CIA, and America's power establishment. It *was* the old Allen, but tempered by his Buddhist meditation, his growing awareness of the other guy's pain and suffering.

hen again, I also wondered if they were all crazy. I know that
Allen had gone missing once in the mid-fifties, only to turn up
in the deep forests of South America, living with a woman,
Burroughs told me, a woman named Karena Shields. Shields had
portrayed Jane in a couple of early Tarzan films, and I knew from
reading the so-called yagé letters between Allen and Bill that they
were practically subsisting on coca leaves and getting incredibly
fucked up. I knew that Allen had been given a choice in his
younger days between staying at a mental hospital or going back to
college. Were the inmates running the asylum at the Jack Kerouac
School? Or were my hopelessly scaredy-cat, bourgeois roots beginning to show?

Peter got up and took a giant ironing board out of the closet.
He was going to press Allen's shirt and pants for the reading later
that night. For the first time since arriving at Naropa, I was going
to read my poems, along with Gregory, Allen, and a few other students from the dance and Buddhist psychology departments. I was
supposed to be the jewel in their diadem, the student who would
come to represent the Kerouac School, the one they exposed to
Ginsberg and Corso, to Charles Olson and Robert Duncan, to the
New York School of O'Hara, Ashbery, and Koch. And, thanks to
Anne's friends, the younger writers who had taken up the brunt of
my so-called education, I had also read Balzac's *Lost Illusions* and
Flaubert's *Sentimental Education*, as well as the "grumps," as Corso
called them, Céline and Ezra Pound. The writer Michael Brownstein, Anne's former lover (the one who usurped her husband,
Lewis, while he had gone around the corner for the evening newspapers), taught me those books in one of my classes at Naropa. So
while Peter laid out Allen's pants one leg at a time on the ironing
board, spitting on the iron like my grandmother used to do in the
basement when she came to visit us, Allen continued his spiel
about Cointelpro.

Allen said that Naropa could be finished before it even started.
He said that I should be on the lookout for anyone suspicious, any-

one who doesn't seem really interested in poetry. (It didn't occur to me at the time that that included just about everyone.) He said that I should keep an eye out at the reading tonight for anyone who looked lost, or hopelessly straight. I thought about how I felt lost and hopelessly straight myself, even though my heart practically leaped like a gazelle in the Song of Songs whenever I found myself sitting in Allen's place or struggling with Gregory over his poems.

I said I would do my best.

I was nervous that night at the reading, which was held in the living room of a beautiful home on a street filled with old trees, which had to be a hundred years old and gave wonderful shade. I walked to the reading with Gregory. I told him about what Allen had said, about Cointelpro, about how the government might have sent a spy to attend classes at the Kerouac School.

"Maybe it's Allen," Gregory said. "He seems to be getting a lot of official recognition, and he always seems to have money. He even knows the police chief of Chiapas," Gregory reminded me. It was Burroughs who told me that, to a stupid person, Allen looks like a communist.

When we arrived the living room was filled. There must've been about two hundred people throughout the house, which was owned by one of Rinpoche's most devoted followers, a young woman whom Gregory pointed out to me as the heiress to a discount department store fortune. She welcomed everyone and then she introduced Allen, who was going to be the master of ceremonies. Anne was there, of course, with her contingent of exotic-looking women and pretty men. I noticed Anne's manager, Linda Louie, her husband Mickey, and their baby Hadrian, named after the emperor or the wall—whichever came first. A young woman with dark hair in an old-fashioned hat pinned with a veil was seated between Linda and Mickey. She was eccentrically dressed. She wore a kilt. She had a round pleasant face and reminded me of

A

S

P

Y

in the House of Love

C

O

O

L

Brenda Vaccaro, an actress no one hears about these days. She was Jon Voight's girlfriend for a while, or at least that's what I'd heard.

Allen was a real *jambon* when it came to an audience. It's why he seemed to love teaching so much. It was hard for him to leave the stage. Originally he was only going to read a small poem, something he had dashed off in the minutes after supper before he and Peter got dressed for the reading. Allen called them his "porch haikus" because he wrote them on the porch as the sun was going down. He read one porch haiku about a guy who cuts up his girl-friend with an ax. I thought haikus were supposed to be about the moon awakening and stuff like that. I guess I was wrong. Encouraged by wild applause, Allen read for another half hour. He read "Punk Rock Your My Big Crybaby"—the crowd cheered when Allen read "Fuck me in the ass! Suck me! Come in my ears! Promise you'll murder me in the gutter with orgasms!"

After that, I was no longer sure they would like me, or sit still for my love poems, written like French surrealism, with titles like "Portrait of Orpheus as a Young Horticulturist" or "The Water Lily Is Doomed."

Allen wouldn't get off the stage. They had to carry his chair away from the front of the room with him in it, like he was the groom at his own Jewish wedding. Gregory finally had to say something.

"Ginzy, that's great but give the kid a chance. Miss Christ, we're all gonna be two thousand years old by the time you run out of breath!" It's true that Allen's meditation practice had given him even more of a barrel chest, even more lung power.

Gregory read next. He recited a poem that I had heard before. He never said it the same way twice. The poem was about how Gregory had met this guy in a bar who had asked Gregory what poetry was. It wasn't an existential or a philosophical question. He was just a guy, Gregory said, who had come into some tavern who didn't know what poetry meant.

"I told him," Gregory said in his poem, which he called "I Met

/ 181 /

This Guy Who Died." "Happy tipsy one night," Gregory takes the man home so that they both might admire his baby asleep in his crib. When all of a sudden, "A great sorrow overcame him / 'O Gregory,' he moaned / 'you brought up something to die.' " That's all he read. It was obvious it was one of Gregory's favorite poems. Later that night, Gregory whispered to me that it wasn't just any guy. It was Kerouac, drunk with mortality, who had peered into the baby's crib.

Like the tiny coffin Gregory had written about seeing when he was a young kid on the Lower East Side, being taken away by all those big Cadillacs, Gregory wrote tiny poems about great big subjects like death and time. He had memorized the poem. I was supposed to hold the crib sheet, in case he got it wrong. He didn't.

Then he introduced me, as a poet, as his friend, as someone bathed in that from which he, Gregory, and Allen also bathed: the healing waters of poesy. He said something like that.

I almost fainted with joy. I didn't think my poems were very good. I apologized for them in advance. I read a few. I heard applause. I dared to look up. I read another. I read the one poem of mine Allen seemed to like, even though I had to explain to him who Donny and Marie were. It was a poem about imagining myself a construction worker, taking The Donny and Marie Show lunchbox with me to work and sitting out on a girder of an unfinished New York City skyscraper. It was meant to be funny. People laughed. They positively howled with laughter. It doesn't seem that funny now, the poem. It got old fast. But it was new then and people loved it.

Peter saw me after the reading. He said I was a star. People milled around me afterward, those too shy to go up to Allen or Gregory. I was grateful. They asked questions I couldn't answer in a thousand years about poems I hadn't taken very long to write. I was happy. I was sweating. Then a dark-haired woman came up and put a napkin in a glass of water and wiped my forehead. She didn't introduce herself right away. She was grinning and said,

A

S

P

Y

in the House of Love

"You were wonderful." She lifted her veil. Anne and Linda Louie came over to me. Anne said, very tightly, "That was good." Linda Louie was more generous, and she introduced her veiled friend. Her name was Carla Fannetti.

I'd only had one serious girlfriend so far, so I didn't know a lot about men and women coming together. But this attractive woman who had just mopped my brow looked like she was in love, and she was gazing in my direction. I looked around; there was no one standing behind me.

32. The Six Realms

A few of us—Allen, Anne, Burroughs, Gregory, and I—walked over to Tom's Tavern after the reading. Carla came along with Linda Louie; Linda's husband had taken the baby home.

I never met the Tom of Tom's Tavern. I don't know if he even existed. The tavern was a place where college kids from the University of Colorado came to get drunk, and men who lived in bombed-out cars or in shacks up in the mountains came down whenever they scraped a few bucks together to make a night out of it with a hamburger and some beers.

We all squeezed into a booth. I sat across from Carla. I could really see her for the first time. She had style and sense. She owned her own import-export business. She often had to make business trips to Thailand. Apparently, Rinpoche encouraged his students to start their own businesses. He would often step slowly out of the back of his black BMW, helped by the Vadjra guards, and walk into a community business and make some kind of blessing over it. Then he would look over the merchandise. Sometimes he would buy something as a kind of benediction for the success of the establishment. His aides would come by later and pay for it.

I asked Carla what Rinpoche bought at her store. She thought it was a hand-painted tie or something that he bought as a gift, maybe some "Flash Gordon soap," which is what Gregory called the oval, scented soaps on display in strangers' bathrooms.

In the smoky and darkened tavern, Carla turned to me and asked how long I'd been at Naropa. She explained that she had come to Boulder because she was a student of Rinpoche's and she wanted to be around other practitioners. She said that she started to "sit" in Scotland, which is where Rinpoche had spent time at a meditation center in the highlands.

I found out that Carla had a past. She had lived with a famous violinist, who was the son of an even more famous violinist, and had traveled the world with him.

I asked if she and the violinist were still together. She said no. She said that studying Buddhism had changed the way she saw relationships. She said that Rinpoche practiced something called "crazy wisdom."

I had already heard about crazy wisdom from Allen, but I let her explain it to me. She said it meant giving in to your desire so you didn't have desire anymore. I started thinking that Carla wanted to give in to her desire. And that she wanted to give in to her desire to be with me—tonight. Crazy wisdom didn't seem so crazy, but it did seem dangerous—dangerous in unenlightened hands, which included mine, and probably Carla's. The more I heard about crazy wisdom, the more I felt like someone was shaking my hands with a hand buzzer and wouldn't let go. But I was intrigued.

As the poets and their hangers-on huddled together at Tom's, I remembered something Phil Ochs once said. Ochs was a folksinger Allen admired who became a suicide. He once said, "To the losers go the hang-ups, to the victors go the hangers-on." I basked in the feeling of being included among the poets; it felt good to be chosen for something. It didn't happen too often. In high school, I never made the honor roll, but my sister made it every year. I did get to be president of my junior high school class,

C

O

O

L

but that was for all the wrong reasons. I think it was because I once had a pizza delivered to the middle of my seventh-grade algebra class, or was it because I had ridden my bicycle down the hall, or because I wore an American flag tie that got me called to the principal's office until my parents came? Or was it because I once fell inside a baby grand piano at a school assembly when I was trying to imitate Jerry Lee Lewis? (The assistant principal had to pull me out by my legs, cautioning me by saying that I had to be protected from myself.) So I felt that being elected class president was like when the people of Paris made Quasimodo the mayor. I even ducked out of the prom, my one ceremonial duty as president, so that I could watch Bob Dylan come out of seclusion to sing on *The Johnny Cash Show*.

Carla said that Rinpoche was always surrounded by a court. Because he had grown up in England instead of Tibet, he had come to admire the English system, and he modeled his spiritual kingdom, called Shambhala, after the English court. Rinpoche's wife actually had ladies-in-waiting and he took some of them to his bed, although some of his consorts were married to his students and members of his court. Carla told me that most of the men whose wives Rinpoche had slept with considered it an honor that Rinpoche had chosen them. Carla said that she wasn't interested in Rinpoche in that way, but she still considered him a great man and enlightened. She said that Rinpoche had helped her with her fears, and she did seem unafraid of the world.

One of her shoulder straps slid off her shoulders. It was a thin black cord and it looked sexy where it had fallen. She had a voluptuous figure. She seemed more interested in me than in the famous writers at the table. She had a youthful face, although she said she was thirty, which made her practically a wizard of age in my eyes. She had raven hair and a strong jawline that gave her a look of maturity and dignity. Hers was a face full of contrasts—listening quietly when Burroughs was holding forth, then becoming animated when Gregory said something outlandish to Anne.

As usual, Carla wasn't making a big impression on Allen or

Peter or Bill. They wouldn't have been interested in her anyway. I liked that.

Carla asked if I was having a good time. She asked me what I thought of my teachers, with most of them sitting right there. Carla had that quality that F. Scott Fitzgerald gave to his flapper heroines: she had "moxie." That was the word I thought of when I looked at her. She also seemed to be jumping out of her skin just to talk to me.

Carla took out a leopard-skin wallet to pay for her drinks. I noticed that she had on black fishnet stockings and a jacket with a faux leopard collar. I felt like I had discovered the illegitimate daughter of Mike Hammer and his secretary Velma, the one he was always flirting with and promising to settle down and marry. The one he tries to save before the world blows up in *Murder My Sweet*. Then it hit me. Through all the chatter at the table, I remembered the French movie director Jean-Luc Godard. One of my teachers, Michael Brownstein, had handed out a mimeographed copy of an interview with him in English; he said it was essential reading. It was a great interview. In it, Godard gave his formula for love: it was time + poetry = love.

We had a black waiter that night in Tom's Tavern, which was rare for Boulder. When he walked away with our order, Burroughs suddenly said, "Did you know that Warren Harding was a quadroon? Did you know that, Allen?"

Allen mentioned that Bill wasn't drinking these days, but I had seen him drunk and weepy in his room. Jubal was a bad influence on Burroughs, I thought. He seemed to be keeping him under his thumb, which was easier to do with bottles of whiskey and the drugs that Jubal brought into the house. Perversely, Jubal kept a set of "works"—spoon and needle—wrapped in a Buddhist prayer cloth. He kept it hidden in Bill's house. I wanted to tell Allen, because I feared it could wind up getting Bill arrested, humiliated in his old age. But Jubal said Bill needed heroin to survive because he'd been dependent on it for so long, and to stop now would kill him. Jubal said Bill's doctors knew all about it.

C

O

O

L

Carla told Burroughs that she had spent a lot of time in Tangier, buying things for her store. She said it was a magical place. Once she was in her hotel room and couldn't sleep and so she opened the window to let the night air in. Suddenly, she heard a sound like no other she'd ever heard; she looked out and saw a wild horse running on the beach.

Burroughs answered her, thank god. I was afraid the women at the table were all going to be ignored, because Allen and Burroughs usually ignored them. Except for Anne, who was paying attention to her friends, to Nanette and Calliope and Kitty.

Burroughs told Carla that Tangier was his dream town. "In the mid-forties," Burroughs said, "I had a dream in which I came into a harbor. When I looked around, I felt completely at home; I knew instinctively in my dream that that was the place I wanted to be."

The waiter came back and placed a small shot glass in front of Bill. Burroughs finished the story by saying that toward the end of his time in Tangier, he went rowing on a lake and came into a harbor he recognized as the one in his dream.

Gregory, his glasses flying from the lariat around his neck, suddenly got up and left the table, with Calliope following him out the door. Too many people crowded the booth, I thought; too close quarters. Gregory's fear of crowds—his fear, Bill says, of death in the moment—must have kicked in, and he was out the door.

"Why doesn't he just have a good cry?" Anne asked when Gregory bolted. "We're all here to comfort him," she said, laughing. It sounded like a good idea to me.

"Did you know," Bill drawled, "that tears rid the body of poisonous wastes, like sweat and urine? In jaundice, your tears are bright yellow. In short, grief or despair causes metabolic poisons to accumulate. The old idea that someone who is greatly afflicted must cry or die has a sound basis in human biology."

The conversation jumped from Caryl Chessman to the Scottsboro boys to Allen's writing of "Kaddish," which was provoked by someone at the table asking for ketchup, which led to someone else talking about tomatoes, which resulted in a question for Allen about the reference to the "first poisonous tomatoes in America" in that poem. Allen said that it was a reference to Russian immigrants, like my grandmother, at the turn of the century who had never seen tomatoes before; they stayed away from tomatoes, thinking they were poison.

It suddenly occurred to me: the best minds of Allen's generation were sitting at Tom's Tavern, and I was sitting with them, included by all except Anne, who hardly spoke to me.

My triumph at the reading that night seemed to annoy Anne. She didn't seem to feel about it the way I thought she would, that I was representing the good work of the Jack Kerouac School and that people seemed to respond to my poems. I thought she would take some teacherly pride in that, but I was wrong. Anne's circle of exotic women and exotically pretty boys seemed impenetrable to me. She spent most the evening talking about what a sensation her two handsome protégés, Stephen Low and Brad Gooch, had been back in New York at the St. Mark's Poetry Project. It seemed like she was going out of her way to say that my achievement here at the Kerouac School somehow didn't count.

I walked Carla home. I asked her if she'd heard Anne on the subject of the St. Mark's reading, hoping that Carla wasn't also discounting my triumph. She answered me by telling me about the Six Worlds. She said it was a Buddhist concept that helped to explain human nature. Carla said that the Six Worlds, or Six Realms, were Heaven, Human, Hungry Ghost, Hell, Animal, and Angry Warrior Realm, that they were all held together in the delusion of time by things like pride, anger, and ignorance. She explained vanity was one of them, and that Anne, like all of us, suffered from that. Carla said she had a Buddhist painting of all the realms, and she'd like to show it to me.

My vanity realm wanted to come up and see it, but my fear realm held me back.

I said it was late and that I'd already taken up too much of her time with my poetry.

C

O

O

L

She asked me if I'd like to go out with her to a Mexican restaurant one night, in a nearby town, with a beautiful cherrywood bar from the old cowboy days of Colorado. She would drive us.

Before I had a chance to answer, we came to a street filled with older homes and Carla stopped beside a carriage house. "This is where I live," she said. She kissed me. She touched the back of my head with her small hand and brought my head a little closer to hers. And then she disappeared into her house.

I walked home through the dark, empty streets of Boulder. A breeze from the mountains seemed to push me home a little faster. In a few days I would go to Carla's place of business, sit in a rattan chair with a price tag on it, and watch her conduct business in the human world—a realm I knew so little about.

The next morning I was supposed to go to Billy Burroughs's apartment to pick him up for lunch with his father. He had asked me to come along, but I didn't want to. Gregory and his wife were going to come by, with Max, and we had planned to drive into Denver to a museum. Gregory wanted to see a show with paintings about warfare, depicting soldiers from Achilles to General Patton. I didn't want to miss the chance to go with them.

Besides, I preferred playing with Max to spending time with Billy and Bill Burroughs. Max wasn't famous. He wasn't crazy. He didn't make me nervous. He was just a little boy who liked to make funny noises, who thought I was funny without having to be witty.

Around eleven-thirty in the morning I went by Billy's apartment. He was drunk or stoned, or both. He said he didn't want to go and have lunch with his father.

"Old Bill can be a prick. He's just a shitkicker," Billy said. "My father should've been an overseer at a plantation. He missed his calling." Billy suddenly switched to a Southern accent, saying, "The smell of magnolias pervades the old manse and I see Old Bill sittin' outside with a shotgun pickin' off pickaninnies."

I didn't know if I could handle this. We walked over to Burroughs's apartment and then to the New York Deli. On the way, I walked between father and son, who had nothing to say to each other. At the deli, we scrambled into a booth. That is, I scrambled and Billy folded himself into the seat, practically putting his head on the table and rubbing the menus together like he was trying to start a fire with them, Boy Scout style. "Old Bill" took his time, seating himself with his customary arthritic abandon, leaning his cane against the side of the table.

"Where's Harry Belafonte?" Bill growled, referring to the handsome, light-skinned black waiter we had had at Tom's the night before. Burroughs was mixed up about what restaurant we were in. It was the first time I wanted Gregory to show up on time and take me with him.

I told both Burroughses about Allen's theory that there might be a spy coming to Naropa, or one already here at the Kerouac School. Bill said with authority that it was unlikely. He said that George Lincoln Rockwell, who had been the head of the American Nazi Party, probably spoke at rallies made up of nothing but Jews from the D.A.'s office and FBI agents, goose-stepping and giving him the fascist salute. Billy laughed.

"He's probably got about two real followers; one's completely deaf and the other is marginally literate and thinks the swastika is an Aztec symbol," Burroughs added.

I saw what passed for a smile cross Burroughs's face. It was like the crack in a mummy that appears after a thousand years. Burroughs had the newspaper with him. I think the pope was in Poland. Burroughs started to talk about communism. He said it was doomed to failure because it was being run like the phone company. Then there was silence. Silence for a long time. Our food arrived, and the two men started eating across from each other, Billy staring into his bowl of matzoh ball soup and Bill looking at his Reuben sandwich, unwilling to take it on.

"I am seized with the panic of one buried alive," Burroughs said, in his best W. C. Fields imitation. He pushed the sandwich aside. It occurred to me that I'd never really seen Burroughs eat anything. Like a vampire, he sat staring at his food. I expected him to say, "I only drink . . . wine."

T
H
E

S
I
X

Realms

C

O

O

L

To my relief, Gregory appeared, rolling through the skinny aisle between the elevated booths on one side and the counter on the other, holding Max and looking like he'd gotten some sleep for a change. He appeared at our table, saving me from the cone of silence I was trapped under. Suddenly, I felt sad at having to leave the two of them alone in the restaurant, gulping down all that dead air. Gregory reached out to pull off some of the melted cheese from Bill's sandwich. He ate some and fed some to Max.

"Bill," Gregory said to Burroughs, "you are always Bill and always will be. We are the Daddies of the age."

As if summoned by the Muse, I followed Gregory out the door, like Sabu following Ganesh's curled trunk away from the mountains and toward the teeming city.

33. "The Death of General Wolfe"

I wasn't prepared for what awaited me in the car Gregory had shanghai'd for our trip to the Denver museum. The car contained all the chaos of Gregory's life. Gregory had had three children and four wives, plus his current girlfriend, Calliope. There was Max, climbing out of his mother Lisa's lap to recline in the well above the backseat like that famous Manet painting of Olympia. Like Olympia, Max didn't have any clothes on—Lisa had just removed them, probably because they were wet. Calliope was also there; she was going to drive us. Miranda, one of Gregory's two daughters from an earlier marriage, was also in the car. Miranda was Gregory's New York daughter. (He had recently started writing poems about her. "She walks in grace like a sharp New Yorker," Gregory said. He wanted me to put that into one of his poems. He really dug "her proud walk.")

I squeezed myself into this leaky lifeboat, and soon we were bouncing along while thermoses of lemonade and whiskey, not to mention Max's bottle, were passed around the overheated, noisy car.

Gregory saw himself in some way as a Romantic poet; it wasn't just the nineteenth-century diction that he loved, but the epic battles, the grottoes of hell, quarreling gods. He wasn't ashamed to talk about the poet as a Great Messenger. Gregory believed in his calling as a poet. I was starting to feel that it gave him permission to live this messy and hopped-up life, one that, in some ways, was exciting to be around. Around Gregory, I sometimes felt drawn into a whirlpool, undone by my own curiosity to find out what it would be like inside the belly of the whale, to strap on Mercury's sandals and jump not just into the symbols of life but into life itself.

The trust-fund Buddhists I was meeting in Boulder, who kept talking about crazy wisdom, well, it was as if they were just looking for an excuse to misbehave. Sad to leave college, they needed another reason to go crazy in the world. But Gregory seemed like crazy wisdom incarnate—or was he just crazy?

To Gregory, the gods were real. Looking at himself in the rearview mirror, sitting beside Calliope, Gregory spouted, "Hermes, you orphan god! Behold Nunzio, Behold Gregory . . . I take back all you took! My beautiful hair is dead." Gregory was intoning his old poem as he checked the gray hairs sprouting on his scalp, like someone checking his garden after a rainstorm.

Gregory, I thought to myself, you don't have to worry about your hair, you still have so much of it, and you're sitting here in this chariot with your wife and your girlfriend—not many men I know could say that.

I know that Gregory believed that time was robbing him. His street-kid life was no more. He was becoming more and more preoccupied with time passing. He kept referring to himself as "a penniless legend." He was feeling more and more like Villon, his brother in crime and poesy. Both orphans, both altar boys "attending the priest's skirt."

Gregory wanted to know how much it would cost to get into the museum. "Kerouac, you know, said that line, how 'everything

"THE DEATH

of General Wolfe"

is his, everything belongs to him because he's poor.' It's bullshit!"
Gregory said. *"Nothing* is mine. Here I am, a prince of poetry and
I'm made to roam the world, with women and Jews."

Gregory scrunched up his face and snorted out a laugh. He
liked to insult me, or at least see how much I could take. And he
really hated it when I tried to be nice to him.

We arrived at the museum. I didn't care what Gregory thought,
or how much I'd pay for it later in abuse, so I paid for everyone,
and everyone followed me inside.

Gregory and I moved faster than the wind through every wing of
the museum, like that scene in Godard's *Band of Outsiders* where the
three friends break a record hurtling through the Louvre, a record
set by an eleven-year-old American boy named Jimmy Johnson.
Max, to Gregory's delight, climbed up on a bust of Homer, unnoticed by the guards, and waved "bye-bye" at a group of Japanese
tourists with cameras around their necks. Lisa rescued a shrieking
Max from falling.

Gregory took my elbow and we scurried into the room with
paintings of Greek and Roman warriors. Gregory stopped and
admired them.

"Growing old is nothing new," he said suddenly, "but I don't
know what it feels like yet. I'm not old, you know, not really. Lisa is
younger than you!" Apparently, he was still thinking about the
gray hairs sprouting on his head. Actually, Lisa was in her early
twenties and thus somewhat older than I, but I didn't correct
Gregory.

"My son is just two and a half. I will be young for some time to
come," he said, reassuring himself, stealing from his own poetry.
"But in twenty years, that's the hard part of the ball game. Lisa'll
be in her forties and Max will be in his early twenties. But that's
the year 2000. The twenty-first century. Achilles will always be
young. I see him that way," Gregory said. "You see with old eyes,"
Gregory admonished me. "You shouldn't worship old poetmen."

"Look at that," his old eyes brightening as he stood in front of a
painting of a Greek soldier. "Look at that shield and helmet of a

Greek warrior! It might have been Alexander, curly hair hanging around muscular shoulders, leading infantry across a tented landscape!"

Gregory fell out amid all that glorious sacrifice. There was a full moon in the painting that seemed to light up the armor. Gregory said he had always loved going to the Metropolitan Museum in New York to see the knights on their horses, but his friends had made fun of him for going, so he went in secret to admire the ancient power of the knights errant. "I think of wars," Gregory recited to me in the empty gallery, "tales of mythical wars flowing from the wrinkled mouths of bards."

Gregory seemed like a man who found himself lucky to still be alive. He usually wrote a lot of poems around the time of his birthdays. Allen said it would be like that. His birthdays would make him think more about his life, his death, the lives and deaths of those around him. It also made him want to have babies. Gregory loved children, or at least the idea of children. He thought each child was a kind of second coming.

Gregory said that he used to dream of dying romantically, like Shelley, but now he was glad he didn't. "Shelley missed a lot," Gregory said.

Then we found it: a painting Gregory had seen as a boy that he had fallen in love with, the painting he had come here to find. It was *The Death of General Wolfe,* by Benjamin West. Gregory had once seen a reproduction of it in school. It was a painting of a battle in which the British army defeated the French on the Plains of Abraham and effectively took control of North America. The painting depicts the victorious British commander, James Wolfe, dying in the arms of his soldiers.

I knew that painting. My mother had brought it back from the A&P in a hardcover book, *The American Heritage History of America,* volume one. I remembered seeing that painting, spread out over two pages: General Wolfe, his lifeblood spilling out on the ground and the weeping soldiers who loved him. It seemed too corny to tell Gregory at the time that I, too, loved that painting. I thought

"THE DEATH

of General Wolfe"

he would think I was copying him, or trying to butter him up or something, so I let it go. But it made me feel close to him.

I knew how much of a trial school had been for Gregory. How when Carmine had made him laugh at the planetarium during a class trip, the teacher punished the whole class and denied Gregory and his classmates the stars. I knew Gregory had heroes like Lincoln and Alexander Hamilton, schoolboy crushes he carried with him to this day. All this made sense to me now. That's why it was so hard to get down to work with him—writing down and organizing his poems was too much like school. It's why his output was so scant, especially as compared to Allen's endless production of poems. "But a lot of it is very bad," Gregory told me, when I asked why he can't just sit down and think of writing poems as his job, the way Allen does it. "Because Allen writes a lot of bad poems," Gregory said. "And when I am good—I am great. Allen writes because he's afraid to die. I *don't* write, because I want to live."

We drove home at night through Denver streets, passing nuns coming out of a convent and growling drunks leaning over a highway bridge. Was this the music of America on its two hundredth birthday? Max leaned out the window, his nose in the wind like a dog sniffing the air, looking at the night sky. "Stars," he shrieked, "star-food!"

Gregory looked happy.

34. Father Death

Allen was going home. He and Peter had to fly back to Paterson, New Jersey, because Allen's father was dying. Six, maybe seven months earlier, Allen's father had been diagnosed with liver cancer. I couldn't stand to even hear about it. I knew Allen was a Buddhist and that Rinpoche had prepared him for his father's death. He told

Allen and Peter what to do. He said that Allen's father had taught him how to live in the world, and now he was given the opportunity to teach Allen and Peter about leaving it.

Paterson had been the lifelong home of William Carlos Williams, the country doctor–poet Allen had sought out as a young man, the poet Allen had asked to bless *Howl and Other Poems* with an introduction. But another poet had lived in Paterson, in William Carlos Williams's shadow. It was Allen's father, Louis Ginsberg.

So Allen had to leave on the next day's flight to Newark. Allen didn't like to fly, and Peter absolutely hated it. They usually ordered lots of those little bottles to drink on the flight and were both completely snockered by the time they landed. But this time they were drinking before the flight.

On the day of his departure, Allen told me he was going to be with his father. I told him how sad I was to hear about his illness, how I wanted everyone's parents to live forever. He said not to worry. Death was poetry's final subject.

"You're going to die one day," he said. "Get used to it."

Peter added reassuringly, "Not for a long time."

I felt better then. The last time Allen had gone back to Paterson it was winter. Snow had covered all the monuments of Allen's youth—Paterson City Hall, the tennis courts in Eastside Park; there was even ice in the Passaic River.

Apparently, Allen's father was too tired to move and required someone with a strong back to lift him. That job, of course, fell to Peter, the nurse in the family. It was Peter who would pull Louis up out of the bath and dress him after they arrived at the house. Allen later told me that while Peter was helping Allen's father get dressed at the edge of the bed, Louis looked up at Peter and with a rueful smile told him, "Don't ever grow old."

Allen's father had come to Boulder once, soon after I'd arrived, when he was still well enough to travel. Allen had taken him to the Flagstaff House, a restaurant high above the town, and as the first poetry student of the Kerouac School I was invited to go along.

F
A
T
H
E
R

Death

From the elevation of the restaurant, you could see the lights of the town coming on; you felt even closer to the stars that high up in the mountains. Rinpoche was also present that night. We all felt pleasantly tired after a big dinner and sat quietly watching the lights of Boulder through the wraparound glass window. Louis talked. Allen called it bantering.

I liked Louis. He reminded me of my father, if my father had been a poet. He wasn't. He was a window shade salesman. He played the harmonica, picking up cowboy tunes on the radio when he was a boy, so he could play "Streets of Laredo" and "Down in the Valley." He liked to play the harmonica while driving up to the Catskills, which he dutifully did every other weekend when I was a boy, to visit my mother's mother. He was a good sport about it. I know he secretly didn't want to do it. I was always astonished by how he could drive the car, steer it with his elbows, and play the harmonica. Other motorists would stare at us on the thruway. On the way, we'd stop at the Red Apple Motel and Restaurant for cafeteria-style meals. It was open twenty-four hours a day; I loved the idea of it being open all night.

Allen said he loved twenty-four-hour cafeterias, too. He said Louis would take him to one after visiting his mother in the mental hospital, but they wouldn't talk very much.

My father wasn't a poet, but he had the soul of an artist. He was gentle, quiet, thoughtful. Maybe now I would say his thoughtfulness could have been depression, at least some of the time. Louis seemed like that, too—depressed in a quiet, thoughtful way, not in a can't-get-out-of-bed-or-wash-my-face-to-go-to-work sort of way. My father loved to draw, to make caricatures of people in restaurants. He kept a small memo pad like the ones I used to take to school to write down homework assignments, and he kept his window shade orders in them, but most of the pages were torn out so that he could hand out the caricatures he made of people. When I was older and home from college, he was still doing it. Most of the time people were flattered by the drawings and came over to ask if he were an artist. "No," he'd say, "I'm not an artist—I like to eat. This is my son, he's the artist, he's a poet."

I always felt embarrassed when he said that. It also made me feel like I would never succeed, that I would be a failure if I became an artist, because artists never make any money and often go hungry. I thought of that whenever Gregory talked about himself as "a penniless legend," someone who has to go through life begging for money.

At the Flagstaff House overlooking the lights of Boulder, Allen's father was talking, remembering something Allen did that he thought was funny and Allen remembered as embarrassing. Louis let out a long sigh. "Is life worth living?"

"Depends on the liver," Allen replied.

It was an old joke, but Rinpoche thought it was funny; he and his secretary, David Rome, both smiled. "Fathers are the same everywhere," Rinpoche told Allen on the way out of the restaurant.

Louis had seemed sad and philosophical that night. Now his liver—or was it his pancreas?—was killing him. Allen had always had a difficult relationship with him. Was it jealousy? Sometimes I used to wonder what my father thought about my living in Boulder with the Beats, that he worked so hard and they had this reputation, unfairly earned and simply not true, of hardly working, of being deadbeats. In fact, Allen worked harder than anyone I ever knew. He worked like a one-man poetry factory, and when he wasn't doing that he was promoting the work of his friends, and promoting the Kerouac School. But here was Louis, a serious poet of a different time, and his son had become an icon, a cultural hero, a famous, notorious legend, and, like Gregory had said, one of "the Daddies of the age." How did that make Louis Ginsberg feel?

Allen loved Louis's second wife. She was probably what Allen's mother would have been like if she hadn't become schizophrenic at age forty—"croaking up her soul," as Allen called it, varicose-veined, fat, doomed, hiding outside the apartment door near the elevator calling the police, locking herself in the bathroom with razor and iodine, her chosen weapons of self-murder, "coughing in tears at the sink." In contrast, Allen's stepmother was a kind of Jewish angel who gave Allen and Louis much love. They were lucky, I thought, to have her.

When I first met Louis, I thought he might be hard to love. Behind his thick eyeglasses, he seemed lost. I know that he never quite understood Allen; some of Allen's fame bothered him. He might have been embarrassed by it. One night Allen told me that he had lunged at Louis when he was a much younger man and they'd had a fight. He thought he would kill him; it was like a psychotic break, but they never talked about it afterward.

Louis was eighty years old when Allen and Peter flew back to be with him. Allen said he thought his father looked frail the last time he'd seen him, "his cheek bonier than I'd remembered." Allen wrote me a few postcards from Paterson; they were very sweet and sad. He seemed changed by the experience of caring for his father. He said it was an ordeal just to get Louis ready for bed, but that Peter was strong and determined to make him comfortable. Once they got him into bed or into his easy chair, "from which it was harder and harder to get up," Allen wrote in his postcard, Allen would read to his father from Wordsworth's "Intimations of Immortality": ". . . trailing clouds of glory do we come / from God, who is our home . . ."

"That's beautiful," Louis told Allen, "but it's not true."

Rinpoche loved that story when Allen told it to him. I told my parents about it, reading them Allen's card over the phone.

"Sad," my mother said, "not to be able to feel that way on your deathbed."

Louis died, and Allen came back in some ways a different man. I saw it in the poems he was writing, poems about love and loss, not just about caring for his father in those last weeks but poems about lovers, about growing old as a lover, about not being able to get it up, worrying about going to bed alone. And I think that Peter's search for a girlfriend and his desire to have a family was beginning to worry Allen. He felt it was a fantasy of Peter's that they would all live like the Sleepytime Tea bears, cozy in a little cave in the Rocky Mountains. So Allen returned from burying his father frightened of being alone.

When I next saw Allen, I wanted to comfort him. I wanted to tell him how much he meant to me. I thought that if ever there was a moment to kiss him and hold him, this was it. But I didn't want to have sex with Allen. I wanted to please him, but had always turned down his advances. I hadn't yet made it into the hot tub with Allen and Peter, like the young dancers and meditation students who thought nothing of taking off their clothes and diving in, kissing Peter and soul kissing Allen. I felt like the shy one at the orgy.

I helped put Allen to bed that night. He was drunk from all those tiny bottles of alcohol he and Peter must've had on the plane. I took his clothes off the way Peter must've done for Louis to get him ready for bed. Then I went downstairs. Allen's poem of a few weeks later, given to me to type, read, "Now I lie alone, and a youth / Stalks my house, he won't in truth / Come to bed with me, instead / Loves the thoughts inside my head." Was that about me?

Allen thought it was so American, so crazy, so gridlocked that his father would be buried in a family plot near Newark Airport under a Winston Cigarettes sign off Exit 14 of the New Jersey Turnpike, in B'Nai Israel Cemetery, which used to be a paint factory. Nearby were some farms, with the wires of the Penn Central Power Station buzzing overhead.

"What's to be done about death?" Allen wrote in his notebook. "Nothing. Nothing? Stop going to school No. 6, Paterson, N.J., in 1937? Freeze time tonight, with a headache, at quarter to 2 A.M.? / Not go to father's funeral tomorrow morn? / Not go back to Naropa teach Buddhist poetics all summer? / Not be buried in the cemetery near Newark Airport some day?"

Flying home, somewhere over Lake Michigan Allen had thought about Rinpoche's advice to realize that death is one of the aspects of impermanence, and that the life his father had given him was not a bad thing for the world. He said that Louis had been a teacher his whole life; death would make him more of a teacher.

Allen said he had written "a blues" while flying back from seeing his father. He said he thought the blues was the only way to talk about death and grief, so he wrote his "Father Death Blues" sitting in the airplane, like a prince of Shambhala above the clouds.

Back in his apartment, Allen took out his harmonium, a musical instrument like a little church organ, and placed it on his lap. The harmonium case had stickers from all the places it had been with him. Wearing a T-shirt and boxer shorts, Allen played the harmonium by pressing the hand pedal toward him and pumping it with air. He started to sing. "Hey Father Death, I'm flying home / Hey poor man, you're all alone / Hey old daddy, I know where I'm going. Father Death, Don't cry any more / Mama's there, underneath the floor / Brother Death, please mind the store . . . Pain is gone, tears take the rest."

35. Going to Bed with Carla

It was my first winter at the Kerouac School. Kerouac himself, for a guy who had grown up in New England, who was buried in his hometown of Lowell, who—in Allen's words—would always have leaves falling on his grave, had hated cold weather. Huddled at a bus stop, waiting for someone to come and sell him drugs, Gregory told me that that was why Jack loved Mexico: it was romantic because it was warm.

I, on the other hand, loved the winter. I wasn't discontented at all. My teachers, the younger ones like Mike Brownstein, who lived up in the mountains, hated coming down to teach in the winter months. For two reasons: I think Brownstein hated teaching, period, and also he nearly drove off a cliff due to the snow and ice. It was like the Alps up there, even though everyone kept telling me it was just the foothills of the Rockies.

For a long time I was afraid to go to bed with Carla. She seemed like such a woman of the world. She had lived with a man, she had been to Macao, which was as close as you could get to China in those days. She knew French and even some Gaelic; she knew things like how Gaelic and one of the Chinese dialects—I forget which one—had words in common. She had danced at the Mudd Club in lower Manhattan; she knew the bouncers. She said the best way to learn a foreign language was in bed.

We seemed to go out every evening during that winter. It became a ritual, my coming by her store as she closed up, meeting her other girlfriends at the Hotel Boulderado for drinks. Sometimes we split off so she could attend her Buddhist studies class or sit for an hour in the shrine room. That's when I would prowl the mall.

Allen seemed increasingly short with me, irritated. I thought maybe it was because I was spending so much time with Carla and maybe he was becoming a little jealous. He found fault with my work; my typing didn't please him anymore. Allen apologized once after yelling at me, saying every day was lost time if I couldn't handle his correspondence. He got a lot of junk mail. I told Allen that we were learning all about "found poems" in Larry Fagin's class, poems that were the literary equivalent of Marcel Duchamp's readymades, everyday objects hung up on a wall and labeled as art, like a black shovel, or a bicycle seat, or, most famously, a urinal. I told Allen he should take all the junk mail and turn it into a found poem.

He looked at me like I was crazy. He was still fuming about something else.

Six months later, after he had come back from a trip to New York, he came home all excited about a new poem he had written in longhand that he wanted to read to me, called "Junk Mail." He

G O I N G

to Bed with Carla

C

O

O

L

either never remembered it had been my suggestion or he just didn't feel like sharing the credit. I didn't tell him that, in his absence, I had written a new poem called "Junk Mail: Canyon Street Apartment" (which was my address). I stuck my poem in a drawer and instead typed out Allen's, which he published in the City Lights book he was working on. Great poets get to do that.

Not long after we began seeing each other, Carla invited me up to her carriage house apartment. I had never been inside. It was part of a private house but had its own entrance. Her apartment looked like that of a sophisticated undergraduate or a bohemian who had decorated the place by scouring yard sales and vintage clothing stores. It was full of contradictions: English tea cozies and dish towels with pictures of the Queen Mother on them, and leopard-skin bedsheets and pillowcases. Part of it looked like a twenties-era parlor—the rooms of a flapper—with silk scarves thrown over the lamps and pictures of matinee idols framed on the walls, although in Carla's case it was a picture of Bryan Ferry and one of Johnny Rotten with green teeth.

Carla put a Brian Eno record on the stereo, and then played me a song she said was called "Love Is the Drug," by Roxy Music.

That night we were supposed to go to a party in a house up in the hills that Jubal had rented, or more likely had gotten someone to lend him for the evening. It was a very modern-looking house that someone said had been used in Woody Allen's movie *Sleeper*; it looked like a giant egg with a window, perched on a ledge in the mountains, as if a prehistoric bird had left it there to hatch.

Just as we were getting ready to go out, Carla barred the door and wouldn't let me out. "Why won't you fuck me?" she said. "You're turning my ovaries blue."

My brain was swimming in my head, bobbing there like a child's toy in a bathtub. It's hard to say what I wanted to do then. It was usually Carla who made the decisions. I made a step toward her.

We stayed in her apartment until five in the morning. We made love, and then she stopped and crawled as far away from me in her bed as she could get. Then we made love again, and then she'd wander off again. This went on for hours, until she got hungry and at five in the morning we went out for steak and eggs.

I saw her bathroom that morning for the first time. On one wall was a nude drawing of Carla, drawn in sharp lines. She said she hated that drawing but the artist was a famous German (I hadn't heard of him), so she couldn't part with it.

Carla put on a kind of kimono before we went out for breakfast. She said she had something to tell me, but it could wait until she knew me better. Meanwhile, she wanted to give me a key to her apartment.

The weeks flew by, and I found myself watching the first snows of winter outside Carla's bedroom window. We spent a lot of time making love, or sometimes I would just watch her sleep; by midwinter, whenever I answered her phone, no one was surprised to hear my voice. No wonder I started not to care so much about the Kerouac School, about Allen's poems, about the Beats. I was safely away from them, and I could now ask myself why I had worried so much about them. Why did I care what they thought about me every minute? They began to fade from my memory, even though I still saw them every day and had their books to read, their classes to attend, and their work to do. And for the first time, though it's hard to explain what I felt, I could tell that Allen was beginning to feel deserted. He never asked me about Carla, and when I brought the two of them together, he pretty much ignored her. It was as if anything she'd have to say couldn't possibly interest him, which I found incredible, considering how fascinating she seemed to me and how much I loved being with her. Of course, a lot of that was sex.

I had never had that much sex before. Carla was the answer to a prayer I barely knew I had formulated at those moments when Billy seemed unable to stand up, or Burroughs cried about Jack

G
O
I
N
G

to Bed with Carla

C

O

O

L

London, or Allen offered his toweled body to me and I had to make some excuse why I couldn't sleep with him. It was the answer to the prayer "Get me out of here," a prayer that surprised me when I made it, because I had wanted so badly to be there.

Burroughs once told me that the very moment someone is shot, the pain is slower in coming than the realization of what had just happened. But now the pain had come: these are just men, I realized, they have faults. They have bad days. They paid a price for storming the ramparts; they paid a price for fame; it's just that not all of their scars showed.

One day Carla asked me if I would stay at her place while she was out of town. I asked if she was making a business trip to the Philippines to buy some furniture or batik dresses. She said no, that it was her partner who was on a buying spree in Asia. I found out that Carla worked for Linda Louie and her husband, Mickey. She said that Anne's manager didn't have any close friends, that she never made any close friendships with other women, that in fact she disliked most women but trusted Carla. At last she told me what she had promised to tell me after the first time we'd made love. She said that Linda and Mickey Louie needed someone who could bring money to Florida and drive back with a car filled with marijuana. That was the trip she'd planned.

I asked Carla if Anne Waldman knew about Linda and Mickey Louie's activities. She said she thought so. That's how Linda Louie was able to pay for Anne's demo tapes and all the work that went into trying to make Anne a rock star. (Carla said she thought Linda Louie was wasting her money. That's what I liked about Carla: she could be extremely realistic in her observations.)

I asked Carla about her upcoming trip; I wanted to know if her work was dangerous. She said that Calliope's work was more dangerous. I didn't know what she meant by that, so I let the remark pass. You couldn't make Carla tell you something she wasn't prepared to tell you. But I wasn't just afraid for her. What about me?

What if some druglord came looking for Carla and found me in her bed? These were the charitable thoughts I had.

She usually left early in the morning, sometimes with Mickey Louie. They went together to Florida and Carla came back by herself. She got paid about a thousand dollars for each run. We'd celebrate whenever she came home by going out. She started to bring me back presents, souvenirs of her travels. After a few months, I was keeping my money in an alligator wallet, wearing a hand-painted tie with a flamingo on it. Her trips were turning me into a sleazy dresser without my realizing it.

Alone in Carla's apartment, I played her Graham Parker album *Sparks Fly Upward,* softly in the dark. Her watch, her rings, a few of her bracelets lay on the night table.

When I finally asked her why she was willing to make these trips, she explained that before she became a student of Rinpoche, she didn't know who she was. She was drifting through identities like a spy. Then, when she took her refuge vows, Rinpoche had given her a Buddhist name. (I don't remember what it was, except that in translation it had the word "mirror" in it, as if her name had become a mirror to help her see herself as she really was.) Now that she knew who she was, she wanted to make as much money as she could in a short period of time. That's why she was working for Linda Louie.

For a long time, I had been able to keep the two things separate: my real life and my Beat life at the Kerouac School. But I realized now, now that I was involved with Carla the Bohemian Drug Smuggler, the two worlds had blurred. My life had become as complicated, as messy, as everyone else's at Naropa. If I had read about this back home in my bedroom on Long Island, I would have thought it was cool, but living it filled me with anxiety.

After each trip, Carla and I resumed our romantic life. She told me that she came from an Italian family in Brooklyn, though her mother and father had separated long ago. Her mother was so angry at her father, who was a trader on Wall Street, that one day when she came home from school, her mother had taken hundreds

G
O
I
N
G

to Bed with Carla

of family photographs and cut her father's face out of every one of them. Now her father's face was missing from every picture. She said that it was a very Sicilian thing to do. She had a brother who was an actor in New York, and every summer he played "Charlie's Aunt" in summer stock. His name was Dean. Carla said that Dean and his mother had a fight one day and hadn't spoken to each other in eight years.

Her other brother was named Frank. Once when I was staying alone in Carla's apartment, Frankie called in tears, saying someone had been in his house and robbed him. I tried to reach Carla but she didn't always tell me where she was staying. And sometimes she traveled under an assumed name, "Mrs. Jenkins."

Hearing about all of this hideous family history of Carla's seemed to go hand in hand with the new life I was living. It was as if the sweetness of my own family had to be killed off by this early frost so that I might feel differently and not so useless. It seemed at the time the only way to grow up.

36. Death Is a Friend

Since becoming involved with Carla I was starting to cut even William Burroughs's class. One day, Burroughs summoned me to his place. That really scared me. In high school the worst that could happen was when they called your parents; in college you'd simply flunk the course, or maybe you'd get a warning. But cutting Burroughs's class—that could be serious. After all, if you're the only student, even William Burroughs is liable to notice you're not showing up.

Burroughs was always a scary figure to me. I didn't see what Allen was talking about when he spoke of how "angelic," how "grandfatherly" Old Bill had become. I wondered what Burroughs had been like before his transformation. Burroughs still told jokes in which the punch lines were things like, "and then they found a lump," or "French Canadian bean soup." To me, he was anonymous and spectral. And like many comics (which I think is what essentially he was), he was a Buster Keaton sad sack, with a view of the world that at first didn't seem to make sense at a school that wanted to be the first Buddhist college in the Western world. But Billy Jr. said his father's writing was very Buddhist in that he was someone totally without illusions, who accepted the first noble truth that life is suffering. In that way, Billy said, Old Bill was "very much with the program."

I stepped into Burroughs's apartment, sparsely furnished with a few metal filing cabinets, his orgone box, and two dueling pistols hanging on the wall. (They worked.) A photograph of Wilhelm Reich and his family was Scotch-taped to one of the kitchen cabinet doors. The apartment looked even more depressing than when he had first rented it. As in *The Portrait of Dorian Gray*, it looked like the room where you could completely obliterate an identity. Burroughs was teaching two courses that semester; I forget which one I was cutting, but I think it was his cartography course, his "map of imaginary places." In it, we created maps of Kafka's castle and the place where Beast kept Beauty. We looked at old pirate treasure maps and maps of Wild West towns. He had a lot of those. He and Jubal were going through a Western phase. They wrote about gunfights in the center of nearly deserted towns filled with dust. After a lifetime of getting high, Burroughs had become obsessed with *High Noon*. He said Gary Cooper could have played him in the movies. While everyone thought that was Burroughs being facetious, it really wasn't such a terrible idea. Toward the end of his life Cooper's face had aged and thinned out, his voice taking on a monosyllabic croak—it could have worked.

I sat on the couch and then Bill came out of the bathroom, buckling his pants. He was starting to wear his pants up around his sternum like a lot of old guys, even though he was as thin as Lincoln. I started to make up some excuse why I hadn't been going to Imaginary Maps class. He stopped me before I could even start to lie.

"So who do you think he is, provided he isn't a she?" Bill asked. Visiting Burroughs made me feel like I had found Kurtz in *Heart of Darkness*; it was like negotiating with a ghost. I wasn't sure what he was driving at.

"I have had good relations with some narcotics agents," Burroughs continued, "but they are recognizable because they are small-minded and give themselves away by asking inane questions. Have you seen anyone like that lurking around?"

I said no.

"I don't think we should be alarmed," Burroughs said. "We'll invite all the suspicious-looking characters to tea, see who makes indecent proposals, and we'll know. If we knew any policemen here, we could compromise one of them and turn it to our advantage. A rogue cop will spill on everyone in town."

Then it dawned on me. Burroughs was talking about the spy that Allen thought had infiltrated Naropa.

The idea began to take hold of me. I told Burroughs that because I go out to eat a lot, I see things. I saw one guy who'd been to every one of Rinpoche's talks. "I saw him at Allen's reading," I said. "He likes to meet a bunch of guys who look like Rotarians. They get together at Pelican Pete's and sometimes I see him talking to guys in cars in front of the post office." I was very proud to offer this information.

Burroughs looked interested, and said that my next assignment was to befriend this fellow and to see if I could bring him over to Burroughs's apartment.

"I will function as security," he said. "I will see what caliber of man this is. If he's a threat, we expose his weakness, although I can't see what the government would want with a bunch of international homos sitting around hatching cancers of the prostate. But there you have it. It's the price of fame, laddie. W. B. Yeats said it best: 'God keep me from ever being a wise old man praised of all.' You may leave now."

Great, I thought. Now I had to spy on the few friends I had. He hadn't said a thing about those missed classes. Did he even know? Would he be sympathetic if he knew why I had cut his classes, to be with Carla? Had William Burroughs ever been in love?

Carla continued to make her out-of-town trips, and I spent days and weekends in her empty apartment. I developed a taste for having a glass of wine by myself while sitting alone in her place, playing her records. I felt grown-up. It felt like I was living in Gregory's poem "Marriage," when he contemplates that "pleasant prison dream" of living in a penthouse with a beautiful woman smoking a cigarette from a long cigarette holder. I felt sophisticated.

On one such evening I went out to replenish Carla's supply of wine. In the liquor store I saw a newspaper headline that the song-writer Johnny Mercer had just died. Most of my friends had no idea who he was, but I loved his music, especially a kind of corny song called "Accentuate the Positive." He was one of the founders of Capitol Records. He was a swinger. As much as I loved the Beats, I also loved Sammy Davis Jr., the Sands Hotel, 1960s-era show business. I grew up watching my parents sitting with their friends in the living room listening to comedy records, watching Barbra Streisand specials. Mercer had written some great tunes. He wasn't Bob Dylan or Crosby, Stills and Nash, but I secretly loved his music.

I looked up from the newspaper and saw Gregory sauntering into the liquor store. I bought the paper. Gregory took it from me and saw that Mercer had died.

"He was great!" Gregory said, surprising me. "He was a poet, too. We should remember him. I heard all those songs—Greek cabdrivers know them. They have a great power. Lovers of life know how wonderful those songs are! Johnny Mercer's lyre quieted by death."

C

O

O

L

I followed Gregory outside. He told me to come with him. We walked for a long time, Gregory lost in thought. He was half humming, half talking to himself. He was a little frightening, drinking my wine out of the bottle by now. The only building in sight was a hotel, far out on Arapahoe Street, like a Ramada Inn. We went inside, but I was afraid we were going to get thrown out. The electric doors opened for Gregory, but they got stuck for me. He went back and stomped on the rubber mat and opened the door.

It was evening and the lounge was in full swing. An older woman was playing the piano. "Johnny Mercer is dead!" Gregory declared to the dozen or so salesmen and tourist couples sitting at the bar. "What dies, dies in beauty; what dies in beauty dies in me!"

He sat down and started writing. A new poem for the book?

"Hold this," he said as he handed the piece of paper back to me, and I saw that it was not a poem, not a Gregory Corso poem at any rate. It was a crib sheet of song lyrics, the words—most of them, anyway (some he got wrong or had made up)—to Johnny Mercer's "Come Rain or Come Shine." Gregory whispered something to the rather masculine-looking woman at the piano, who was dressed in a suit and tie. She began to play Mercer's song. Gregory stood in front of the piano, his hand over his heart, and I understood I was to prompt him, like in his readings, if he should get something wrong. He prided himself on memorizing his poems and he hated to get it wrong.

"Happy together? Unhappy together / and won't it be fine / Days may be cloudy or sunny"—Gregory blew the hair out of his eyes, and went on in a sweet but breaking voice—"we're in or we're out of the money, but I'm with you always—" ("Did I get it right?" he asked interrupting himself, and spoiling the moment, which we are all carried away by)—"I'm with you rain or shine!" He looked up at the word "shine" and I saw that his eyes had filled with tears.

I glanced around the room. Everyone in the place was crying or trying not to. I was getting a headache because I didn't want to feel sentimental about it. Gregory would only make fun of me later. He then asked the lady pianist if she knew "Blues in the Night," because I'd told him that that was my favorite. She did and he sang it, sweetly but a little off key.

"How'd I do?" Gregory asked me when the song was over.

"You were great!"

"Fuck off, no I wasn't! Why do you have to suck up to me all the time? I'd like to see you do that. You'd pee your pants."

I should've known. I should've told him he couldn't sing for shit, then I'd have his respect. Another beautiful night ruined.

On the way home Gregory apologized. He told me that he was writing a play for Halloween, about different people who meet death on the subway platform at Astor Place. He asked me if I'd like to be in it.

"You can play Death," Gregory said.

"Why me, Gregory? Why do you want me to play the role of death, what did I do?"

"Because Death is a friend," Gregory explained. "You need Death to be a friend. Death's got to be a friend." I suppose that was his way of apologizing, of letting me know that I was still his friend.

I got the part.

37. "First Thought, Best Thought"?

I had Calliope's address book.

I found it in the shrine room, the only place big enough to accommodate the crowds when Rinpoche gave one of his public talks. By now I was familiar with the routine—the long wait, the arrival of the Vadjra guards to secure the space, sweeping it for "undesirables," which I always thought was pretty funny, considering that among

C

O

O

L

Rinpoche's students sat Allen Ginsberg, Peter Orlovsky, William Burroughs, Gregory Corso, Charlie Haden, and, during the last couple of weeks, Allen's old friend Carl Solomon, a guy with thick eyeglasses to whom "Howl" was dedicated. (In the third section of the poem, a long catalogue begins each new line with "Carl Solomon I'm with you in Rockland where you're madder than I am . . . I'm with you in Rockland where you imitate the shade of my mother . . . I'm with you in Rockland where you've murdered your twelve secretaries . . .")

Carl had come to Boulder for a purpose. A very odd purpose. Yes, he was friends with Allen, and yes, he wanted to get out of the Bronx for a vacation. But when Carl heard that Allen had been asked to prepare for publication an annotated version of "Howl"— kind of like the Gettysburg Address in all its drafts and versions— he wanted to come and set the record straight. I thought Allen was going to have a stroke when he was on the phone with Carl, who apparently wanted Allen to tamper with his masterpiece. For example, Carl hadn't really been in Rockland Hospital for mental illness.

"Allen knows full well it was the Columbia Psychiatric Institute. He should know," Carl told me shortly after his arrival at Naropa, "because that's where I met Allen!" Carl also said that he wasn't given electric shock treatments when Allen said he had had them. "That was six years later at Pilgrim State, for crissakes!" He also was upset that Allen had gotten the story of the thrown potato salad all wrong. "It was off campus," Carl said, irritated with what he called Allen's bad reporting, "but I know why he did it—only it's too important to get it wrong."

I didn't know what he was going on about until I recalled the first section of "Howl," where Allen wrote that Carl "threw potato salad at CCNY lecturers on Dadaism and subsequently presented themselves on the granite steps of the madhouse with shaven heads and harlequin speech of suicide, demanding instantaneous lobotomy."

A sullen fifteen, I loved Kerouac's *On the Road* but refused to take driver's ed. *(Courtesy of the author)*

From left: My sister, Gella; my uncle Joe; my father, Seymour Kashner; and my mother, Marion. They didn't really know why I wanted to study with the Beats, but I had their blessing— and my father's Diner's Club card. *(Courtesy of the author)*

The poet Gregory Corso *(left)* and Allen. Once, after Allen published a poem about being robbed, Gregory groused, "The *New York Times* paid him $400 for a $60 mugging!" Allen loved him. *(Photograph by Gordon Ball. Copyright © Gordon Ball.)*

Allen Ginsberg with William Burroughs—the Kerouac School's "professor of language as a virus"—by the pool at the Varsity Apartments in Boulder, July 1976. *(Photograph by Gordon Ball. Copyright © Gordon Ball.)*

By the time I met Ginsberg, he had been famous for a quarter of a century. He was like a rock star of the poetry world. But he often complained about sleeping alone. *(Photograph by Gordon Ball. Copyright © Gordon Ball.)*

A triptych of modern saints in Allen's apartment at 437 East 12th Street in New York: Arthur Rimbaud *(left)*, Allen's Buddhist teacher Chogyam Trungpa *(center)*, and Walt Whitman *(right)*. Some of the greatest artists of the second half of the twentieth century passed through that door. I cleaned up after them. *(Photograph by Gordon Ball. Copyright © Gordon Ball.)*

The spirit of Bob Dylan hovered over the Kerouac School. Allen and the other directors even considered asking Dylan for a huge donation when the school needed a cash infusion. *(Elsa Dorfmann)*

For all his outrageousness, William Burroughs was a conservative dresser. He hated my fashion sense. He called these the "suspenders of disbelief." They were purple. *(Edie Baskin)*

Allen gave me a pair of leather pants to wear for this reading. It was hot that night and I almost fainted. I peeled them off and gave the reading in my boxer shorts. *(Courtesy of the author)*

Peter Orlovsky *(right)*, Allen's lover for twenty-seven years, taught poetry at the Kerouac School. On the first day of class, he asked, "Who here thinks that pussy tastes like strawberry jam? Raise your hand." *(Photograph by Gordon Ball. Copyright © Gordon Ball.)*

Last Gasp &/or Gasm

POETRY READING & SOCK HOP

Poetics Department Benefit

ALLEN GINSBERG ANNE WALDMAN
JACK COLLOM LARRY FAGIN
PAT DONEGAN PETER ORLOVSKY
SAM KASHNER SUSAN EDWARDS
REED BYE MICHAEL BROWNSTEIN

2 Live Bands

Welcome Camarillo   The Help

Wednesday, August 11 7pm

$5 general admission
$4 students

Naropa Institute
1111 Pearl Street
444-0202

William Burroughs in Keds sneakers. He and his son, Billy, drove me up into the mountains to help harvest the marijuana crop they raised at an old mine. *(Photograph by Gordon Ball. Copyright © Gordon Ball.)*

With scarves flowing and bracelets clanging, Anne Waldman was like Isadora Duncan on speed. Here she is in a rare pensive moment with Allen. *(Photograph by Gordon Ball. Copyright © Gordon Ball.)*

Anne and Allen on stage at Naropa with Chogyam Trungpa Rinpoche. He was the perfect guru for Beatniks. The former Buddhist monk liked to smoke, drink, and seduce women. *(Photograph by Gordon Ball. Copyright © Gordon Ball.)*

Allen noticed this drawing of me when he visited Williamsburg, Virginia. "It's missing your arm hair," he said. And he filled it in. He didn't miss much. *(Courtesy of the author)*

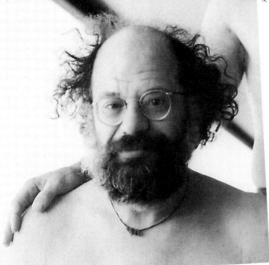

Allen never lost his childlike sense of curiosity. Even as he grew frail, he never seemed old. He celebrated his fiftieth birthday with the Clash and his sixtieth with Sonic Youth. *(Photograph by Gordon Ball. Copyright © Gordon Ball.)*

After I married the poet Nancy Schoenberger, we moved to Colonial Williamsburg, Virginia, so she could teach at a college. It was an even weirder place than the Kerouac School. *(Courtesy of the author)*

When Allen visited us, with his harmonium in tow, we had aging Beatniks, kids in Nirvana T-shirts, and dropouts of all kinds on our doorstep. Nancy was both amused and horrified. At a reading, I introduced Allen to a huge audience as the "father of my country." It would be the last time I saw him. *(Photograph by Gordon Ball. Copyright © Gordon Ball.)*

"You are the tape deck / in the car of my life," began the first poem at my big reading just before graduation from the Kerouac School. *(Gella Meyerhoff)*

I graduated "in the Earth Horse Year," whenever that was. *(Courtesy of the author)*

Naropa Institute

A Division of Nalanda Foundation at Boulder in the State of Colo

The President and Board of Directors
of the Nalanda Foundation
Meeting together in the ASSEMBLY HALL of Naropa Institute
on the Sixteenth Day of August, Nineteen Hundred Seventy-eight,
the Thirteenth Day of the Sixth Month
in the Earth Horse Year,
Did, upon Recommendation of the Faculty of Naropa Institute, Award

Samuel Jacob Kashner

A Certificate in

Poetry

PRESIDENT,
NALANDA FOUNDATION

EXECUTIVE VICE-PRESIDENT,
NALANDA FOUNDATION

VICE PRESIDENT,
NAROPA INSTITUTE

ACADEMIC DEAN
NAROPA INSTITUTE

REGISTRAR,
NAROPA INSTITUTE

AS WITNESS MY HAND THIS 16TH DAY OF AUGUST, 1978

Carl felt that Allen had taken his personal life, had garbled its history, and had gotten it all wrong, simply to write a poem. The fact that the poem might be one of the few true masterpieces of twentieth-century American literature didn't seem to make a difference to him at all.

"First, it was Brooklyn College, not CCNY," he explained to anyone who would listen. "I'd never go to CCNY, and anyway, the incident was off campus, so already it was a different type of protest!" Carl said that throwing the potato salad had been an act of Dadaism, something done in jest to impress Carl's girlfriend on her birthday. "For twenty years I've been wanting to tell Al that in the second part of that line about Metrazol and shock treatments—*no way!* I didn't have electroshock therapy until I was committed to Pilgrim State, and that was six years later! It all sounds good, but, sorry, Al, I was diagnosed as a neurotic, I wasn't catatonic." Carl felt Allen should've consulted with him more. The fact that "Howl" was written while Carl Solomon was in the bughouse and Allen was in San Francisco, three thousand miles from Carl's hospital room, didn't bother him, though.

"He can set the record straight now," Carl said.

Carl and I were sitting next to each other in the shrine room, waiting for Rinpoche to arrive to give one of his enigmatic lectures. Carl, uncomfortable on his red meditation cushion, had heard from Allen that my family came from Jerome Avenue in the Bronx. He started to tell me about his growing up there, in a private house, where his big, noisy, opinionated extended family read Marx and Freud, and rooted for the Yankees. "By the time I was your age," Carl said, "I had already dropped out of Brooklyn College. I shipped out as a Merchant Marine. When I met Allen, he admired my collection of books I had picked up in Paris: Artaud, Genet, *Tropic of Cancer*, Lautréamont. We talked about things."

I got the feeling that Carl was more hurt than flattered that

C

O

O

L

Allen had told his story to the whole world in "Howl," that it became a famous poem and that all of Carl's pain and suffering had become public, and not just public but a work of art, a kind of private mythology. Carl Solomon was Allen's Dean Moriarty, his Neal Cassady. Cassady, by most accounts, seemed to dig the notoriety, but I don't think Carl did. The fact that he had come to Boulder ("There's nothing to do here," he groused to Allen after about twelve hours in Boulder, "and those mountains give me claustrophobia. At least in the Catskills, you can go fishing"), traveling all this way to a place he didn't like, just to help Allen get the details right about "Howl" for Allen's *Collected Poems,* made me think he hadn't really forgiven him. But now he was stuck. He knew "Howl" was a famous work, a masterpiece, even. He was trapped with a variation on his own past inside a great work of literature.

What a strange problem to have, I thought.

I wondered what Carl, this Dadaist-anarchist, would make of Rinpoche and the Vadjra guards patting down the shrine room. Allen, after all these years, still saw Carl as he must have twenty-five years earlier, as if he were still capable of some Artaud-like "crime." Would he throw another plate of potato salad at Rinpoche? I started to worry when Rinpoche came out and sat before a microphone, accepting the deep bows of the crowd.

Fanning himself in the overheated room, Rinpoche began to talk about poetry as a meditative discipline, how a poem develops from "ground, to path, to fruition." Allen and Anne were taking notes; a lot of people were writing things down. Carl wasn't. He pulled one of his shirttails out and started cleaning his eyeglasses. I considered the fact that I was sitting next to a man who had stolen a peanut butter sandwich from the Brooklyn College cafeteria and then surrendered himself to a policeman and wound up on the sixth floor of Columbia Psychiatric.

Rinpoche talked about the poetry he had written as a young man upon the deaths of his teachers. He said they were never sad poems. He talked about direct experience, about writing what you see, about a direct path to the mind. He spoke in a kind of rasping whisper. It was hard to follow. We all perked up when he mentioned the Jack Kerouac School. He said the school was becoming possible because of a spiritual breakthrough, because America was freaking out and this was a good thing. He invited Allen to come up and share the stage with him. Gregory was applauding and whistling for Ginzy to go up onstage, as if he had just won at bingo.

Allen took the stage and began to talk about the Kerouac School. It was becoming obvious to me that they had planned this bit of spontaneous poetics because they needed to pitch the Kerouac School to a full house. It made me sad. I didn't want any other students to come. I wanted the Beats to myself, but I knew other students would be coming. In fact, some of them were already here and would be around for the spring semester, scattered among the meditation students and flower-arranging students. I felt jealous about sharing Gregory's put-downs with anyone else. It was the Stockholm syndrome, all right. I didn't want anyone to come and rescue me, not even my parents.

Allen spoke to the throng about the school. He said that Kerouac had taken LSD in Allen's apartment and that Allen had asked him what he had thought about, if he had had any psychological breakthroughs while on acid. "Walking on water wasn't built in a day," Kerouac had said.

"We are just beginning," Allen continued. Then he said that the Kerouac School was different from every other writing school in that it would teach, as well as practice, writing that reflected the mind and nature observed during actual composition: creating poetry "out of mind," in "spontaneous and unrevised utterances." As in "first thought, best thought."

Rinpoche interrupted Allen. " 'First thought, best thought'— that was an idea I expressed to you, Allen, to help explain the idea of purity of thought, being helpful to describe the shapeliness of mind."

"F

I

R

S

T

Thought, Best Thought"?

C

O

O

L

"But it's a Kerouacian idea," Allen countered, beginning to pout a little. "It's even in 'Belief and Technique in Modern Prose,' number twenty-one: 'struggle to sketch the flow that already exists intact in mind.' "

"Allen," Rinpoche said, "you are so quick to apply what you have learned, and you are so arrogant and humble and resourceful, I'm sure you will remember, even teachers can have problems with appropriation of materials and self-satisfaction."

Carl looked at me. I looked at Carl. "This is like the fight at a board of directors meeting at Temple Emanuel," Carl whispered to me. I couldn't believe it. Allen and Rinpoche were fighting over who was the first one to think up "first thought, best thought." Was it Allen, Rinpoche, or Kerouac?

"I'm not sure first thought *is* best thought," Carl said to me in a stage whisper that everyone could hear.

Then Rinpoche started laughing. Allen started to laugh. The whole shrine room seemed to shift a little uncomfortably. We had been sitting a long time on our cushions anyway (I still didn't have the hang of it). At last Trungpa got up to leave. We stood up, as when a judge leaves the courtroom. The Vadjra guards followed him out. There was a collective sigh from the crowd in the shrine room. Allen walked back to our group.

"Does anyone think I took a wrong turn?" Allen asked. "Did I make the wrong decision, spiritually, I mean?"

Anne said you never contradict the teacher.

Gregory said, "Trungpa loves it when people give him a hard time."

Carl said it was good theater and that it'll give him something to think about when he goes back home and sits under the City Island Bridge, in his rowboat, fishing. "I'll ask the fish: do I take you home and fry you or throw you back? First thought or best thought?" I laughed at that, but nobody else did.

After everyone had left, I found a little black book, with a blue ribbon for marking your place, lying next to me on the floor of the shrine room. I looked inside. It was Calliope's. I looked through it. I shouldn't have. But I still had Burroughs's and Allen's assignment. There was a spy among us. I had to do my homework.

38. Billy at the Boulderado

Have you ever slapped a dead man? That's how it felt trying to wake up William Burroughs Jr. It was already dusk, but I needed to talk to Billy, who was sleeping through the days and waking up at night. I knew I would get the truth from him. He had been through so much nuttiness in his life. He was the only one in and around the Kerouac School who was at all cynical about the place. He was also the only one with a genuine sense of humor. He liked reading S. J. Perelman, the *New Yorker* writer whom Allen dismissed with the wave of his hand as if he were swatting away a fly. Not unlike his father, Billy had a deadpan style, a sarcastic, witless wit.

Billy shuffled along the halls of the Buddhist rooming house like an old man. Like a Parkinsonian, Billy's hands shook when he held anything except a shot glass, which he forcefully brought to his lips. The rest of the time, though, he was the most passive guy I ever knew. He still seemed shell-shocked, like someone whose willpower had been sucked out of him while he slept.

Billy had a job now, working in a ski shop for a born-again Christian ski instructor and his wife. He took people's skis and planed them, made them sharp for the slopes. Billy himself hated skiing. He didn't even like snow. I visited him once at the shop, which was tucked away on one of the side streets off the Pearl Street mall. There was a big cross, made out of two skis, on a wall of the shop. This was one in a series of odd jobs Billy had in his

C

O

O

L

life, and it was just his luck that all of Billy's bosses seemed crazy. He had a knack for finding them.

I had stopped by Billy's apartment one evening after another snowfall to show him the address book I'd picked up from the shrine room floor. I wanted to tell him about Old Bill's assignment: to bring in a spy, the one Allen said might be planted here by Cointelpro to sabotage the Jack Kerouac School. I thought he might know something.

As usual, Billy's apartment was a mess. There was ancient beef stew on the burner, and ancient, uneaten dinners now covered over with what looked like ice but what was actually congealed fat. His rooms smelled like hashish. Billy kept moving his couch, which he used as his bed. It was never in the same place two nights in a row. He kept thinking the location of his bed would help him sleep better, because Billy had bad dreams. He dreamed a lot about his wife, Karen. They weren't together anymore; they had broken up just before Billy had moved to Boulder. He had met Karen at a school for kids with problems where Billy's grandparents had sent him when he was younger. Every kid has problems, but Billy went to a special school for his. He said it was worse than the farm they'd sent him to in order to get off drugs. That's where Billy said he had learned to grow pot.

Karen was a wild girl and had kept Billy in trouble. That seemed to be the family pattern. Allen once said that Billy's deceased mother, Joan, was far wilder than Burroughs himself. "He was the Rock of Gibraltar next to Joan," Allen had said.

I woke up Billy, who was burrowed into the cushions of his couch, which had been moved to the center of the living room. I showed him Calliope's address book, admitting that I had pawed through it. It even had a little poem of Gregory's that he had written in the front of it, with a funny drawing of Calliope and Gregory in bed. I would have stolen it for that reason alone, but instead I came to Billy with the book.

Calliope's notebook didn't just have phone numbers in it. It had appointments. And, curiously, almost every name was a man's.

Straight-sounding names, like Bob Doan, or Chris Korshak. Well, it's true, "Chris" could be a woman, but I noticed how Calliope seemed to have an appointment every few hours, and only with men. FBI men?

I asked Billy what he thought. Could Gregory's girlfriend be a spy? "Then clever to woo Gregory," I said.

"You knucklehead," Billy answered. "She's a call girl! A prosti-tutie. Didn't you see *Klute?*"

I didn't know what to say. "And Gregory knows?" I asked finally.

"He's probably making all the business arrangements," Billy explained. "You must be here on one of those 'born yesterday' scholarships the Jack Kerouac School gives out."

I decided to let that pass. "Who are these men?" I asked. "Where do they come from?"

"From their mother's wombs," he said. "And they all got there from fucking—we all got here from fucking."

"I know. But why did you have to tell me that a week from my mother's birthday?" It would be Marion's first birthday with me in captivity at the Kerouac School, I thought. Birthdays weren't a big deal to the Beats. Except for Allen. He called his stepmother every Sunday. Deep down, Allen was a nice Jewish boy. No wonder I felt safe in Allen's house—safe and unsafe, familiar and strange.

"Well, now that I took it, how can I just casually give it back to her?" I asked Billy about Calliope's address book. "And where does she do this? Does she go to their houses?"

Billy sat up wearily and bent over to put on his shoes—moccasins, really—which were underneath the couch. He was dressed; he had slept in his clothes. He got up, rubbed his eyes, and we shuffled off to Pearl Street. Billy said he would show me the ropes.

"Someday, my boy," he said, imitating W. C. Fields, "all these ropes will be yours."

We arrived at the Boulderado Hotel just as the sun was going down. We noticed Anne holding court on the veranda. Her

B
I
L
L
Y

at the Boulderado

bracelets sliding up and down her long arms made a clicking sound I liked. I liked almost everything about Anne. I wondered why she didn't like me.

We went over to say hello. Anne looked up but mostly made eye contact with Billy. Who's famous son do you have to be to get attention around here? I thought to myself. After a few minutes, Billy said we had to go. He ordered a drink and took it with him up to the second floor. I followed.

On the second floor were two dark rooms connected by French doors. Two or three men sat around reading the *Daily Camera*, Boulder's newspaper. I thought to myself, the *Daily Camera* is missing a big story: there's a brothel right here in the Boulderado Hotel. The madam was the head of the stewardess school for American Airlines. She recruited her girlfriends; it was being done more for fun than for profit. A friend had loaned them antiques from her antiques shop in town—antimacassars, highboys, night tables. The madam greeted Billy more affectionately than any mother. I think it was the most affection he'd ever gotten. I suddenly felt like the Goody Two-shoes brother in *East of Eden*, who gets taken by James Dean to meet his mother, played by Jo Van Fleet, at her house of ill repute. Someone was playing David Bowie's *Low* on a tape player, then the music stopped, and Carla's friend Kitty came out. She was wearing a red slip. She looked beautiful and utterly beyond my depth. I didn't even know she knew Billy.

Billy whispered something in her ear that made her laugh. She came over and gave me a kiss on the cheek. Kitty said that Nanette and Monica would be ready to come downstairs soon and join us for a drink. I discovered that most of the women in Anne's court seemed to be working here. Her sirens were calling men up to the second floor of the Boulderado.

Later on, when Allen Ginsberg and Daniel Ellsberg tried to shut down the Rocky Flats nuclear facility, which manufactured the triggers for nuclear weapons, the women from the bordello sat down on the railroad tracks. The protest was successful—the girls all had their days free.

Billy must have explained how surprised I was to find out there was a bordello right in the middle of town, so Nanette told me that she loved the work. "In fact, it isn't work," she said. Kitty, it seemed, had two jobs—cutting hair and sleeping with men. She said that she was learning to live on exhaustion. Monica, the last to show up, was a large woman with very blond, almost white, hair. She had a little upturned nose and looked like she was always looking up, like a dolphin under the ice. Monica said that she had just had her first customer ever.

"And you know what?" she asked. "I came for the first time!"

"You girls are lucky," Billy said. "Someone actually pays you to have sex. I wish someone would pay me to have sex, or not to have sex."

"We have some of those, too," Kitty said. All the girls laughed.

I felt almost delirious. I felt that now it was impossible to fulfill my original mission, which was to somehow give Calliope back her address book.

"It doesn't matter now, does it?" Billy said, almost reading my thoughts.

I told Calliope, who had come downstairs holding hands with Monica, that I had something that could help her keep her appointments, something that fell out on the shrine room floor during Rinpoche's last talk, something she might need. "It probably fell out while you were meditating," I said.

Calliope was excited to get it back, for it had all the girls' appointments in it, not just Calliope's. Apparently, she was their manager. The madam who had greeted Billy so tenderly a few minutes earlier was just the day manager. Calliope worked the nights.

Monica asked us to come see her room. She said you could hear crickets outside and that, at first, her guy couldn't get it up because he knew those crickets could hear everything. Billy thought that was funny as hell. I never saw him so happy. Billy said he liked to come here to work, that it was the only place he could write. Things were starting to look up for Billy, I thought.

B
I
L
L
Y

Too bad he was starting to die.

On the way out of the Boulderado, Billy casually mentioned that Allen and Anne had finally taken him to a real doctor, a liver specialist whose practice was in a suburb of Denver. He told me that when he had walked into the doctor's waiting room, he'd looked around and asked, "How often do they kill people around here?" Nobody laughed.

"He was probably a quack," Billy said, "but at least he wasn't a veterinarian, like the guy my father found for me."

This doctor told Billy that he needed a liver transplant, and he needed it soon. His liver had had it.

"I need somebody to wipe out on their motorcycle," Billy told me. "That's what it'll take to keep the party going."

39. Dream Lunch

Toward the end of the fall semester, Ginzy and Burroughs were going to let me meet them for what Allen called their "dream lunch." They started it when the two had first come to Boulder to teach at the Kerouac School. They'd meet at a restaurant off the mall so that they wouldn't be bothered. They were an interesting pair to look at now, walking the street together, Allen with broad shoulders, growing his gray-grizzled beard back, his Greek fisherman's shoulder bag always full of poems, one or two tomes, and his ubiquitous appointment book. And Burroughs, long and thin, dressed like a banker, a bony formality about him. He even wore a hat—straw in the summertime (a boater) and a bowler in the fall. Dressed like the last modernist stranded among the Beats.

I walked a little ahead of them, slower, on purpose, than I would have. I learned the pace from walking down Central Park

West with my grandmother. "I'm like Nerval's lobster," I told Allen, "on a blue leash." Why was I so happy to make an obscure literary reference like that to these two giants who ruled my world at the Jack Kerouac School? Because it delighted Allen and Bill, who were just crazy enough to know what I was talking about. (The nineteenth-century French poet Gerard de Nerval was said to walk a lobster on a blue leash through the Tuileries, his lobster setting the pace. Nerval would later hang himself from a lamppost and, in his suicide letter, say that he was hanging from the Queen of Sheba's garter belt.)

I didn't really want Allen or Bill to think of me as a lobster tethered to their leash, but I wanted to say something clever, and that was the best I could do. Conversation wasn't equal, not even after nearly a year at the Kerouac School.

The thing of it is, though, I had just learned about Nerval and his lobster from Michael Brownstein. Michael had been to Paris on a Fulbright scholarship, where he had gone to translate the prose poems of Max Jacob. Michael was a good-looking guy with delicate eyeglasses and long black hair. He wore a strand of elephant's hair made into a bracelet, and he lived in the mountains. He had a lot of girlfriends. He was what you'd call sardonic. He had written a book that all the other teachers, especially his old girlfriend from New York—Anne Waldman—considered a masterpiece. It was called *Country Cousins*. Mike Brownstein treated Allen like he was a pain-in-the-ass grandfather who was always complaining about something, but whom he never failed to kiss on the forehead when he said good-bye. I dug Mike. I wanted to be him, but he was already there.

When I told Mike and Gregory that I was going to join Allen and Bill for a lunch in which they were going to tell each other their dreams, Gregory looked over at Mike and said, "Ahh, they make all that shit up anyway. Well, children will hear what they must hear." And as I left Corso added behind my back, "I can see you, going to join the fairies!" He and Mike laughed. But I didn't care what Gregory thought. He was just jealous that he wasn't invited.

Allen and Bill sat across from each other in a darkened booth of Sage's restaurant, an imitation Tiffany lamp hanging over their heads. Drinking hot cider through straws, Allen and Bill looked like chaperones at some demented sock hop. They were talking about "oneself and the other," and Bill answered with something about "what is needed is direct action against the regime." I wondered if they thought, these two, whether or not they had won a kind of victory against the squares. After all, they were famous, legendary even. Did they assume that victory was theirs? Were they now getting down to molding a world to their measure? I wasn't sure that outside of Boulder or the Kerouac School anyone even cared anymore. Or did Allen and Bill think this was a war they had lost, that the squares had in fact won? And they, in retreat, had ended up here in the mountains, safe only among each other? Even the loveliest hallucinations fade away—hadn't Allen taught me that?—leaving one that much sadder for having glimpsed paradise and lost it.

I remember only one dream from that lunch. It was Allen's dream. He said that in his dream, he put all of Kerouac's books and letters into a kind of steamer trunk and dragged it to a harbor by the sea. With great effort, he pushed the trunk into the sea and the water swallowed it up. When Allen got back to his apartment, in the dream, Kerouac was waiting for him. He asked Allen, "Why did you do that? I thought you loved me. That was my life's work."

"But now that you're dead," Allen had said, "you don't need to make any dust. Books just gather dust."

"Maybe," Bill said, "you just needed to get Jack's work out of the way, to make room on the shelf for you." Old Bill, a Freudian to the last.

40. A Bathing Suit in the Hot Tub

In spite of everything, I always went back to Gregory. I didn't like the abuse, but I always felt that I learned something talking to him. He seemed completely himself. Everyone else was so happy to hide from you, and maybe if you lived long enough you'd discover something about who they really were, but not Gregorio Nunzio. He would get you there faster than a bus. He would always tell you what the ball game was, though you could never tell how far he'd go in his frankness.

Gregory had a terrible habit. A disgusting habit. Maybe it stemmed from the days when he had his nose pressed up against the glass, the street urchin of Little Italy, or from his life after prison, feeling that he had to *be* bad because he *was* bad. Whenever we went for a walk down Pearl Street, Gregory would stop in front of a fancy restaurant, especially one with a window that looked out onto the sidewalk, where you could see the people enjoying their dinners and they could look out onto the street. Gregory would stop and stand there and start picking his nose—deeply, fiendishly, until he was completely sure that everyone in the restaurant could see him. He wouldn't stop until some of them put down their forks and knives and tried shooing him away like a mangy cat. I could never bring myself to laugh at Gregory's prank. I liked eating out too much. It made my gorge rise just to see it. I felt for the people inside the restaurant. Gregory said that he used to do it as a boy in New York City. If he couldn't afford a nice meal, he didn't want anyone else to have one either.

"Everything you do," Gregory told me on one such stroll in Pearl Street, "can be *beat*, every face you meet is a beat kind of face."

"Every face?" I asked.

"There's inconceivable heartache in every face," Gregory said. "It just doesn't come out until, like, six o'clock at night. Some people can't tell the difference, but I can."

Another day Gregory and I were walking out on the strand, or at least what passes for the strand in Boulder, Colorado, and Gregory stopped in front of Pelican Pete's restaurant. He started picking his nose. Who should come rushing out but Allen.

"Gregory, what are you doing?"

"I'm sorry, Ginzy, I didn't see you. This climate, man, it dries out my nose."

Allen hadn't come out to chastise Gregory for being disgusting, but to ask what had happened to him. He'd missed the last three faculty meetings. (Gregory had successfully managed to avoid almost every faculty meeting at the Kerouac School for the two years I was there.) Allen either hadn't noticed Gregory's revolting stunt or he didn't think it was worth commenting on. Or maybe he didn't think there was anything wrong with it because Allen was so magnificently blind, so wall-eyed about the flaws of his lifelong friends. What for Ginsberg was a definition of friendship, the embracing of social dissonance, would have been for me a defining moment in a relationship— the beginning of the end. But the Beats seemed interested in my opinion only if it was exactly like their own.

So your own ideas, your own feelings, went underground. You drifted. You waited for their approval. You wanted to go through their rites, their rituals and procedures, you wanted to be one of them, but then (I had a terrible thought): Do they know who *they* are?

Allen, on the other hand, was much more careful—and more socially acceptable—than Gregory. In a way, Allen was the exact opposite of his image, the one I had imagined for him when climbing the walls of Bookmasters on Third Avenue looking for Allen's City Lights books. People always think of Allen Ginsberg as the outrageous, out-of-control, scatological, nudist-loving, free-speech advocate who smoked pot for breakfast and took LSD the way other people take Tums, whose work and life ushered in the hippie movement and prefigured punk. To be honest, Allen encouraged that image, in countless public readings, and in his musical collaborations with Dylan, the Clash, Sonic Youth, and others. Even in interviews Allen liked to push the envelope, bearding the lion in his den, such as in his famous television interview with William F. Buckley on *Firing Line*, chanting and playing the harmonium inches away from Buckley's darting tongue. None of that was very hard for Allen to do, because he really did have those qualities in him.

By the time I was Allen's apprentice, though, he had changed. If he hadn't changed, then he had finally managed to come into the personality he had always had: the soul of an actuary, not a wild man. He loved keeping lists and files and filling notebooks as if they were ledgers, his dreams charted and monitored like stocks. He rarely if ever cursed. He could be the most polite of men. He often wore a bathing suit in the hot tub. He liked to take pictures when he traveled, like any bourgeois tourist, and he was an incessant labeler. Everything had to have a name or a lineage attached to it. For example, I was the third-generation, New York School poet, descended from Samuel Greenberg (a young Jewish immigrant poet who died of consumption and was an influence on Hart Crane's "The Bridge"). Allen went to bed late only if he couldn't fall asleep, and he didn't care for bohemian espresso pits; in fact, he tried to get me to stop drinking coffee. So twixt the image and the cup, Allen was a very different person. Still, despite all his European influences, from Apollinaire to Zukofsy, Allen was an American poet. He was a JAP: a Jewish American Poet. He was a whiner who howled.

A

B

A

T

H

I

N

G

Suit in the Hot Tub

41. Kidnapped by Poetry

"It's always a bad day for someone," Gregory liked to say. Here's what happened toward the end of the fall semester, when I was looking forward to getting away from everybody, returning to Long Island for the holidays. Christmas break was coming to the first Buddhist college in America.

I was walking home from a party at Jane and Batan's (the couple who taught tai chi at Naropa). Gregory was living there now, sleeping on the couch, after Lisa, Max's mom, had thrown him out. She usually took him back after their fights, but this time she'd left, taking little Max with her and heading back to San Francisco. Jane and Batan loved Gregory.

I liked Jane and Batan, and I loved to watch them performing tai chi; it looked so calm. It's a discipline that tries to slow down the speedy confusion of the world. It was strange to think that Batan and Jane would welcome Gregory into their home, but they did. They accepted the chaos he brought with him.

I noticed that even as Gregory brought the whirlwind with him, he also seemed to carry prison around with him wherever he went. He set up his prison life, so no matter how much space he was given, he seemed to choose a tiny area in which to live. He was never free of it. He had roped off a little corner of Jane and Batan's living room, and that's where he was living now.

Even though Gregory suffered from panic attacks, he once said that one of the things that bothered him about me was my fear, that I was too afraid of everything. Gregory told me that when he was a kid, his heart used to beat like a scared rabbit in a cage—a rib cage. He thought I was like that, too, and he wanted to help me get over it. He said that he had overcome his fear in prison.

Jane and Batan had big, beatnik parties during weekend nights at Naropa—noisy, beat parties that spilled out of the house onto the lawn, the backyard, even into other houses. Allen and Peter were always the first to get naked at those parties, having done so ever since a famous poetry reading in the mid-fifties when some-one in the audience had asked Allen and Gregory what they wanted. Allen had responded by saying, "To be naked, to reveal the truth," and he took off all his clothes. Then Peter took off his pants and started throwing them around his head, as if he were roping a steer. Since then, it didn't take much to get Allen and Peter to take off their clothes.

This night, Carla was away on another run for Linda Louie. I thought she was becoming addicted, not to the drugs she was running for the Louies but to the money and to the idea of herself as an outlaw.

I left the party and walked home. It was cold; there was no moon in Boulder that night, no cars on the road. I couldn't see in front of me. It was one of those dark nights when you felt you could stretch your arm out in front of you and wonder if you would ever get it back. So it was a relief when a car raced past me and its headlights flooded the street. For a moment anyway, I wasn't alone in the dark.

Then the car came back a second time. It passed again. The high-beams sent a silvery light onto the trees before I even heard the motor. I walked along. Now my heart was beating like a warm rabbit in its cage.

As the car slowed down beside me, I heard laughter. It sounded like the kind of laughter that had been going on for a long time. I could feel the heat radiating from the car's engine. I couldn't see inside. A window was rolled down. Thank God, it was Calliope at the wheel, and Gregory was sitting next to her.

"Get in," Gregory said.

"I'm almost home," I told them. "Don't go to any trouble."

"You're always having things explained to you," Gregory said. He sounded like he was starting to get irritated with me. "I have some new poems you have to see. I want to know what you think. They're fucking great poems."

K
I
D
N
A
P
P
E
D

C

O

O

L

"I'm sure they are," I said.

Gregory knew what would get me into the car. I climbed into the backseat. Calliope did a three-point turn and headed down the one-way street the wrong way. It was dark, but I knew we weren't going in the direction of my apartment house. In fact, they had no intention of taking me straight home. We were going up into the mountains.

"What do you think of that?" Gregory said, almost sneering.

"We're going to have him on our hands for the next few days," Calliope complained.

"That's the idea," Gregory said.

"For days?" I said, echoing Calliope. Now I *was* scared.

I was kidnapped by poetry. I would never have gotten into the car if Gregory hadn't offered me the chance to see his new poems, the ones I was desperate to put into the new book, just so we could get it done, so he could get paid and have some money to see him through the rest of the year, and I could justify Allen's confidence in me as an assistant, a helper of the Beats.

Where were they taking me? Just a moment before, I was feeling a little like Jack Kerouac in that line that Gregory hated, when Kerouac says how, because he was poor, everything in the world belonged to him. But walking home that night, I did have everything I wanted. And I had it all to myself. I owned the moon, and Boulder, the mountains, and my thoughts, melancholy though they were. I was thinking about how other poetry students had begun to trickle in, and by next spring a horde of students would join the few of us at the Jack Kerouac School, which made me sad. But I knew it would be good for accreditation, which Allen and Anne so desperately craved, and which I promised my parents would happen any day now, though it didn't look good.

But now I was the owner of an enormous fear, riding up the side of a mountain, farther and farther away from my apartment.

They say you can never really picture your own demise—that's a good thing. I hated Gregory at that moment, lying to me like that. I could tell he was high on heroin again. Whenever he got high, he became a kind of chickenshit god, a tyrant, a Mussolini of poetry, jut-

ting out his almost toothless jaw, in love with his ideas about everything. I knew that he was desperate for money. Lisa and his other
wives were pressuring him for cash, and the Kerouac School wasn't
much help. They couldn't always pay their teachers. It wasn't a problem for someone like Allen, who could make a thousand bucks giving
a poetry reading, but Gregory didn't get that kind of money for readings. And anyway, whenever he did get money, it seemed to go into a
hole in his arm. He was furious with the school for not paying him.

"Forget about this fucking school," Gregory said as we drove
higher up into the mountains. "I'll teach you what you need to
know. I'll be like those angels who brought me books in prison. I'll
be your school—you pay me! No, we'll get your parents to pay.
We'll keep you up in the mountains until they all pay. I'll teach the
fear out of you. Did you know you can learn a lot about human
nature from looking at cats? Cats who are threatened by fire end
up jumping in the river."

Calliope said, "Gregory is the only teacher you'll need. And
anyway, your parents know all about it. They approve of the plan."

"What plan? My parents approve of my being driven up the side
of a mountain, in the middle of the night, by a junkie and his prostitute girlfriend?" There. I'd said it. "Has everyone gone crazy?"

They laughed.

The phone calls, I figured out, were to blame. I didn't want my
parents calling me up every day to see how I was doing; it just made
me more nervous, more homesick. So I had given them Gregory's
phone number, knowing I'd be there at least a few days each week
for class. (Gregory preferred to teach in his apartment, with Max
running around, rather than in a classroom.) What started happening was they'd call when I wasn't around, and Gregory would talk to
them, snowing them, even in the summertime. Junkies are always
charming when they have to be. My parents even invited him, Lisa,
and Max to their house on Long Island! Maybe Marion just liked
being called Minerva.

"Your parents cure homelessness," Gregory told me. "So we're
coming home with you." The idea terrified me. My parents, sweet

K
I
D
N
A
P
P
E
D

by Poetry

as they were, didn't know what they were getting into. I could just see Gregory showing up with Calliope and screwing her in my boyhood bed on Lowell Lane, in Merrick, Long Island.

As we continued up the mountain, it was as if we had reached the end of the world. An enormous darkness swallowed up the road, until we came to a driveway and a little cabin with a flickering porchlight.

"We're here," Gregory said. "We're home."

42. Jailhouse Fear

I saw it written in one of Allen's notebooks: "You can be a virgin in fear the same way you can be a virgin in sex." I thought about that as Gregory pushed me ahead of him into the deserted cabin. Gregory led me into the deserted cabin. It had probably belonged to a miner once upon a time. It had a bed, a table, a chair, and not much else. I got the feeling Gregory had been there before. The bathroom had a single lightbulb hanging from an exposed wire. There was a telephone and a desk with a few books on it. It had a wooden floor, and both Gregory and Calliope seemed to know their way around the cabin.

"It's dark as an asshole in here," Gregory said. He lit a kerosene lamp that I didn't know I was standing next to. I tried to play along for a while, to pretend I wasn't scared. My feelings toward Gregory hadn't changed, really, in spite of everything that was happening. I wanted to understand him, to figure out what could make a poet so brutal. But what I wanted even more was to get the hell out of that shed, because the whole thing looked pretty sinister to me. In a mess like this, with someone like Gregory, I said to myself, there's nothing you can do but clear out.

But Gregory was determined that I lose my virginity as a fearful, protected boy of the Long Island suburbs.

"I never met anyone who looked greener, who looked less

prepared to have something to write about than you," Gregory said. "Where's your subject? If you haven't lived, if you're living through the lives of a few legends like us, you've got to be alone with your fear, like I was. You have to get a pretty good look at her, and then you'll have your subject."

That's how Gregory started a war between us. I don't know if he meant to. He was out to shock me. He really thought he could change me, that he could frighten me out of being a child, like he was frightened as a boy in prison. It's true, I didn't know what men were like, what people were really capable of. "People—nobody loves them, not even people," Gregory liked to say to Allen. "Men are the thing to be afraid of," Gregory told me that night, "always men, and nothing else."

"What about *Long Live Man?*" I asked, referring to one of Gregory's books of poems, the one I had read on the plane, sitting next to my father, coming to Boulder.

"This is serious," Gregory said, lifting the shade to look out the window as if he were expecting company. "This is the real ball game," he said, which is how he usually introduced his serious subjects. "The Beats are no example. They forsook certain habits, a certain way of being, but acquired their own habits. They're as lost as the main flow. The only way out is the death of the way. Americans are a great people," Gregory continued. "Are you an American?" he asked me. He didn't wait for my answer. "I don't need some Chinaman to tell me that."

I wasn't sure what he was talking about, but I think he meant Rinpoche.

"*Man* is the victory of life," he continued, "not life, man."

I was going to have to sleep there. But where? And not with Gregory and Calliope, not the three of us, naked on that cold, park bench of a bed.

Gregory sometimes called Calliope "Poppy" in honor of his favorite plant. She walked out to the car and brought back a set of works. "What thinkest thou the poppy?" Gregory said to me. I knew what Gregory thought of drugs, especially drugs like heroin,

Whe n I Was

peyote, and hash. He felt that most drugs were the poet's preroga-
tive. I knew it from his poems; now I saw it before me. Gregory
had often said that what was good enough for Chatterton,
Coleridge, and Shelley was good enough for him. "Like the poets of
the Lake District," Gregory explained as Poppy held a soup spoon
over the kerosene flame. "It's part of the poet's lineage, the poet's
inheritance, such drugs." Only Coleridge didn't have to go through
a Puerto Rican connection, or flout the law to get it. Gregory
resented that. "It should be a part of every poet's medicine cabinet," he said.

He paced the cabin floor and, telling me to get comfortable,
explained how the law turns farmers of the poppy into gangsters
and prevents the poet from exploring the pain of life. "For me,
there is no Xanadu," Gregory wailed.

I was present, sometime earlier, when Gregory had dictated a
poem about his muse, who asked him, "Do you love drugs more
than you love me?"

"With tearful eyes," Gregory cried back to his muse, "I swear to
you, there is in me yet time / To run back through life and expiate
all that's been sadly done . . . sadly neglected."

Gregory, I wanted to tell him, there is no time like that. No one
is given that much time. It wasn't a muse, it was Gregory's own
intelligence looking back at him that seemed to be saying, "Oh,
Gregorio, Gregorio, you've failed me."

Gregory went to the bathroom, leaving the door open. Calliope
used the noise of his peeing to give me the news that I'd be shooting up with Gregory. I would see through the big lie of life with
him. We would both partake, and the apothecarian earth would
bloom in our veins, or something like that. I would shoot up, then
make love to Poppy. *People have only themselves, and they don't do that
too well,* was one of Gregory's themes. He believed no one person
would give you everything—you had to steal what you needed.

Yet, I thought, many had been kind to Gregory because of his
gift, because his poetry revealed his soul, which seemed both good
and fragile.

I started crying when it looked like I would have to shoot up with Gregory. I thought I would die up there in the mountains. I suddenly envied people who don't have much imagination. When you don't have an imagination, dying probably isn't much to worry about. But if you do have an imagination, then dying is something awful, something to be afraid of. I wasn't really enough of a Buddhist to feel any other way. I entered the shrine room only for classes, or for school dances, never to meditate.

How much longer would this craziness go on? It felt like we'd been up there for hours. When would these lunatics fall asleep, drop off with exhaustion? How long would it last—weeks, months? Would they keep me here for years, until we all died of hunger and exposure?

Pity comes in funny ways. My tears made Gregory stop in his tracks, so to speak. He saw my tears and told me to go outside, to listen to the birds singing at night. There were still some left, up in the mountains. I think he was probably just as glad not to have to share the junk. I suddenly remembered what Charlie Haden had said: that Gregory was the real addict; he was the one to be afraid of.

"In the morning," Gregory said, "we'll call your parents. We'll make our claim."

I waited outside the cabin, listening for the birds whose songs I couldn't hear. The only sound in my head was my own fear. They were naked and rolling in the bed when I came back inside the house.

Poppy told me to approach the bed. She pulled at my tie. (I still had it on.) I felt excited and sick to my stomach. The noise was still in my head—that noiseless noise of fear. Calliope rose to her knees in bed and gave me a long kiss. Gregory was drowsy, his head on the pillow, making small, whimpering noises like a puppy having a bad dream. They were both high.

I walked away from the bed, determined to wait them out. I was waiting for them to fall asleep. When they did, I would be the one to call my parents, to have them come and take me out of there. This

C

O

O

L

was a time for daring. Maybe Gregory *had* helped me conquer my fear after all. Anyway, I had nothing to lose.

"What is it?" Gregory asked. "What are you doing?" Gregory had gotten up when Calliope had kissed me. He slurred his words; he was very stoned. He was trembling. I couldn't tell if he was mad or about to have a seizure. I couldn't figure out if he wanted to talk to me, if he wanted to tell us something, or if I was going to see Gregory Corso cry.

At first, Gregory wanted to have some fun with me. Then he changed his instrument, and began playing a different tune. He wanted to teach me something, to give me a night in the jailhouse, a night under the open roof of the Parthenon, where Gregory had once slept. But Gregory misjudged me. For all his talk about self-reliance, he, too, was trading on the heroic romances of the Beats. Gregory thought he could make up new stories on the spot to entertain me, to keep me there. He thought we could share exploits—exploits that verged on the delirious.

I was about to leave, to make that decisive step and bolt from the cabin and take my chances with the cold and the darkness, when who should arrive at that very moment but Mike Brownstein and a girlfriend. It was a double bill, and I was the audience.

It turned out that it was Mike's cabin after all. I ran past him, out the door, into the middle of the dark road. I must have hit something on the way out, because I noticed my arm was bleeding. I didn't even wait for him to ask what was going on, or offer me a ride down the mountain; I just followed the road as best I could until I saw the lights of the city and I could hear the generator of Boulder Hospital humming in the night air. I don't know how long I ran, or if anyone tried to come after me. All I knew was that I was happy, as if I had suddenly seen the mad, flickering lights of a carnival. I was home.

The next day I found out that Gregory and Calliope had gone to Mike's cabin because Gregory had destroyed his apartment after Lisa had left him.

I went with Allen to survey the damage. Gregory was crazy to ruin the one place of his own in Boulder. It looked like he'd started with the furniture, breaking it up and throwing it into the fireplace—chairs, tables, even his writing desk. Apparently, he'd given away everything that wasn't nailed down—plates, cups, saucers, lamps. Anything that wasn't missing was destroyed. Even Max's children's books were shredded.

Allen shook his head when he saw the wrecked apartment. We stood for more than a half hour in the midst of Gregory's mess. It was suddenly like standing inside a cluttered tomb. Life hides everything from people, even what they know to be true about their oldest friends. For the first time, Allen seemed unable to help Gregory. Allen told me he and Peter would have to leave for New York soon. He asked if I would like to come with them and spend New Year's Eve at Anne Waldman's apartment in New York. I asked if Gregory would be there.

Allen said he hoped not, so I said yes.

As far as Allen was concerned, what Gregory had done was unjustifiable. He couldn't save Gregory from himself. Gregory had intelligence, he was incredibly intuitive about people, he even had a weird code of honor. But he had no sense of how to live in the world. That's probably when Allen realized they'd have to get rid of him. The Kerouac School couldn't afford Gregory Corso anymore. So Allen and Anne, and some of the younger poets who were better at tolerating Gregory's social dissonances, gathered in executive session in Rinpoche's office to consider Gregory's fate.

As you get older, you can look back on the selfishness of the people you've known in life. You can see it for what it is. It becomes harder to make excuses for it. With Gregory, I certainly tried, but his pain and his cruelty were exhausting all of us. They seemed even stronger than time itself.

Thanks to Allen, though, I'd be going home.

43. Back to New York

The air above Boulder was as unstable as the atmosphere at the Jack Kerouac School. The wings of the plane were flapping as if they were made out of canvas. Allen and Peter were holding hands. I hadn't seen that before, in the whole time I had been at Naropa. I didn't know when I first arrived at the Kerouac School that there was so much unresolved *tristesse* going on among the Beats, to say nothing of the second-generation poets and other characters that Allen and Bill had brought with them to Naropa from the Lower East Side. I didn't know I was in the middle of turbulent affairs and unrequited love: Burroughs for Allen, Allen for Peter (now that Peter had discovered women, or at least the idea of women), Peter for girls, girls for Anne, Anne for Gregory, Gregory for the Muse, Allen for Neal Cassady, as Cassady—now dead—had become an object of veneration in a lot of the poems Allen was handing over to me to work on. And, of course, all of them for Kerouac, whose disembodied spirit held them and our school together.

I had no idea how tormented Allen was by his crushes. He had come back from the Rolling Thunder Revue in love with a skinny, curly-headed violin player named David Mansfield, though I got the feeling that David was straight and a lover of Allen's poetry, which didn't translate to the poet.

Allen had now, it seemed to me, transferred his love of Neal Cassady to the young Neals who were coming up to Naropa's reception desk, "looking for Allen Ginsberg," hoping Allen would help them in their battle for survival, only to reject him if things didn't go well, or if Allen—God forbid—criticized their poems, or became impatient with their standing around waiting for some of his fame to rub off on them. They would instead humiliate him and storm off. Allen's bed was either the most crowded or the most lonesome bed in Boulder—I couldn't decide which.

Allen Ginsberg was the most airplaned of poets. He had crossed America more times by plane than Neal Cassady had driven across the Golden Gate Bridge. Although Allen and Peter hated to fly, Allen liked United Airlines. He said it gave him the idea for his "poems of these states," which he called *The Fall of America.* He was very proud of his National Book Award for that book, the only national literary award he would ever win. Flying United made him feel like an American poet.

"Why not fly American then, Allen?" asked Peter, the most practical man in Allen's chaotic life.

Before we left, Allen admitted to Rinpoche that his ego, which he had tried so hard to rub out with meditation, always came roaring back on an airplane. "I'm too famous to die," Allen shrieked as the plane rocked in turbulence.

I had offered to sit between Allen and Peter on the flight to New York because, compared to the two of them, I was usually a patient and calm flier. If necessary, I could hold both their hands.

The stewardess seemed to know them. She brought them small bottles of alcohol.

I had my first gin and tonic on that flight. Allen ordered it for me. I also had my fourth and fifth gin and tonic on that flight. Somewhere over Michigan, it suddenly dawned on me that Peter and Allen were both smashed. And I had started to slur my words as early as the Grand Canyon.

Then it hit me: something more terrifying even than being drunk for the first time in a rollicking airplane. My father had agreed to pick me up at the airport! He would see two of my teachers completely wasted and their main student—me—on his first bender. Is this what Allen meant, whenever he dragged me from one place to another, when he said that he was going to treat me like Edgar Allan Poe on Election Day, when Poe got taken, Allen explained, from one pub house to another, liquored up by the pols so he could vote repeatedly for the same candidate? (I thought all

B
A
C
K

to New York

C

O

O

L

the bars were closed on Election Day, but Allen never let the facts interfere with a good story, even the story of his life. It's why he was a poet, I guessed, and not in market research, something he actually did in the 1950s until he was let go for rifling through other analysts' desks.)

My father, Seymour Kashner, was going to drive in to JFK from Long Island and find us drunk as sailors on shore leave, walking around and around the bag carousel like Buddhist pilgrims around the stupa.

The plane landed. There is a sigh you sigh when you think you are out of danger, a sigh that commemorates the fact that you are still alive. Peter was the first to make it. Allen was next. Then, a funny thing happened. Allen Ginsberg—the poet who had chanted "Om Mani Padma Hum" in Lincoln Park, Chicago, during the calamitous Democratic convention of 1968, who, in Gregory's phrase, "dropped Hindu for guru" and became an industrial-strength Buddhist practitioner—put his hand on his bald head and uttered the Sh'ma, the Jewish prayer testifying to God's oneness. Every kid in Hebrew school knows that prayer. I guess Allen never forgot it.

Then Peter put his hand over his thick ponytail and said the same thing. Russian Peter saying the Sh'ma? In another life, he would have been a Cossack rounding up Jews for the czar's army. Prayer works, I thought as I stood up and waited for the air to come back into my lungs, teaching myself how to breathe again.

As we left the plane, Allen and Peter wobbled like a couple of ninepins, leaning against me for support. It wasn't a good idea. My own hallucinations were getting in the way. I saw standing at the end of a long corridor—at the very back of a group of people who had come to meet our plane—an older man with eyeglasses wearing a false, long beard hooked over his ears. What can only be described as love beads were worn around his neck, over a dark business suit. He also pretended to be reading a small book of poetry, which he held up for us to see, called *Howl*. The man also happened to look a lot like my father.

Seymour Kashner had come to the airport dressed like Allen

Ginsberg. I don't think my parents, in their planning for this kind of hilarity, counted on Allen being there, too.

My father's appearance stopped Allen in his tracks. He stared at my father, as if he were looking into a mirror. He even held up a hand to see if the mirror image would hold up its hand. It didn't.

"Allen, this is my father. Seymour, meet Allen Ginsberg. Peter, this is my dad."

"You never told us he looks like Allen," Peter said.

"He doesn't," I said. "Not usually."

Seymour unhooked his beard.

"He still looks like Allen!" Peter said. I guess he did.

Allen seemed weirdly flattered that my father had come all this way, dressed like him, to pick us up. It was typical of Allen to misconstrue the whole thing and turn it into an enormous compliment. My father and I looked at each other as if to say, well, maybe it will mean a good grade at the end of the Jack Kerouac School term.

Marion was waiting for us in the car. She seemed a little taken aback by seeing Allen and Peter with me. Seymour got into the front seat and put his fake beard back on. Allen, Peter, and I sat in the backseat and we headed for the airport exit. We crossed the Williamsburg Bridge. My mother said, "You're probably hungry," and she offered to take Allen and Peter to Ratner's, the ancient kosher dairy restaurant on Delancey Street in lower Manhattan. To my shock and horror, they accepted. My hip, independent, beatnik world was suddenly turning into a short story by Isaac Bashevis Singer.

I'm a little ashamed to remember how much embarrassment my mother and father had awakened in me, these profoundly good-hearted people who were treating my teachers to a late-night meal at Ratner's.

Once we'd arrived and were shown to a table by one of the sourpussed, argumentative waiters, Allen told Seymour that he hadn't been in Ratner's in maybe twenty years. Marion ordered for everyone, while Allen explained how the last time he was in this restaurant he'd had a vision after taking peyote and copulating with a man from the U.S. Army—a male nurse who had the face of an angelic creature. Allen said he had seen a vision of Baudelaire, right there in Ratner's, who told him to change his life, to devote himself to poetry, to music, to singing the blues in life.

The vegetarian chopped liver came. My father told Allen to try it. Allen ate practically the whole thing.

"Don't they feed you at the Jack Kerouac School?" my father asked. It was like being with Allen's father, Louis, and Allen's brother, Gene, only worse. I didn't want anyone at Naropa to know I came from parents. Hadn't Bob Dylan told people he was an orphan, that he'd been raised by circus performers? Allen noticed my discomfort and told me, sotto voce, not to worry. He said he liked my parents. He even said I was lucky.

At the end of our midnight supper, before heading for East Twelfth Street to drop off Allen and Peter, Allen told Marion that she reminded him of Mitzi Gaynor. It made my mother's night.

44. Anne's Party

It was cold in New York, but a few days after landing in Merrick I started going into the city (as we who lived on Long Island called Manhattan) every day, to walk the East Village, knowing Allen and Peter were waking up on East Twelfth Street. Now I could really see them, even though in some way they were sewn back up into their own lives.

I called Allen from the pay phone on the corner of First Avenue and told him I was in town. If you stood in front of the building where he and Peter lived, Allen would lean out of his window and throw down the key to you. Richard Hell and his girlfriend lived in the same building. Anne Waldman lived practically around the corner; her window looked out over Eighth Street. I knew that W. H.

Auden had lived farther down Eighth, across from the St. Mark's Cinema, a tiny blue grotto of a theater that played old films. Ted Berrigan, who would be coming to Naropa in a few months, lived here too. In the 1960s, when I was still in elementary school, he and his poet friends were walking the amphetamine-soaked streets of the East Village. It seemed impossible to compete with them for Allen's ear; they seemed to know him well enough to treat him like some annoying uncle. Anne and Michael Brownstein were always making gentle fun of Allen—his baggy pants, his hissy fits. They kept telling him that he was taking on too much work and stress. They even, behind his back, made fun of his high blood pressure.

I would never know Allen well enough to tease him like this, I thought.

When I was in high school, the East Village was like something out of the *Arabian Nights* romances. The Fillmore East was still in existence, and there was the St. Mark's Bookshop, with its picture of Allen in a huge oval frame hanging off a nail downstairs. I once saw Auden shuffling into the Gem Spa in his satiny bedroom slippers on a rainy Saturday night, where he had gone for an egg cream and the Sunday *New York Times*. It was a place where I knew that Allen and his friends were lurking, that confidences were taking place—but where, exactly, were these gloomy zones of melancholy? I was still groping my way around Avenue A, a little uncertain in some of the same places where Allen moved so effortlessly. I once lied to my parents about coming here to the East Village on the Long Island Rail Road, telling them I was studying for a test with a friend. That night, I brought home a drum major's uniform complete with epaulets that I'd bought at a vintage clothing store on Eighth Street. My parents had already called my friend's house and found out I wasn't there. The drum major's uniform and I were met with "the treatment"—my father's not talking to me for twenty-four hours—and the confiscation of what he finally called my "doorman's uniform." I had seen the Beatles inside the foldout of *Sgt. Pepper's Lonely Hearts Club Band* seated in those uniforms, and I wanted one.

Somehow everything was different now that I knew the Beats,

ANNE'S

C

O

O

L

or thought I did. My visions of Allen and Burroughs had become real, even to me. My visions didn't fail me, as I walked down Second Avenue with Allen and Peter, and Larry Fagin (one of the younger teachers at Naropa) and his girlfriend Susan Noel (the whitest woman I ever saw, from Kentucky, who looked like Mia Farrow in *Rosemary's Baby*).

We were headed toward Anne's apartment on New Year's Eve, midway through my first year at the Jack Kerouac School. I had the feeling in this bitter cold that the rest of the world had gone away.

Here they were, all together in one room, or, more accurately, spread out over the several rooms of Anne's railroad apartment. Most of the guests—Ginsberg, Burroughs, Larry Fagin, Reed Bye— were in the club car (the living room), holding drinks and smoking cigarettes in groups of twos and threes, like the cocktail hour in a Frank O'Hara poem. There was Edwin Denby (bearded, delicate, whippet-thin, with the fragile whiteness of a ghost, smiling). His lively eyes looked around the room. I was hoping Larry Fagin would introduce us, as they were friends. He never did. Instead, Allen brought him over. He left us standing together in front of Anne's window, which looked out over Eighth Street. I saw the snow starting to fall.

"It's snowing," I said.

"Just wait till summer. Have a little patience," Edwin Denby said. After that, it was only our two voices on the verge of saying what voices always seem about to say, but never do. So here they were, the last free men, I thought. The ones who stormed the hills of bourgeois complacency. The ones who were going to restore humanity to itself, freeing it from encrusted, outdated inhibitions and fears. The ones who would spear all the two-legged sharks who walked the earth.

But that was before Peter freaked out.

A few minutes before midnight, Anne recited her long poem "Fast Talking Woman," a command performance that put an exhausted

Allen to sleep. "I'm the celebrity woman / I'm the luminary woman / I'm the student woman / I'm the braggart woman . . . / where will I go? . . . / who will save me? . . ."

Anne wrote a poem for Allen, which she read that night. Anne loved Allen, but I think she was a little jealous of his fame; a lot of Allen's friends were. In her poem, she told Allen to go to Rinpoche's meditation center and park his ego. Allen came to life when he heard his name spoken. "Go disappear," Anne advised him, "and meditate, just be Allen the janitor, go clean the stove." She told him to "stop telling everyone what to do, then act meek."

Away from Boulder, it seemed that the younger poets were getting back at Allen for running the show. It reminded me of those Dean Martin "roasts" on television, which I loved, with Don Rickles poking good-natured fun at Frank Sinatra. Only there was no laugh track in Anne's apartment. Perhaps the younger poets thought Allen was just a madman who thought he was Allen Ginsberg.

"Don't eat that terrible food, empty that soda down the drain," Anne continued. Her poem was a kind of rant, a bill of particulars laying out what bugged the younger poets about Allen. I'd heard it before at the Kerouac School, whenever the younger teachers got together and began tearing into the boss. "If the phone rings," Anne continued, "don't answer it. Say 'no.' I dare you."

Wow. Even Allen's big heart was starting to get on their nerves.

"Don't be so hungry for young boy meat," Anne recited. "Don't worry about / what everyone else is thinking about you. / No one's smarter or more enlightened or more famous. / For heaven's sake, Allen, pull up those baggy pants!"

I looked over at Allen. Guess what? He wasn't laughing. I knew he was hurt. As much as he had designed the Kerouac School as a kind of protective retreat from his own fame and the craziness of his own life, he was giving the last bit of his health to the place. And here were these younger poets who didn't seem grateful for the chance Allen was giving them even to *be* artists at all. It just seemed to me to be bad manners. I was so grateful to be there, and they seemed to take it all for granted.

C

O

O

L

Allen had a lot to contend with lately. Recently, a young poet had showed up at a reading at the Kerouac School and told Allen that he was going to commit suicide and name Allen as his literary executor. His estate consisted of two tremendous shopping bags filled with his poetry. Allen already felt in some way responsible for his own mother's shock therapy and death. Allen had started jumping up and down and yelling, shaking his fists in the air, throwing a tantrum, whining and screaming at this kid. The kid looked terrified of Allen. I thought Allen was going to have a stroke. Everyone told him to watch his temper, to deal with his anger, to watch his blood pressure.

Allen didn't have a great sense of humor about himself, but he was learning. The tricks of his ego and his regard for his own reputation were starting to make him laugh, just a little. Rinpoche had already put that bee in Allen's bonnet, and he was the only person Allen seemed to listen to about any of this. Rinpoche was giving Allen a real inner life, a life not just made up of Allen's own thoughts and ideas, but one of ego-lessness. "It's the only thing," Allen once told me, "that can melt the glacier inside of me, the one that's been building up for fifty years."

Incredibly, I don't think Allen really minded the barrage of criticism because, after all, it was about *him*. Allen hadn't lost his ego at all—it was still intact. In fact, I noticed that Anne and Allen were now talking about meditation, and had planned a retreat together. There was a lot of talk about losing your ego, about taking refuge in the dharma. Didn't anyone around here realize that this was the sixth day of Chanukah? In fact, the threat of ego-lessness was the reason I had stayed out of the shrine room. I liked my ego. I always made up an excuse for not joining Peter and Allen when they went off to meditate. I was afraid of emptying myself out, afraid I'd have no serious reason for living. I once asked Allen, "Aren't you afraid of disintegrating, of having nothing left to write about?" There was Allen's old friend Philip Whalen (the poet who'd told his wife on their honeymoon that he had just taken vows to become a Buddhist monk), who was writing nothing but poems about how he couldn't write since he started meditating. Most of Rinpoche's students, those who seemed to spend all their time sitting, were in danger of sinking into an irresistible boredom, the human equivalent of torpor. Who was it who said human beings are such timid creatures that only our amusements can stop us from dying for real? That's why Gregory always flew off to the movies.

I'd known something was wrong with Peter as early as the car ride with my parents and our late-night dinner at Ratner's. Peter was a man who shouldn't be drinking. He had seemed manic to me, even in the car, petting my mother's hair. (She told me later he was using a little too much force, pressing down on the back of her head, as if he were trying to flatten the flip in her hairdo.) He was like a kid in the backseat who had had too much chocolate. He was slapping Allen on the wrist and pulling pages out of Allen's notebook and making them flap around out the window, threatening to let them go.

Peter started drinking at Anne's party right from the beginning and wouldn't stop. He seemed to become even more agitated, more profane. At Naropa before we'd left, Allen asked Peter to sit in for him and teach a few of his classes while Allen went out of town to give a poetry reading. I remember one of those classes: Peter had looked around the room and called on one of the newer students, an intense, serious-looking woman who had come to class prepared (well, she had brought a notebook and some pens). Peter asked her, "Do you like to have your pussy eaten?" followed by, "Who here likes to eat pussy?"

One shy girl I had danced with once at a Kerouac School party held her hand up at half-mast, looked around meekly, and then quickly withdrew her hand.

"Does it taste like strawberry jam?" Peter demanded. "It should taste like strawberry jam."

Then Peter turned to me. "Your assignment, Mr. Sam," he said, "is to eat the pussy of some girl in the class and tell us if tastes like strawberry jam."

C

O

O

L

I pretended to write down the assignment in my memo pad.

Peter never taught again, at least not that class. After Peter had confided to Allen that he'd had suicidal thoughts, Allen had taken Peter to a doctor who put him on antidepressants. Peter was now going around saying that he was really straight, and had been duped by Allen into being queer.

At Anne's party on Eighth Street, Peter kept saying that he didn't want to be gay anymore. "It's because you had such a strong personality," Peter told Allen. I didn't really believe it. I thought it was just the alcohol talking, the pills, even Peter's illness. But in front of all these people, on New Year's Eve, Peter kept going on about how Allen had tricked him.

Peter was eyeing a carving knife Anne had laid out for cutting the New Year's cake she had bought in Little Italy. I touched Peter tenderly on the shoulder and moved between him and the table. I liberated the knife and brought it back into Anne's kitchen. Allen threatened Peter with sending him to Bellevue. I feared that Peter wouldn't be making just a weekend visit to the nuthouse. One more act of madness and Peter would probably never, ever get out. I was afraid for him. If gentle Peter, who let tiny birds perch on his finger, was doomed, then everyone was doomed. Even Allen. Even Rinpoche. Even me.

Peter was now starting to take off his clothes. I could tell he was getting ready to throw himself into the arms of a monster—a madness that, in time, would perhaps subside, but you never knew when. You could threaten Peter, like Allen did, with the drip-drip of a drug that would quiet him in the hospital—and maybe that was the only way—or you could try to understand Peter's dilemma. Sweet and care-taking, his outward gentleness seemed to mask a hatred of the people closest to him.

When you saw Peter's zombie brothers, who would both come out to Boulder for a visit during the spring term, you saw what the problem was. The problem was Peter's fate. This was Peter trying to escape his own private sorrow. Burroughs said that in the end Peter, like Ezra Pound, would probably choose silence.

Peter was upsetting all of Anne's plans for New Year's Eve.

Midnight had come and gone. Peter was being calmed down on the couch, or, rather, held down. Suddenly, he sat upright and jumped off the couch. I thought I recognized Philip Glass trying to hold him back, like a policeman. Like a Russian bear at the picnic, Peter was chasing away all of Anne's friends.

Larry and his girlfriend asked if I wanted to leave, and we went to Raoul's for a late dinner. Larry ordered caviar and an expensive wine. He got me to pay with my father's Diner's Club card, which I still had. I had too much caviar. Walking toward Penn Station alone, I threw up in the snow. It was black.

I knew my parents would eventually see the bill for dinner—$300 for the three of us. I didn't want to face them. I didn't want a temperance lecture from my father. I felt bad. I just wanted to take my body off to somewhere else. I had been locked up with the crazy Beats long enough, but I was always nice to crazy people. That was my problem. I thought you had to live on the edge of craziness to be a poet, and I wanted to be a poet more than anything. At the Jack Kerouac School and around Rinpoche himself, I felt as if I were in an almost constant state of danger and excitement, as if the Beats themselves had lured me into this unknown city, a city where everything is wreckage but you stay as long as you can. You keep looking with fascination, not for a way out but for a way in—even deeper. It had happened to Allen, Gregory, and even old Bill. It was happening to me.

"They fell in front of a cracked mirror, Sam," Billy Jr. said when I called him from my parents' house the next morning to wish him a happy new year. He sounded stoned—very stoned—as I told him what had happened at Anne's. "And they fell in love with that cracked image. They'll just stare at it until they die."

45. Birdbrain

When I told my folks about Peter's freakout at Anne Waldman's, my father said it could have been worse. I could have had William Burroughs as a father. He was right, although I was a little embarrassed when Seymour and Marion showed up just after New Year's at the Ukrainian Meeting Hall on Second Avenue on the Lower East Side to see Allen perform his new poem "Birdbrain," which he talked / sang to a rock band accompaniment. "Like Rex Harrison in *My Fair Lady*," Marion generously critiqued.

The Ukrainian Hall was packed, but not with Ukrainians. Allen was signing copies of "Birdbrain," the 45 rpm record that a small, independent label had just put out. The band Loud Fast Rules was going to perform too. Most of the members lived in Allen's building around the corner on East Twelfth Street. It was the first time my father saw green hair. He himself was bald, had been since his twenties. Seeing a lot of hair always made my father think about how he'd woken up one day, dragged a brush through his hair, and found most of his hair on the brush. It wouldn't happen that way for me. My receding hairline would creep up on me, like the erosion of the continental shelf. In high school, I had wanted to call my garage band Male Pattern Baldness, which horrified the other musicians. Instead, we called ourselves the Glitters, but because the "l" and the "i" were so close together on my drum kit we kept getting introduced as the Gutters. We broke up.

Allen loved to perform. He was like most Jewish entertainers, a real ham. There were rumors that the legendary English punk rock band the Clash might show up and jam with Allen. In the early 1980s, Allen would appear in a music video for "Combat Rock." Joe Strummer, the lead singer for the Clash, apparently liked visiting

Allen on Twelfth Street. Anne Waldman later floated the idea to Strummer that he take over the music department of the Jack Kerouac School. He turned her down.

My father played the harmonica. He'd picked it up as a little boy listening to Gene Autry and Tex Ritter on the radio. It was cheaper than piano lessons, and what's the use of piano lessons if you can't afford a piano? He played "Cielito Lindo" ("My Beautiful Heaven"), which he said was his father's favorite song, and "Home on the Range," FDR's favorite song. My father's repertoire consisted of other people's favorite songs, mostly cowboy songs and ballads. I didn't think he knew anything more contemporary than "Streets of Laredo."

My father saw the band setting up onstage and asked them if they needed a harmonica player. He was only half kidding, but Loud Fast Rules thought that was a great idea. They weren't embarrassed. They weren't horrified. He wasn't their father. The lead singer told Allen that my father had offered to "back them up" on the harmonica. Allen looked very interested. They talked about harmonicas—Hohner's versus Marine Band. My father said that Bob Dylan couldn't play the harmonica. Allen said he could. (I loved Bob Dylan's harmonica playing. I thought it sounded like Dylan's soul blowing through his harmonica.) Seymour mentioned Larry Adler and Johnny Puleo, the midget harmonica player. "Now those are harmonica players," he said.

When Allen asked Seymour if he was going to play, my father said he didn't want to "ruin the evening." But everyone started to insist that he play with Allen during the premiere of "Birdbrain." I went up to a few people and told them how embarrassed I was, but they kept telling me how cool it was that this old guy was going to play the harp for Allen.

By the time Seymour took the stage, dressed like he was going to work in a brown suit and tie with a fedora and his plastic shoes, look-ing like nothing so much as a precursor to one of the Blues Brothers, the rumor had spread that my father had just come off the road with Johnny Winter. In fact, the only public performance Seymour had ever given was to play "Happy Birthday" to children in restaurants.

B
I
R
D
B
R
A
I
N

C

O

O

L

Allen introduced him as my father, Seymour Kashner. He then played "My Beautiful Heaven." That night, this jaded, hip crowd of Lower East Siders belonged to my father. For an encore, he played "Blowin' in the Wind." He had been listening to my records after all! He winked at Allen. Allen smiled back; he seemed to actually enjoy sharing the stage with my father. It wasn't so long ago that Louis, Allen's own father, had died.

Seymour got a standing ovation, which wasn't hard seeing that there were no chairs, but they were really digging him. I was embarrassed, but I was also secretly proud of my father.

I suddenly saw Gregory Corso across the room, mingling with the crowd. None of us knew he was even in New York. He just appeared, like a genie out of some discarded kerosene lamp. I wondered if he'd still be teaching at the Kerouac School when the new semester began.

Gregory sidled up to Seymour and told him that he played the harp like a Negro, then he asked him for ten bucks. Seymour gave it to him. That night my father met all the people who had been wining and dining on his credit card the past year. He spied William Burroughs, settled in the only chair at a table near us, but Seymour thought he was the actor Dean Jagger. I didn't correct him. Someone asked Burroughs what he thought about my father's harmonica playing. Bill said a terse "no comment," then added that Allen always had a soft spot for vaudeville. I thought that was a cruel remark. I didn't understand why Burroughs had this mean streak in him. After two years at Naropa, I would still feel that Burroughs didn't have any feelings, any tenderness. No wonder Billy was drinking himself to death back in Boulder. What had Burroughs done with his heart? I didn't defend Seymour. I was too afraid of Bill, and anyway, I probably wasn't supposed to hear his remark. But I could hear the whole room that night. I could hear the whole world.

I didn't so much feel proud of my father that night as I felt relieved. Relieved that he somehow had managed to keep up with the non-melody of "Birdbrain" and that the crowd didn't pelt him with unlit Gauloises, forcing him to leave the stage. Why was I embarrassed by this good man? Allen was often far more embarrassing.

Later that night I would drive back home to Long Island with my parents, riding on my father's coattails along the L.I.E.

The Clash never showed up at the Ukrainian Meeting Hall, but on my way out to the car I saw Joe Strummer in black combat boots, wearing a blue jean jacket, smoking a cigarette, skulking in the doorway of the social club.

"Nice job," he said, bowing slightly to my father. "That was beautiful, man."

I couldn't believe it. I waited for Seymour to say something. For an exquisite moment I stood between Joe Strummer, punk rocker, and Seymour Kashner, window shade salesman.

"Do you know who that was?" I asked.

"A bum?" my father said. "The Bowery is home to a lot of men like that. You have to have your wits about you around here. Did he ask you for money?"

Our car was parked in front of the Kiev, a restaurant off East Seventh Street. With its Polish churches and restaurants, its onion domes and its onion rolls, the Lower East Side appealed to my father, the son of Jewish immigrants from Warsaw. "How about some blintzes?" he asked. "You get hungry performing."

As we headed for the Kiev, a few people seemed to recognize him on the street. There's a thin line between pride and humiliation, like two countries sharing a common border. That night, I seemed to move between the two like a double agent whose loyalty was only to himself.

As Gregory once said after Allen had called him on some particularly egregious behavior, it isn't a pretty picture, but there it is, hanging on the wall for everyone to see.

The next morning my father asked me, "What are you writing at the Jack Kerouac School?" We were all sitting down together at the kitchen table; that's where all the momentous and trivial moments of our life together were traversed. I started to read some of the poems I had written during the past year at Naropa. My mother

C

O

O

L

thought all my poems were beautiful. My father said, "Well, I don't understand them, but they sound very nice, very pretty."

That's exactly what Allen had said to me about John Ashbery's poetry, so I took it as a kind of compliment. I remembered what Charlie Haden had said about the problem of having hip parents—there was nothing to rebel against. I read a few more of my poems, and the phone rang upstairs. My mother went to answer it. She didn't want to interrupt the poetry reading.

"It's Allen Ginsberg on the phone. Al-len Gins-berg," she said, turning it into an English-sounding name. She wasn't making fun; it was her way of saying someone distinguished was on the phone for her son.

It felt good to take the call. Allen said he would be going back to Boulder earlier than planned. He said something had taken place that could ruin everything, something involving Rinpoche that could destroy the Jack Kerouac School. We had to go back. He asked me to come along. He said that it was important to show people that Naropa wasn't some kind of cult, and that he might have to put me on exhibit at the Kerouac School in order to save it.

Allen said he had been walking around with a secret about Naropa that he couldn't tell anyone. Now, he said, because of a story ferreted out by his friend the poet Tom Clark, everyone would know. But it was a rotten time to have to go back.

I had returned home to Long Island with a secret of my own. Carla was pregnant. I didn't tell anyone, either. It came as a big surprise, especially to Carla. She said a doctor had once told her that she couldn't have children. She had once lived with a musician—a drummer for the Mothers of Invention, Frank Zappa's group—who wanted children, and he'd left her when the doctor told Carla it just wouldn't happen. Now it did.

She told me she was pregnant as we walked home after a Barbara Dilley dance performance at Naropa, in which Barbara had given birth to a giant medicine ball onstage to music by Gordon Lightfoot. I sensed something had changed in our relationship; she seemed happy and angry at the same time. When I asked what she was going to do, she said she wasn't about to raise two babies, meaning me and the real baby. I also felt two things at the same time: I felt insulted and relieved. Insulted that she didn't think I was grown up enough to have a baby with her; and relieved because I wasn't really able to grasp the idea of having a baby with Carla. I thought of my folks. They had sent me to Naropa to become a poet, not a father.

But I was trying to be a grown-up, maybe I was trying too hard, trying to act as if this had all happened to me before. In truth, I was trying to hide the fact that I was scared to death.

I offered, in a whisper, to get married. Carla just laughed, and then she cried. I asked if she needed money. A big mistake. "Look," she said, "it's not your problem."

Carla was pretending to be tough, the way I was pretending to be unfazed.

I tried to see her after that, but she avoided me. She said some cruel things. She said I'd get over it. She said the sex wasn't all that great anyway. And here I was, thinking it had been the greatest sex of my life. She said I was just too attached to her, and she quoted something Rinpoche had said about neurotic attachments and how my love for her was just an extension of my ego. I wept over the phone, but she was unmoved. She said in ten years I wouldn't even remember her name. She was wrong.

On the phone, I asked Allen what had happened, why we had to run back to the Jack Kerouac School. What could be so awful? If it wasn't because of Gregory or Burroughs or Billy, what was left?

Allen said it involved a poet named W. S. Merwin. The name made me think of Merlin, King Arthur's teacher. Allen said not everyone understood "crazy wisdom," and that what happened to Merwin and the woman he was with could ruin everything. This was the incident that Rinpoche's detractors were waiting for, to bring down the first Buddhist college in America. That Tom Clark, a fellow poet and a friend of theirs, had done this, Allen said, hurt even more.

C

O

O

L

Clark was one of those second-generation poets, a former poetry editor of *The Paris Review* who had recently moved to Boulder where he was editing the *Boulder Monthly*. His wife, a delicate-boned beauty who had wanted to move to the mountains with her young children, made Tom go to work, so he began editing the magazine, looking for a big scandal to make his mark. He found it in Rinpoche's kingdom of Shambhala.

Tom Clark prefigured the grunge look, wearing a wool cap over his receding hairline. He was tall and exceedingly lanky, like the baseball pitchers he admired, the kooks of the mound like Stan Lee, whom they called "the Spaceman," and Mark Fidrych, the eccentric pitcher for the Detroit Tigers known as "Big Bird" who during games had intense little conversations with his pitching mound. Tom Clark loved these guys.

Allen believed that Clark was going to succeed in doing what Cointelpro had, up to now, been unable to do: disembowel the Jack Kerouac School of Disembodied Poetics.

So I flew back to Boulder with Allen and Peter. Carla shunned me. Because I've never been able to seriously think about killing myself, I spent a lot of time at the movies. I preferred the lies of the movies to my own.

One day I saw Burroughs on the street. I asked about Billy. He said Billy spent most of the time in his apartment. It reminded him of a thieves' den in Marrakech. He said Billy didn't know what to do next about his fading health. Old Bill said Billy Jr. was reading up on Doc Holliday, the tubercular gunman at the OK Corral. Old Bill thought that was a bad sign, but in fact it was something that these two men—father and son—had in common, a romance with the Old West. I wondered if they ever knew that about each other.

I saw a lot of movies that winter. I went with Gregory and Calliope, who seemed to have completely forgotten that they had kidnapped me a few months earlier. Gregory was still living with the Faigos, taking tai chi. He was trying to stay away from drugs, but I couldn't keep the same kind of eye on him that I had before. He still hadn't finished his book, and his money was running out; he looked like one soul Allen could not save.

Gregory said that, for him, going to the movies was like going to church. He liked the flood of light radiating from the screen. We saw a lot of old films on Pearl Street. Gregory liked Frank Capra's movies, and films like *Macao* with Jane Russell and Robert Mitchum. He thought Russell had "unforgettable tits and shoulders. Her shoulders are even bigger and sexier than her tits," Gregory said. He loved the fact that actors don't grow old. Well, not on the screen they don't. Also, he liked to say that the poor see the same things the rich see when they go to the movies.

"The rich can't save Tara from burning," he said. "They can't rescue the Count of Monte Cristo."

One night I saw Carla in the movie theater. She looked right at me, but then walked away. Gregory put his arm around me. It gave me courage, even before the lights came all the way on in the theater. I'd taken on some of the courage—or whatever it was—that helped Gregory get from one day to the next. It's a funny thing, but Carla's contempt for me, her anger, didn't hurt as much. I thought of Gregory watching Laurence Olivier and Vivien Leigh in *That Hamilton Woman*. That's what was playing the night I saw Carla.

"Just let yourself get pulled in," Gregory said when we slunk into our seats. "In the movies, the world is love. It's like being in your mother's womb, and you can see your father—his shadow—as he comes into the room, and you know your mother is glad to see him."

It was a pretty weird thing to say to me at the time, but somehow it worked. I felt almost like myself again.

W. S. Merwin was a well-known poet, for what that's worth in America, which means he still must feel pretty lonely—an ant

BIRDBRAIN

crawling up an American anthill. It can be pretty discouraging. Allen was fond of quoting Shelley about how poets were "the unacknowledged legislators of the world." I was discovering, however, that poets could be a pretty resentful bunch, possessors of bad attitudes. "Heap Big Jackasses," Billy Jr. had said about the poets who came and went through the Jack Kerouac School. The most sensitive poets seemed capable of cruelty, just like anybody else. And even when you think they should be sticking together, they stick out like a bunch of sore thumbs in the eye of the great American night. Geniuses and artists banding together—that was the idea behind the Kerouac School, though Allen was now starting to get a lot of criticism from the poets more acceptable to the academy, Merwin being one of them. Some said Allen was just using Naropa to find jobs for his friends. "What's wrong with that?" Allen cried out when he heard that the National Endowment for the Arts had refused his application for money for the Kerouac School. "Do they want to punish me because my friends happen to be some of the greatest writers and poets of the twentieth century?" Allen seemed really perplexed. I couldn't tell if he was asking me or telling me.

I tried to cheer him up with a Sam Goldwyn story that I had read about in Oscar Levant's autobiography, *Memoirs of an Amnesiac,* a book that Jack Kerouac had loved, all about Levant's famous breakdowns and his legendary nicotine habit and coffee drinking (up to fifty cups a day, like Voltaire). He was an addict of everything. "I'm going to hold my hand over my heart," Kerouac used to say, "like Oscar Levant faking a heart attack." The story was that lawyers hired by Sam Goldwyn told him that he couldn't keep hiring his relatives for high positions at MGM because he would be accused of nepotism. "You mean they have a word for that?" Goldwyn had asked, incredulously.

Allen was in no mood for jokes. I'm not sure he even got it, any more than Sam Goldwyn had. All I knew was that this business with Rinpoche and W. S. Merwin had something to do with sex.

46. Allen's Secret

People wondered about Trungpa's love life. Allen said you had to do what the teacher told you. That was part of crazy wisdom. He said that you had to trust the teaching.

Merwin had a beautiful girlfriend. The previous summer they had gone on a retreat with Rinpoche and other Buddhist practitioners. Merwin had requested permission to attend Rinpoche's seminary, a kind of sleep-away camp for his most advanced students. Besides Allen and Peter, Merwin was the only other poet to have attended one of Rinpoche's seminaries. Merwin had been to Naropa before, as Allen's guest, but he was totally unfamiliar with Buddhist teachers, and his Hawaiian girlfriend, a woman named Dana Naone, knew even less. Trungpa evaluated applications to his seminaries like a college admissions officer. He apparently took great pleasure in turning people down. But Merwin's application was approved, and for a $550 tuition fee he was invited to join the seminary, which would gather at a remote ski lodge in the Colorado Rockies.

Something apparently had happened between Merwin and Rinpoche at that retreat. Something had also happened between Dana Naone and Rinpoche. But what? Some people said that Rinpoche had wanted Merwin and his girlfriend to take off their clothes. One friend of Merwin's said it was like Kristall-nacht. He said there was a lot of yelling and broken glass. He said it had nothing to do with crazy wisdom or the teachings, just that Rinpoche was just crazy and drunk with power. I heard that a lot when I came back to Naropa for the spring semester of 1977.

* * *

It was as if a key had been turned and a door was opened, through which a lot of Allen's enemies now felt free to walk. I came to the Kerouac School unconvinced that Allen could do any wrong. I didn't think much about Rinpoche. He just seemed like the incomprehensible, spooky father of a girl you really liked. But I was starting to think there must be something powerful about what he was talking about, because a lot of powerful, strong-willed personalities were responding to it. They were hanging on his every whispered word, his enigmatic talks, his chronic lateness, his air of gentle menace.

"Here's the ball game," Gregory said to me one night in the Boulderado Hotel, waiting for Poppy to come to him after earning some money in the big double rooms off the second floor. "Allen's like Jack. They need teachers. They don't think they've got the goods. Jack needed Neal. He said, 'Here's my teacher.' Jack's first religious instruction—it came from Neal, not the nuns of Lowell," Gregory said. "Ginzy needed a teacher, too," Gregory explained. "He'd spent his life rebelling against authority, but secretly Allen admired his professors at Columbia. He could have had that kind of life. Instead, he found something to follow both in Rinpoche and Neal Cassady. Rinpoche is something of an intellectual, with the soul of a voyeur, and Neal? Neal was an exhibitionist with an insatiable thirst for knowledge—and words." And for Allen and Jack both, Neal's prison-yard torso, his muscles bulging out of rolled-up sleeves, didn't hamper their adoration.

Allen had often mentioned Neal as a kind of teacher to him and to Kerouac. Allen said that Kerouac had once received a letter from Neal about a football game that turned into a letter about his life in Denver. It had thirty, maybe forty thousand words in it. Allen said it became a sacred document to Jack. It was almost as if that letter freed Kerouac to write his great works. It gave him the gift of Neal's style—his relentless, fascinating jabber.

I didn't really understand Neal Cassady. In fact, I found him a little scary, the idea of him, anyway. He reminded me of Jimmy

Gordon, a high school kid who let his girlfriend play with my hair during assembly, who couldn't wait to drop out of school. Jimmy and I were in general math class together, that is, eighth grade math but in high school. I was pretty stupid about numbers. Jimmy was so much older than the rest of us, on account of his being left back so much, that he actually had a job, with benefits, in the ninth grade. And he stole cars, like Neal. I figured that I would have been afraid of Neal Cassady. But Allen and Jack were in love with him.

The end of Neal's life sounded pathetic. He took a lot of psychedelic drugs and drove Ken Kesey's bus, hanging out with hippies half his age. He lifted weights. He tried to talk up his legend, while Kerouac, the artist, ran away from his. Neal had had a kind of scandalous love life. One of his wives was only fifteen years old. The Beats, my teachers, had learned to live with some very complicated romantic situations. Rinpoche's court, for example. This idea of being a courtier in the kingdom of Shambhala was not a problem for Allen, or for Anne.

Rinpoche didn't make any bones about the fact that he wasn't a monk anymore. He had a wife and a couple of young kids, three sons, in fact. Rinpoche's wife, Diana Pybus, was the first woman from America ever to attend the famous Spanish riding school of Vienna. Rinpoche was once warned by one of his teachers about exceeding the limits of familiarity with Occidentals. But that was a long time ago.

Rinpoche and Diana lived in their beautiful mansion on a hill in Boulder, "the wedding cake house." It had a lot of rooms. I should know. I had to vacuum them all, as part of my job as Allen's assistant at the Kerouac School. He also had a home in Nova Scotia, and property elsewhere in Colorado. The Vadjra guards took care of his every need. I started to think that it must be good to be reincarnated.

Allen believed that I was making a big mistake in not availing myself of the teachings. He thought I should try to meditate, and learn about the Four Noble Truths. Allen had even put the Four Noble Truths to music. He'd get his audiences to sing along with

ALLEN'S

Secret

C

O

O

L

him: "Born in this world, you've got to suffer. You die when you die, die when you die." And so on. It was catchy and upsetting at the same time.

In the weeks following what was becoming known as "the Merwin incident," the Kerouac School was in an anxious state. Mike Brownstein and Anne Waldman tried to deal with it by first asking Tom Clark what he thought he'd accomplish by publishing a story about something outsiders could never hope to understand. But the horse was not only out of the barn, it was off and running, setting records at Churchill Downs. And the barn? The barn was on fire. Something had to be done. While no one knew exactly what had happened to Merwin and Dana on that retreat, the intermezzo wasn't pretty.

Allen had other troubles. By now he and Peter had moved from the apartment complex on Broadway to an old wooden house on Mapleton. But if that move had been intended to give Peter more of a gemütlich sense of family, it didn't work. Allen's life companion of twenty years had met a woman. Peter Orlovsky was in love.

Juanita Lieberman arrived at the Kerouac School during one of the registration periods for the spring semester. She was painfully shy. I was meeting prospective applicants for the next summer session at Naropa. Peter's class was still mentioned in the catalogue, even though, after his crash course in cunnilingus and strawberry jam, his class had been canceled. Nonetheless, Juanita expressed an interest in it.

She was the daughter of a Park Avenue psychiatrist. She was plainly—almost shabbily—dressed, wearing a torn green sweater, dungarees that came down only to her ankles, and old tennis shoes. Her appearance made no secret of the fact that she hated makeup and wasn't dressing for the pleasure of men. She had a sad face. It was always a little red, as if she had just been crying. She looked like she was suffering from some invincible melancholy. I waved Peter over and introduced them.

I left the two of them alone in the hallway of Sacred Heart, the parochial school where the Naropa registrations always took place. That was the whole story. That evening, during Allen's poetry reading welcoming the new inmates to Naropa, I saw Juanita napping on Peter's shoulder. Like two bedraggled immigrants staring into the sea, Peter and Juanita sat there oblivious to everything. Juanita didn't even seem interested in the other writers who had come to see Allen, even the presence of Ken Kesey, who had driven out from Oregon with his friend Ken Babbs in a big Cadillac to visit a woman named Felice Duncan, with whom Kesey was having a "same time, next year" love affair that had been going on for twenty years.

As soon as Kesey arrived at Allen's house on Mapleton, he went into the bathroom. We all just sat there and listened to him pee; it took forever. Then someone broke the silence by saying that Kesey urinated with a sense of eternity, like a sailor.

Felice lived in Boulder and had become a Trungpa student. At first, I felt badly for her. I thought she lived for these visits from Kesey. They were both big, tall as trees, powerfully built—a good-looking couple. Kesey made Felice Duncan wait a long time for their night together, but she never griped about it. She waited for her lover with all the forbearance you see on those Mexicans waiting for a bus in Los Angeles, with the patience of saints. I wondered if Felice dreamed about Kesey, satisfied with not going to the bottom of life with him. Well, I guess life sometimes throws you off the path, and you just have to change your plans.

Gregory was right again, the disgraced Gregory. "You have to hurry—death is chasing you and it's closer than you think. There's a lot to do in a short time." So I didn't blame either Felice or Juanita. They had all those noises inside them, too.

Peter was practically living with Juanita by the end of the first week of classes. Was Allen going to have to support Peter and Juanita, and maybe a baby? First he had to worry about losing the Kerouac School, and now Peter. What about their pact, the one they had made to look

ALLEN'S

Secret

C

O

O

L

after each other, even in paradise? I guess Peter must have decided that paradise will have to wait, while he searched for it on earth. Of course, Peter never had any intention of leaving Allen—it would have to be the three of them, or the four of them. I know that Allen didn't like to go to bed alone, and Peter was beginning to spend less and less time at home and more and more time sleeping with Juanita and going out with her friends. When you saw them all together, Peter looked like Hercules attended by the maidens.

I would have done almost anything to please Allen. I had arrived at the Jack Kerouac School wanting to learn how I could become Allen Ginsberg; but I ended up wanting to take care of him. We hardly spoke about not going to bed together. Early on, when I'd had my chance, I always left. I always walked home in the evening, wondering what Allen was thinking after I'd left him alone. I had seen the poems he was writing now, the things he was confiding in his journals, his fears about Peter leaving him, about getting older, about not being attractive. Relying on his fame to take boys to bed. I didn't want him to take my refusals as some form of rejection. It was like a wound we had to keep dressing every time I said no.

One night after Allen asked me to stay, he started to cry. He seemed lost in his private darkness. The big, two-bedroom house was empty except for the two of us.

Allen was already in bed when he called out to me to come in and sit on the bed and talk. He reached out and hooked his fingers through one of the empty belt loops on my pants and pulled me closer to him. He kissed me on the mouth. I gently pushed him back on the bed and tried to say something sweet, something to comfort him. At the time, it felt like the end of the world, as if we were the only two people left, with no one else to confide in. All of his fame seemed to disappear for me inside his own unhappiness.

A time comes when you are just alone. No wonder it had been hard for Allen to do what Rinpoche asked—shave off that beard, stop wearing black, buy white shirts and a tie, go on retreat, and just be the Allen who takes out the garbage. At moments like this, I'm sure he sought comfort in retracing his steps as a great man in the world, returning to those moments when he was more certain of who he was and what the world expected of him. Peter's taking up with Juanita, and my rejection of Allen, must have left him feeling like someone fated to go back over his life, again and again, in the lonesome dark.

I kissed Allen's hand and let it go.

47. A Woman with No Heart

I failed. My first year at the Kerouac School was coming to an end, and I flunked the first assignment Allen had given me at the Jack Kerouac School of Disembodied Poetics: I couldn't keep Gregory away from his drug dealer. I had tried. I tried everything. I tried talking him out of going into Denver and spending all his money. I told him, "What if something happens to you? Think of your kids if you have an overdose." It didn't really occur to me that as far as Gregory was concerned, getting high was the only place in the world where he felt comfortable, now that he was forgotten, or not as famous as his famous friends Ginzy and Burroughs. It was also a way for Gregory to have a kind of permanent vacation from the slavery of having to make a living. Gregory's boss-hating attitude was the most extreme I had ever seen. It didn't help that Allen was making the Kerouac faculty plow their money back into Naropa, especially now that the scandal involving Rinpoche and W. S. Merwin might hurt future enrollment. It would be a happy miracle if Gregory could only finish his book; there was more money in it for him if he could.

Gregory had been a beautiful young man. Anne Waldman had told me that when she used to see him walking along MacDougal Street, his black curly hair and impish smile would take her breath away. Allen was always saying what a gorgeous kid Gregory was. But the years of wandering and drug taking had taken something out of him. Butterflies in youth, maggots at the end.

C

O

O

L

It wasn't envy, really, that Gregory felt toward Allen, but whatever it was it seemed like a pendulum that swung between aggression and depression. I didn't like hearing Gregory swearing at Allen behind his back, or calling him names. If Gregory could have been a ghost, free to haunt Allen and Bill, he would have shown his resentment in boundless mischief. As it was, he acted out in front of Allen, accusing him of abusing his authority at the Kerouac School and not promoting his friends' work so much as using it as a way to control them, a way of supervising how famous *they* could get.

I couldn't stand up to him anymore. He said if I let him go down into the hole of his addiction one more time, he promised me he would finish the book, and even write a letter of apology ("you could write it, I'll sign it," he said) to the entire Kerouac School faculty, apologizing for trashing the apartment they had given him. It seemed too good to be true.

It was. If Allen found out, I would be one dead poetry student. They would never trust me again. Nonetheless, I decided to go with Gregory—at least I could sit in the car so he wouldn't be given a parking ticket, proof that I had let him return to the junkies' trading post, a place as exotic in my imagination as any jungle in the Amazon, crawling with strange animals and natives with blow darts. Besides, I was curious to see what it was really like. I wouldn't have to avoid talking about it with Gregory, *I would know*. If a swindle took place, or if he lost some serious money to these people, he would be able to talk to me about it. Maybe he'd have more respect for me. I wouldn't seem like such a virgin to him. That was, after all, the big difference between us. Gregory's past had everything in it, whereas my biggest setback occurred when my high school guidance counselor had left a packet of vocational school brochures for me just at the time when I was starting to think about applying to colleges.

We set out at night, Gregory looking for a church. The semester was almost over and summer was just around the corner—you could smell its hot breath hovering in the air. "A church," he said, "with a tin roof." Allen or Neal, maybe it was, had taken him there one night. We found it. As we pulled up to the curb, the car scraped the sidewalk as if we had hit a sandbar.

I thought I would just stay in the car and wait for Gregory to get his drugs, but he told me to go instead. He said he had a bad feeling about what would happen if he went in, so he sent me. I couldn't believe his gall. I looked over at Gregory. I must've looked like I wanted to kill him; I certainly felt like it.

I got out of the car. Gregory said that the guy I was looking for would probably see me first and come out of church or around the corner. Gregory said that he was expecting me.

That's when I realized this had all been planned in advance. Gregory said that the guy I was looking for was very nervous about these kinds of transactions, and that I should try not to blink or look nervous. Suddenly, my eyelid started twitching like mad. It had never done that before.

I approached my destination. No one appeared. I walked into the church. Sanctuary! No one was going to kill me there, I thought.

The church was very hot. I could hardly breathe in the little alcove. There were a lot of candles burning in little glasses. I was alone. The altar of the church looked like a horizon very far away.

Suddenly, someone put his arm on my shoulder from behind. There was a small space between the candles and the door. I turned around. It wasn't a priest or someone who had come to say his prayers at the end of the day. It was a sandy-haired guy with blue eyes who smelled like he had been working under the hood of a car. He smiled and his gold tooth caught the light from the burning candles. I recognized him. He was one of Billy Jr.'s friends, one of the Westies.

This was Gregory's drug dealer? I never had much respect for Billy's friends. Billy was so smart; he loved to read; he wanted to be Mark Twain. The Westies seemed like idiots—the more they drank, the more drink they poured into Billy, and the more idiotic they seemed.

C

O

O

L

The Westie was staring at me. He didn't seem too interested in his money or in giving me the glassine envelope with Gregory's ticket to paradise in it. "How much is that worth?" he asked, pointing to the chain around my neck. "What is it anyway?" He put out his hand, and I leaned back. "You don't have to be afraid of me. I'm not going to hurt you. Fuuuuck." He must've added that for reassurance.

I never liked wearing jewelry. My father never even wore a watch or his wedding band. I'm not sure he even had one. But my parents had given me a mezuzah, which I sometimes wore on a chain around my neck.

"What's in it? What's it for?" the Westie asked.

"There's a tiny scroll in it," I said. "It has Hebrew writing inside. I wear it for good luck. It's like a Jewish rabbit's foot."

"Is it valuable?"

"Some are. This one isn't."

I wondered if he also noticed the veins in my neck throbbing with fear.

"I want it," he said. He was going to try to tear it off my neck. I could feel the chain getting hot as he began to pull, as if he could pass the chain right through my neck. I tried not to look at him. I looked at his tropical shirt instead: hula girls standing on the backs of dolphins. I wanted to run out of the church, but he held the chain of the mezuzah in his hand.

I don't know why but for some reason, when I left Gregory in the car, I'd taken with me a small bag of things I just bought at a drugstore—shaving cream, toothpaste, that sort of thing. I managed to get out a can of deodorant and I sprayed it in the Westie's face. I sprayed him up and down and from left to right. It was like I was making the sign of the cross in deodorant spray.

He let go of the mezuzah. I left him sprawled out like Thomas Becket on the floor of the church, with all the candles burning. I ran back to the car. I pounded on the window for Gregory to let me in.

Back in the car, Gregory said I was a lucky bastard because that particular Westie was "not a Corsican." In Gregory-speak, that meant that he wasn't any good. I didn't bring up the fact that

Gregory had set me up with this creep to begin with, who could've had a gun with him for all I knew. Finally, out of sheer exhaustion, I told Gregory that for someone who was always complaining about not having enough money, his habit was sucking him dry.

"Just think of the money you'd have if you didn't spend it on drugs," I told him. "And by the way, you've got a windfall coming because I ran out of the church without handing over the money."

Gregory looked through his money as if he had just won the lottery, as if he couldn't believe his good fortune. When we got back to Boulder, he used the cash to have flowers sent to his wife, and to Calliope, and he took me to a great dinner at John's restaurant, with its white tablecloths and fresh-cut flowers on the table. Gregory ordered an expensive wine, and for once I wouldn't have to use my father's credit card to pay for the meal.

Seated comfortably and enjoying our meal, Gregory started talking about drugs. He said, "Drugs aren't beat" (though Gregory had never really liked the word "beat"). "The problem with drugs is that they're like a woman with no heart. You keep trying to appeal to her, but she doesn't hear you. She doesn't really return your affections, not for very long."

Gregory got treated like a great man at John's. He sat at the table swathed in a kind of Roman dignity. I couldn't figure out if it was because he seemed to suddenly have come into a lot of money or if they knew who he was: a great poet, for that's what his face looked like by the restaurant's candlelight.

48. King of the Cats

Like Jean Marais, the man in Jean Cocteau's *Orpheus* who sat in his car and listened to messages from the underworld, Billy sat in his room like the incarnation of a hookah in an abandoned harem. Billy sat alone with his thoughts bubbling to the surface. I noticed that all his furniture was missing. He didn't even have a nail left from which to hang himself.

Billy had huge gambling debts. He was drinking so much by now that his apartment looked like a liquor store filled with empty bottles. He was turning into a character from Dostoyevsky. In fact, Billy was turning into Dostoyevsky himself, a genius of waste and sorrows. His creditors had come and taken everything out of the apartment, even Billy's beloved couch, what he referred to lovingly as his "barge of sufferings." His favorite hat had disappeared into the couch and he'd forgotten to retrieve it, so even his hat didn't belong to him anymore.

When I first met him, certain things used to make him come alive. A good joke, James Cagney on television, his memory of the owls he'd once seen swooping through Grand Central Station. I thought that my telling him about spraying one of the Westies with deodorant would cheer him up, but even that failed to register on his Dead End Kid face. He was like one of those Central Park carriage horses at the end of its usefulness, unresponsive to the crop, impervious to any thrill.

Billy had taken to gambling out of desperation. It was the last vice he could find. He awaited his nightly poker games the way other men wait for love, nervously, impatiently. He bet on horses. Offtrack betting had just come to Denver.

He even bet on bicycle races, including the one sponsored by Celestial Seasonings, the tea company that was started in Boulder in Mo Siegel's backyard garden. I think that even if Billy had had a run of good luck as a gambler, he would have given the money away, or spent it on booze and pot. He seemed to like the fellow-ship of losers. Billy was a realist, though, even for a gambler. He believed in the healing power of calamity, the idea that you leave yourself without any safety net, that you run away from the demon that's chasing you by climbing up a tree and sawing off the limb you're hanging on to. Billy was the collateral damage, the refugee in the war against himself. He sat in his damp, empty room with a pack of cards and let Allen and Old Bill arrange to get his furniture back.

When it came, Billy just got up from the floor and let them put the couch back where it had been before. He looked for the hat. There it was, beneath the huge pillow—his threadbare cap. He pulled it over his head, a strange look in his eyes. His pale, unhealthy pallor looked even worse in the nearly empty room.

And then I saw it: the bitter smile. Some part of him liked doing this to Allen and Old Bill. He was punishing his father. Here was this undiscovered genius whom the poets seemed to recognize. But what did it matter? They were unable to help him. Billy was a prince of the Beat tribe. Anne certainly treated him this way. I was a lot nicer to her than Billy, but she could hardly give me the time of day. Billy, with his mute eloquence and his shabby clothes—he was going to be Old Bill's heir.

I wouldn't bet on it.

Billy said that while I was in New York he had heard that they were closing down the operation at the Boulderado. Some of the women were becoming emotionally involved with the men who came to see them, and that was too much for Lydia, the madam I'd met at one of Carla's parties. She was a Holocaust survivor, so it was hard to dislike her, but I did.

Lydia didn't like the emotional entanglements that were getting in the way of her business. "It's because they're babies, they're not professionals," she complained to Billy about her girls. "They have orgasms while they're working, for Chrissake!" But it didn't sound like a house of pleasure, not anymore.

Billy said that he couldn't afford to go there anyway, but that now there'd be no place to work. He had always liked to go there to write. "It was Yaddo," he said, referring to the famous artists' colony in upstate New York, "only with pussy." Not that it mattered to Billy Jr. He seemed to care only about the pack of cards fluttering inside his chest. That would be his ticket out—the World Series of Poker in Las Vegas. That's what he was preparing for.

Allen had talked Burroughs into allowing for Billy to receive a kind of stipend from some of Bill's books. Jubal, Bill's scary assistant, didn't like the idea. Naturally, they wanted *me* to tell Jubal about their plan. So I went over to Burroughs's apartment and knocked on the door.

Jubal had never liked me. I always felt he was just waiting for an excuse to kill me; now he'd have it. I was relieved when Calliope opened the door. When she wasn't with Gregory, Calliope was with Jubal. I looked at her for a moment in the doorway. "Good-bye," I said.

"Good-bye?" she replied. "Wait, where are you going?"

"I came to see Jubal, but he's not here, so I'll go. I have a taxi waiting at the corner." That was going to be my excuse for getting out of that house, and to discourage Jubal from killing me.

It was starting to rain. It did that a lot in Boulder in the late spring, especially when you were stuck outside. Suddenly, the sky would become as dark as the inside of a hat and the rain would come. Calliope invited me in. Now my hope of not finding Jubal at home was in ruins.

"He's upstairs. He's practicing darts and polishing William's guns."

"Don't bother him, Poppy," I said. "Just tell him that Allen's going to talk to Bill about setting up a little trust fund for Billy so that he can pay some of his bills. Just think, he'll be able to buy breakfast with the proceeds of *Naked Lunch.*" I didn't realize how dumb that sounded until I'd said it. Calliope smiled at me, but it was the mocking smile of a statue, one that could have been called, "Beauty Looks at an Idiot."

Walking home through the rain—I didn't really have a cab waiting for me—I noticed the mountains of Boulder. I had forgotten about the mountains. I was surrounded by them, but I'd never really seen them. They were brown with black rings of earth that reminded me of my father's fedora, the hat he liked to wear to work. I know they were only foothills, but they were mysterious, jutting up into the sky, full of foxes and fugitives eating scraps left by hikers, and mountain couples who washed in the creeks and lived, god knows where, in abandoned shacks that had once housed miners cooking trout in a iron skillet. (I don't think I'd yet seen an iron skillet. I grew up surrounded by Teflon.) I was so blinded by Allen's fame and Burroughs's scary reputation that I couldn't see the mountains for the giants that were living at the base camp, which is what Boulder really was, a place to live before you went up into the ever thinning air.

When I got home the phone was ringing. It was Jubal, and he was angry. He shouted into the phone that he didn't care how Bill threw away his money. He claimed that he saw right through Allen and Bill, Billy Jr. and me. Jubal told me that his mother had been killed by his father, and that his father had shot himself, leaving Jubal in possession of a secret for making a fortune. Jubal said that his wishes came true at the very moment he utters them. He told me that he was about to wish Billy Jr. dead.

For a few days after that, the slightest sound outside my apartment made me jump. "Take away Jubal's meanness, his talent as a writer of Westerns, his success with women, and what have you got?" I once asked Gregory.

"You've got you!" Gregory said, laughing to himself. "You've got you."

There was a noise at the door. It sounded like a tree branch scratching against the wooden banister on the tiny porch in front of my apartment. Then I heard a short cry. Jubal trying to lure me onto the front porch, so as to plunge one of his darts into my chest? Shoot me with one of Burroughs's brilliantly polished guns?

C

O

O

L

It was a cat. It was Gregory's gray cat, Horace, named for the Roman poet who wrote odes. Under Horace's front paws—one blue and one gray (Civil War paws?)—was a note: "Take care of Horace and he'll take care of you. Don't let him die, or I will have sex with your mother. Love, Gregory." I took Horace inside. I had a terrible allergy to cats. Horace always made my eyes tear and a scarlet streak flare up on my neck.

Gregorio Nunzio was a *gattari*—at least, that's what he called himself—a lover, a feeder, a stroker of cats. He fell in love with them while wandering in Rome. Feeding strays in doorways, Gregory would fall asleep among the cats of the Colosseum, before being chased away by the *polizia*. "If Allen is the king of May," Gregory once said, referring to the student coronation of Allen in Czechoslovakia in 1965, "then I declare myself to be the prince of the Piazza Argentia"—the City of Cats Gregory discovered when he lived in Rome, thinking up his poems among the hundreds and thousands of wandering cats scratching and screeching among the marble ruins.

Now Horace was mine. Gregory had left him, as well as something else wedged inside the screen door: his new collection of verse. The book was finished. No title yet. I picked up the manuscript with one hand and held Horace in the other. Horace weighed more than the sum of Gregory's poems.

Gregory claimed he had found Horace as a kitten wandering the English cemetery in Rome, where Keats was buried, that he was purring and pawing Keats's inscription: "One whose name is writ in water." I didn't believe him, but now it didn't matter. I had the finished book he had promised, and I had Horace. I would have to take care of them both.

A few nights earlier, the ax suspended over Gregory finally fell. Gregory got himself and the Kerouac School in trouble again by going with Calliope and Jubal to the Blue Note, a nightclub that had just opened up on the mall on Pearl Street. The Go-Gos were appearing for two nights. Gregory, who knew nothing about pop music and couldn't care less, shouted out that he and the Go-

Gos—all five of them—should have sex in their hotel room. He shouted that having sex with a great poet would only improve their musical abilities and their access to the Muse. He kept interrupting them from his seat. I don't think the Go-Gos knew who he was, just another heckler, another drunk they encountered on the road.

He caused such a ruckus that the businessmen around Rinpoche who were trying to keep Naropa afloat got wind of it and gave Allen the unhappy news that Gregory would have to go. The faculty had almost fired him when he'd trashed his apartment; now they had no other choice. It fell to Allen, his friend of nearly thirty years, to tell him to get lost, to leave the Kerouac School, for the sake of the school itself and its chances for accreditation. He was out.

Where would he go? How would he live? Gregory really had nothing to declare but his genius. The croupier of Gregory's fate seemed to be pushing all of Gregory's chips off the table. He had simply run out of chances.

Gregory would never completely disappear, however. After being let go he still hung around the fringes, occasionally teaching other people's classes; between the cup and the lip, there would always be room for Gregory. He would still appear suddenly at a party or pop up at a reading to heckle the performing poet, a thousand phrases whirling around in his brain and then finding a launching pad out of that nearly toothless mouth.

49. "Consulting I Ching Smoking Pot Listening to the Fugs Sing Blake"

The spring and summer sessions wound to a close and I hung on in Boulder over the break, wondering whom they would get to replace Gregory. The fall semester passed without incident, and the spring term of my second and last year as a student was about to begin when Allen threw a party to welcome Ed Sanders to the Jack Kerouac School.

Allen had summoned Ed Sanders to Boulder to conduct an investigation into what had happened that night between W. S. Merwin and Trungpa Rinpoche. Allen didn't have much choice. Reaction to Tom Clark's story in the *Boulder Monthly* was yet threatening the Kerouac School's very existence. Some people even thought that the bad publicity was making Rinpoche's talks even weirder.

Meanwhile Allen informed me, now that I was a second-year student, that I had to start meditating or I wasn't going to graduate. I got six credits just for showing up in the shrine room and taking off my shoes. It was less humiliating than dodge ball.

Rinpoche usually gave his talks wearing a beautiful blue suit. It shone in the light like the scales of a fish. Blue might have been Trungpa's favorite color. He gave a talk called "The Blue Pancake." It was about crazy wisdom. It was a Chicken Little story with a tantric twist. Rinpoche talked about the sky falling, about the moon and stars falling on your head. During the question-and-answer session someone asked Rinpoche why he was so enthusiastic about having the sky—the blue pancake—fall on everyone's head. Rinpoche started to laugh. "I think it's all a big joke, it's a big message, ladies and gentlemen." I didn't get it.

I walked outside and looked up at the sky. The stars were still there. But I wasn't sure about tomorrow, when I was supposed to join Ed Sanders's official investigation into Rinpoche and the "Merwin incident."

Ed Sanders was a poet and a musician. He had been in a notorious rock band called the Fugs, which had gotten its start in the Lower East Side of New York City. I think they wanted to call themselves "The Fucks," but then they wouldn't be able to advertise their appearances in any newspapers. And so, being made up of writers and a few poets, they changed their name to something that sounded like "fuck" but wasn't. Another story was that the word "fug" came from Norman Mailer, that he'd wanted to be able to say "fuck" in his novels but knew he would never get away with it, so he came up with "fug" instead. I never asked Ed Sanders. In fact, I hardly spoke to him.

In class, Sanders said, "People with shyness problems who want to get into investigations have a big problem." Ed Sanders had written a book about the Mansons called *Family*. I read it by a sliver of bathroom light in my parents' house in Merrick, Long Island. After I read it I kept thinking that Tex Watson (one of Manson's followers) or maybe even Charlie himself would break out of prison and wind up on Long Island, and maybe, just maybe, he'd make his way to my house and kill me. It was a pretty remote possibility that Manson would escape from San Quentin, get to New York's Penn Station, find the Babylon line of the LIRR, know enough not to change trains at Jamaica, then come to Merrick and find our house and kill me. But that didn't discourage me from worrying about it. (I thought the same thing when Richard Speck was at large after he'd killed those student nurses. When I was much younger I must've thought that being a victim of a famous serial killer would make me famous, too. Gregory told me that all poets want fame, but that it's sad because poets cannot be famous anymore, for poetry is not famous anymore.)

Sanders looked like a disheveled version of the painter James Abbott McNeill Whistler, with his downturning Victorian mustache and unruly mop of slightly poofed-up hair. He even wore

"CONSULTING

I Ching Smoking Pot Listening to the Fugs Sing Blake"

C

O

O

L

vests. I knew the poem Allen had written in June of 1966, "Consulting I Ching Smoking Pot Listening to the Fugs Sing Blake," which made Ed Sanders even more mysterious. He had made it into Allen's poetry.

I never figured out why I found it so hard to talk to him; perhaps it was because he seemed so smart and I was shy about what I didn't know about literature. He was putting Sappho's poetry to music. I was unable to give up my Sammy Davis Jr. records. I was still going back to my apartment and listening to *Sammy at the Cocoanut Grove*. He did imitations of movie stars from the 1950s like Jimmy Stewart, Marlon Brando, and Jerry Lewis. I thought it was funny. I had to keep my interest in show business a secret from my teachers at the Kerouac School. I was afraid of what they'd think. I shouldn't have been so insecure. In *Visions of Cody*, Jack Kerouac writes a kind of aria to the Three Stooges. I should've given my teachers a little more credit. On the other hand, I never heard any one of them ever tell an old-fashioned joke. Allen had funny poems, but they were funny in an ironic way. They got big laughs, but with punch lines like, "America, go fuck yourself with your atom bomb." It wasn't the Friars Club.

Allen said that I should follow Ed's lead and pursue the investigation wherever it goes. He said to be careful, though, because other poets were already gunning for Rinpoche and for Allen, too. Their animosity went back to a public reading at the University of Colorado four years earlier. Gary Snyder, Robert Bly, and Allen were all giving a poetry reading to benefit Rinpoche's Meditation Center. Trungpa was there, presiding as master of ceremonies. He was loaded on sake. He kept interrupting the poets; at one point he kept puffing up his cheeks and then collapsing them with his fists, making a kind of farting noise. Robert Bly was getting mad. Allen, who never really liked being upstaged, asked Rinpoche if this was all some kind of religious instruction. At the end of the evening Rinpoche apologized. Not for his behavior but for the poets. "I'm sure they didn't mean what they said." Then Rinpoche started to yell or possibly yodel, and he started banging on a large gong. Allen looked at him and pleaded with Trungpa to tell him if this was really him, or was he acting out of some Buddhist tradition.

"If you think I'm doing this because I'm drunk, you're making a big mistake," Rinpoche said, teetering on the edge of the stage at the school's Macky Auditorium. One of the Vadjra guards reeled Trungpa back and prevented him from falling into the orchestra pit.

"Put it in the report," Ed told the class.

All these unflattering stories. I think Allen believed that the report we were working on in Sanders's class would ultimately absolve Rinpoche and thus Naropa from all suspicions of wrong action. But it wasn't turning out that way. I worried that Allen was going to have a heart attack when he read the report, and that Anne would flay us alive and use our skins for a shawl.

In class, Sanders told us that the principle of "Investigative Poetics" was that "poetry should again assume responsibility for the description of history." He said that we as young poets now had the chance to do this.

So we compiled a series of questions for Trungpa to respond to, but he refused to answer any of our questions when we presented them to him the next day. Through a spokesman, Rinpoche said that he would never cooperate with the class, and that this was the one class at the Kerouac School that was illegitimate. We then invited him to visit the Investigative Poetics workshop in a closed-door session. We took our job very seriously.

I wanted out of the class, but then Anne Waldman called me and said I should stay in and report back to her. Just what I wanted, to be Anne Waldman's spy!

Some of Rinpoche's closest students and advisers, members of the inner sanctum, wanted the investigation to stop. They said that the Buddhist community of Boulder should be on the lookout for what they called "the enemies of the dharma." (Every single time I heard the word "dharma," I thought of stuffed derma, the orangey-looking circle of fat that my grandmother loved to cook. It too had

"CONSULTING

I Ching Smoking Pot Listening to the Fugs Sing Blake"

C

O

O

L

a lot of the teachings within it—just a different tradition—and anyway, Rinpoche always said that Jews made good Buddhists.)

In the midst of the investigation, Robert Bly returned to Boulder, ostensibly to give a poetry reading, but instead he tore into Rinpoche and into the very idea of the Kerouac School. Not surprisingly, he brought up Rinpoche's fight with Merwin. He told the crowded room that the "Kerouac School is doomed."

"Oh, God, not before accreditation," I prayed to myself.

Someone in the audience yelled at Bly, called him a coward and a traitor to Shambhala. All these people started to seem crazy to me, caught up in some warfare that seemed more corporate than anything else. The next thing would be a proxy fight, or a hostile takeover of Naropa by the board of Yeshiva. I was getting mixed up. I think Allen was right. Bly and others saw an opportunity to stick it to Allen and Burroughs and their offspring, people that they never really liked anyway, and here was their big chance to say why.

The investigation dragged on through the spring semester. Merwin agreed to talk with us, and a few students who had actually attended the seminary retreat came forward. I met one of them at an all-night donut shop and took her testimony.

According to her account, it was like that Fatty Arbuckle party in the 1920s—Merwin was not an innocent, at least not at the beginning. He was a gentle guy, but he had tried to get into the spirit of the retreat. He was on the front lines of a terrific snowball fight earlier in the day with the Vadjra guards, and he had hatched a plan to create a little mischief by surprising Rinpoche with laughing gas, but they couldn't get their hands on it—all the dentist offices were closed.

The events in question had occurred at the end of October, when leaves were turning and falling from the trees. All of a sudden it was Halloween, even in the Rocky Mountains. The last month of seminary is supposed to be the hardest. Cabin fever combined with crazy wisdom. The Vadjra guards were throwing a Halloween party: come as your neurosis. This would be the big blow-out before the transmission of some very heavy psychic petting, when the coal of the psyche, under enormous pressure and over time, is transformed into diamond.

Merwin and his companion, Dana, had arrived early at the party, according to my informant. They left early, too. Trungpa came late, and most people thought he was drunk. He was dressed casually in blue jeans and a lumberjack shirt. It was hot inside the ski lodge. It was noisy. It was turning into a typical Naropa party. Rinpoche decided to take off his clothes. He ordered a few of his most trusted guards to lift him up on their shoulders, like a bride at a Jewish wedding, only he was completely naked as they led him through the various rooms of the ski lodge. Everyone looked up. Rinpoche looked down. He noticed that Merwin and Dana were not there. He asked where they were. Someone said they had gone back to their rooms.

"Bring them down," Trungpa said.

"They don't want to come," one of the guards told Rinpoche.

"Bring them anyway! Break down the door if you have to."

But Merwin and Dana refused to open their door. One of the guards decided to smash the plate glass and enter the room. Merwin broke a beer bottle and held it out, threatening to cut anyone who came close to him or Dana. He thinks he might have even cut one or two guards simply by brandishing the broken bottle before throwing it against the wall and allowing himself to be dragged downstairs to the party, where Rinpoche was waiting.

Downstairs, Trungpa urged all his students to expose their neuroses. Then he singled out Merwin and Dana, accusing them of indulging in neurotic violence and aggression. Merwin defended himself. He said that it was Trungpa who was being irresponsible and a traitor to the teachings. Merwin said that Rinpoche was cutting his own throat with the way he was going about teaching crazy wisdom.

Trungpa threw a glass of sake in Merwin's face, then he turned to Dana Naone. "We're both Oriental," he told her. "The Communists ripped off my country. Only another Oriental can understand that."

Dana then called Trungpa a Nazi.

That's when Trungpa suggested that Merwin and Dana take

I Ching Smoking Pot Listening to the Fugs Sing Blake"

their clothes off. After all, he, Rinpoche, was already naked. They turned him down.

When Ed Sanders, during the course of the investigation, spoke with Dana and introduced her evidence into the report, she told him how the Vadjra guards had dragged her off and threw her onto the floor. She could see Merwin struggling too a few feet away. She told Ed, "I fought back and called out to friends, men and women, whose faces I saw in the crowd, to call the police." But no one did.

Only one man, Bill King, broke through the crowd, and while Dana was lying on the ground in front of Trungpa, King spoke up. "Leave her alone," he said. "Stop it." Then Trungpa got out of his chair and surprised Bill King with a punch from his good arm, which was quite strong, and knocked Bill King down, saying that no one else should interfere with what was going on. Another Vadjra guard Dana identified as Richard Assally was trying to pull her clothes off. She said that Trungpa leaned over and hit Assally in the head, urging him to "do it faster." The rest of her clothes were torn off.

Merwin and Dana Naone stood in front of Rinpoche "like Adam and Eve," as one eyewitness described it, and then Merwin spoke up. He challenged everyone else at the seminary to take off their clothes. Everyone did. Belt buckles fell to the floor, shoes were flipped in the air, people slithered out of their clothes like snakes in molting season. Then Rinpoche gave his final order of the evening: "Let's dance."

Someone put on a record, Roxy Music's "Love Is the Drug." Seeing their chance, Merwin and Dana grabbed their clothes and slipped away.

The next morning Rinpoche had a letter placed in everyone's mailbox. "You must offer your neuroses as a feast to celebrate your entrance into the Vadjra teachings. Those of you who wish to leave will not be given a refund [it had cost $550 to go to seminary], but your Karmic debt will continue as the vividness of your memory cannot be forgotten."

I read the letter at the donut shop; it already had a few coffee rings around the edges. The woman who gave it to me liked to come here late at night to think about what had happened. She said that since seminary, it was hard for her to sleep. I added the letter to our "Merwin Incident Report" and took it to the copy shop at the top of the hill near the university, where I had it Xeroxed. I gave it to Allen. We had a copy made for the Naropa library, but someone removed it about a week later.

By the time Sanders left Boulder, he looked like an old man. He'd been through hell. He was living with Tom Clark and his family, who were trying not to answer the phone because threats were coming in. Tom wanted to publish the findings of the Investigative Poetry class in the *Boulder Monthly,* but Allen and Anne really didn't want all of that to come out. The younger poets were angry with Tom that he would even think of doing that. But Tom had no allegiance to Rinpoche or to the Kerouac School. Tom liked Gregory's way of doing things—keeping his distance within the circle. Sleeping with one eye open, even among his friends. I also got the feeling that there was no one Tom wouldn't betray for a good story.

I saw Sanders the day Tom Clark took him to the airport. "Good-bye," was the first thing I ever said to him. We shook hands. Ed was carrying a lot of the paperwork from our investigation in a big shopping bag. We were all a little frightened. Ed had told the class when we first started our investigation that when we opened the file on Rinpoche and Naropa, our first concern should be to define what he called "the area of darkness," and to bring to that darkness "the hard light of Sophocles," or something like that. But it was hard for us; these were our teachers, this was our school, and accreditation, we hoped, was just around the corner.

Just think of me, if you will, as I was then: an overheated imagination, a dangerously susceptible heart, a good-natured kid, maybe even a tender soul with a mind full of poesy, constantly in the presence of some of the flintiest (Burroughs *père*), moodiest (Allen), and chilliest (see Waldman, Anne) temperaments around.

"CONSULTING

I Ching Smoking Pot Listening to the Fugs Sing Blake"

C

O

O

L

Ed's report and the anxiety it was causing Allen put me in a state of despair that seemed only to induce a kind of narcolepsy. I slept like I was still growing. My somber fits had me (when I was awake) playing lots of Bob Dylan records. Playing "Sad-eyed Lady of the Lowlands" more than once a day was a sure sign of my misery. Even when I stepped into a restaurant, the one thing I always loved to do whatever my mood, I felt lost and alone.

I suppose that the reason I was eating myself alive was Ed's report and the unhappiness it was causing the Kerouac School. As my two years at the Kerouac School were drawing to a close, I had stopped calling people up. The investigation had made me slide backwards into shyness and found me returning to my old haunts like an innocent, pretending that I knew no one. I was tormented by the desire for company but unable to pick up the phone. If the Kerouac School had taught me anything, it was to think of my teachers as trusty confidantes, to turn up the radio at a party and climb into the Faigos' hot tub with Allen and Peter and a few girls, even if they laughed when the steam made my eyeglasses fog over. I was able to throw my library card over the garden wall and be a primitive youth, at least in the backyard of a suburban house. Maybe I was worried about what was going to happen to me after I graduated. Would graduating from the Jack Kerouac School make me a poet? Would I start to publish? Would I stay on in Boulder or go back to Merrick? I didn't have a clue.

Yet I knew how upset Allen was, and I was afraid that somehow I had displeased him. Around Allen and Bill, even after all this time, I still felt like a schoolboy. Their every word sounded like it was coming from under a dome of gold, even if it was just Allen exasperated with Peter for putting his dirty underwear back in the drawer.

After a few weeks into my slough of despond, I finally screwed up my courage and called Allen. He told me he had just been to New York to accept an award for his poetry; he was now getting serious attention from more academic poetry circles. I think he liked it. He had a habit of surrounding himself with poets who were never that good. Gregory noticed this right away, how Allen often championed the work of vastly inferior poets, some of them just because they were working-class guys who reminded him of Jack Kerouac. They were solidly built and had hair. "That's not enough," Gregory said, "to let them into Parnassus." (I loved how he said "Parnassus" in that thick New York accent.)

Toward the end of the spring semester, Allen invited me to a party. He said we should talk about Ed's investigation and what else Tom Clark planned to do to ruin the Kerouac School. I went with Allen. It was in a student apartment full of lots of kids trying to act grown up. Almost immediately they began asking questions. "Was it true about Rinpoche and what happened?"

Allen patiently explained to them that the so-called Merwin incident had indeed happened, but that things like individual rights didn't really exist in a situation like that. He surprised me a little by saying that Merwin got what he'd deserved by going there in the first place.

I could tell Allen was getting angry. He said that Trungpa was a revolutionary, in that he was in some sense challenging the foundations of American democracy, and that, anyway, democracy was a failed experiment—the atom bomb proved that. "What Trungpa was up to was a new experiment in monarchy," he said.

I saw Tom Clark at the party. He was listening to Allen, who didn't notice him right away. Tom approached Allen, and it looked like they still might be friends. Tom asked Allen if he would be willing to do an interview about the Merwin problem, about religion and poetry. Allen didn't want to do it. Clark had interviewed Allen once before for *The Paris Review*, an historic interview in fact. Allen wasn't shy, but he didn't want to be interviewed for the *Boulder Monthly*; he wanted his interview in a more respectable forum, like *Playboy*.

That spring semester I had taken a class Allen was teaching on the prophetic books of Blake: *The Book of Urizen, Jerusalem*. A few days after the party, we left class on a night that felt like Yom Kippur. We walked out into the cool mountain air. Tom Clark was waiting. He told Allen that the interview had to be *now*. People wanted to hear from Allen Ginsberg on the Kerouac School's first big scandal. Allen agreed, and we walked back to Allen's house on Mapleton.

Peter was there with his schizophrenic brother Julius, who was visiting that week. Julius roamed through the house like a skinny ghost in a checkered shirt, stopping to stare at something on the wallpaper. I felt like there were two tragedies going on in Allen's house at the same time: one was the pain of the Rinpoche / Merwin incident, the other was Peter.

The Orlovskys never seemed ready for this world; they were like incarnations of its suffering. There were four children raised in poverty by a deaf mother. Julius and Lafcadio had both spent considerable time in psychiatric hospitals. Allen was the one person they seemed to trust. I always thought that Peter would have wound up just like his brothers but for Allen's love and devotion. Allen was able to look after Peter, to "handle" him on Peter's days and weeks of locking himself in the bathroom and crying. Allen had had all that experience with his mother's schizophrenia.

Now that Peter had taken up with Juanita Lieberman, Peter's emotional absences, the weird vacancies that would cross his face, making him unapproachable, almost catatonic like his brothers, became a real crisis for Allen. "Now I'll have two babies to support," he complained, referring to Peter and Juanita's plans to move in with Allen and start a family.

It sounded familiar. That's the same language Carla had used with me after she decided to send me out of her life.

Peter had just made dinner for his brother when we all came into the house. He was doing the dishes and preparing to put out the garbage. Peter cleaned out the house like he was cleaning out the Augean stables, but I understood how he had gotten himself dismissed from the army for "mental disturbance" (when he was asked to clean out his barracks, he had tossed out everything he considered ugly—including guns and helmets—and then hung curtains and painted sunflowers on the soldiers' lockers). Peter sang to himself, but in a very loud voice, while Allen spoke softly into Tom's tape recorder in the living room, driving Tom crazy by making him turn it off and on every few minutes, while Allen considered what he wanted to say, "for posterity."

I liked helping Peter with the dishes; I liked to do the chores that would keep me from having to offer an opinion, anything not to get sucked into the Merwin whirlpool, where I could feel myself getting old just thinking about it.

Sometimes, despite his quiet, reasonable tone of voice, his sane manner, Allen could say some very outrageous things. That was a source of his power—his quiet mania, his well-mannered, apocalyptic thinking.

"I accuse myself all the time of seducing the entire poetry scene, and Merwin, into this impossible submission to some spiritual dictatorship, which they'll never get out of again, and which will ruin American culture forever," he said into Tom's tape recorder. "Anything might happen. We might get taken over and eaten by the Tibetan monsters . . . All the horrific hallucinations of the *Tibetan Book of the Dead* are going to come true right now. Right here in Boulder . . . But with Trungpa . . . you're talking about my love life. My extremely delicate love life, my relations with my teacher. Trungpa said that he was trying to explain to Dana that she should respect her roots by taking part in a classical experience. What he finally told me was, 'This is an opportunity to turn poison into nectar.' I don't know what happened," Allen admitted. "So I went to see Trungpa. It didn't bother me too much, but apparently it bugged a lot of other people."

Allen interrupted the interview to ask Peter to sing a little less loudly while he washed dishes. Julius kept switching a bouquet of flowers from one vase to another; he couldn't quite decide which one "was a better house for the flowers."

Allen then said he thought that Trungpa was being influenced by the teachers at the Kerouac School. Allen said Trungpa had sounded like a character from a Burroughs novel when he'd told

"C
O
N
S
U
L
T
I
N
G

I Ching Smoking Pot Listening to the Fugs Sing Blake"

C

O

O

L

Dana, "You Oriental slick cunt, why are you hanging around with this honky?" Allen told Tom that he was "looking at it sort of as Burroughs-type humor," rather than as anything truly sinister.

It seemed pretty sinister to me. I cringed when I heard Allen sounding like Burroughs.

"Everybody was getting very self-righteous," Allen said, "for Rinpoche to bring up the fact that Dana was hanging around with a white guy. You're not supposed to say things like that. Even if you're a Vajrayana teacher, breaking down all privacy and breaking every possible icon in every mental form, and acting like a poet, no less. I mean you're supposed to out-Gregory Gregory Corso, and out-Burroughs William Burroughs, if you're a Vajrayana teacher."

For Allen the whole incident was like the story of the snake and the rope, where you see a snake coiled up in a basket and, when you look closely at it, it turns out to be a rope. In other words, the entire world is an illusion.

It was getting late. That wasn't an illusion. The kitchen was filling up with students. I tried my best to hide my feelings, but I thought that Allen couldn't win, that we should be making ourselves as inconspicuous as possible. I mean, in a few days our parents would be here for Parents Weekend; didn't we want them to approve of everything?

Tom's being in Allen's house and Peter's brother walking like a zombie between Allen and Tom and the tape recorder weren't helping Allen's mood. Every one of Clark's questions seemed to go against Allen's grain. The whole issue was becoming about as friendly as a hangnail. Allen looked exhausted, but he was incapable of kicking people out. Even more people came into the house, and soon it was overflowing as students and hangers-on gathered in the kitchen, the living room, out on the porch, in the backyard. Allen became more and more angry, as if all the people in the house were feeding off the problem at hand.

It's hard work, I thought, standing up to Clark's questions, his wise-guy remarks, steeped in vinegar, that came flying through the air even over the head of the innocent. Allen said that Merwin had been free to leave and free to stay. Rinpoche put himself in danger by having an inexperienced meditator like Merwin even come into a situation like that. The worst thing Allen could say about Trungpa was that he had put Allen into a situation where he had to go through all this *tsouris*.

"As if I hadn't had enough with LSD and fag liberation, now I've got to go through Vajrayana! And Merwin, whose poetry I don't care about anyway! With Ed Sanders freaking out and saying it's another Manson case! Ed has a large quotient of paranoia," Allen explained to Tom's tape recorder. "He's been studying black magic and Aleister Crowley and playing around with all that. I mean, getting into the Manson thing, and then getting into Vajrayana and Trungpa and Merwin, is just made for Ed Sanders. It's even made for my paranoia, because half the time I think, 'Maybe Trungpa's the CIA.' "

I almost dropped the glass I was drying. Could Rinpoche himself be the spy Allen and Bill were talking about? Allen was on a roll; it just wasn't very pretty. His voice became higher, scratchier, a sign of his irritation and distress. I think he forgot that the tape recorder was on.

"Who are these poets anyway," Allen asked, "who feel that nobody should be above the poets? That the poets have the right to shit on anybody they want to? That they've got the divine right of poetry? They go around and commit suicide. Burroughs commits murder, Gregory Corso borrows money from everybody and shoots up drugs for twenty years, but he's 'divine Gregory.' But poor Trungpa, who's been suffering since he was two years old to teach the dharma, isn't allowed to wave his frankfurter!"

Julius was picking his nose by now, and examining it. I lost interest in Peter's leftovers. Suddenly, a middle-aged couple appeared in Allen's living room.

They looked lost and a little afraid. They were carrying their suitcases. They put them down and asked if they had the right house. They asked for me. I had forgotten that Allen had wanted me to invite the parents who were going to be in charge of Parents

"CONSULTING

C

O

O

L

Weekend to stay with him at the house on Mapleton. There wasn't much I could do to stop them from coming. Now they were here, wiping their feet on the doormat.

Allen had recently played host to his two completely useless nephews, who wore their hair like a curtain so that I never actually saw their faces and who hated everything. They had responded to Allen's suggestions to go out and find a job by telling him how many awful things can happen to you while working—cans of peas falling on your head if you become a stock boy, getting mauled by a vicious dog if you take the civil service exam and become a postman, and so on. He put up with them because Allen liked having family around him. His stepmother, newly widowed, was a frequent guest in Boulder. He could be cranky and become irritated with them, but he liked the fact that they were around. It made him feel like the paterfamilias. Allen Ginsberg, the godfather of poesy!

There was a trickle of blood coming out of Julius's nose. I noticed Allen had come back from the bathroom with his pants unzipped. I looked over at the middle-aged parents who had arrived with their suitcases; a look of misery came over the husband's face. It was as if standing in Allen's foyer had brought back a bad dream. I probably made things worse when, like Lurch, I stepped up to the parents and said, "I'll show you to your room." I had everything but a candelabra.

"Where do you sleep, young man?" the woman asked me.

Her husband interrupted her. "In the dorm, Betty, of course."

"We don't have dorms at the Kerouac School," I replied. "I sleep in my coffin. What a lift it gives you!" Gregory would have been proud of me.

50. Plutonium Blues

My head, like life itself, was in shambles. My parents weren't going to make it to Parents Weekend. It was just as well. The entire weekend ended up being about the Rocky Flats nuclear facility.

Rocky Flats was a big deal. It was owned by the Rockwell Corporation, and Allen was obsessed with it. The facility was in Golden, Colorado, and they made triggers for plutonium bombs. Allen even wrote a poem called "Plutonian Ode" and made it the title of one of his books. No one liked having the Rocky Flats facility so close to Boulder and the Kerouac School. Anne wrote a long poem she liked to perform all about plutonium and what a long shelf life it had. Allen invited Daniel Ellsberg, the revealer of the Pentagon Papers who at one time had helped to design a fail-safe system for our nuclear program, to come to Boulder and get arrested with him out at Rocky Flats. Allen wanted Ellsberg, Anne, and all the other teachers and students at the Kerouac School—even Gregory—to go to the facility and sit on the railroad tracks with him and meditate. He wanted to stop the trains that were carrying nuclear material to Rocky Flats. They called themselves the Rocky Flats Truth Force.

So one morning Allen, Peter, and Ellsberg drove to Rocky Flats, along with most of the students from the Kerouac School and all of the teachers. Allen was going to read "Plutonian Ode" and Anne was going to read her plutonium poem. Before leaving, we all had breakfast together while Allen explained how just ten pounds of plutonium scattered throughout the earth is enough to kill four billion people.

Just as we were about to leave, Ellsberg told Allen that he wanted to change his pants. He was wearing a very expensive pair

C

O

O

L

of white pants, and he didn't want to get them dirty sitting on the railroad tracks. We waited while he changed into blue jeans.

Allen asked if I wanted to go and get arrested. I knew that Anne would be angry with me if I backed out, but I didn't care. I didn't feel like getting arrested, not during Parents Weekend. I asked if it wasn't bad timing to go out to Rocky Flats the same day all the parents would be coming to see the school. Allen thought it was perfect timing, because then it would get more attention. Imagine pictures of parents coming to the Jefferson County jail to bail out their socially conscious children, heroes in the war against death! I had written a poem to be read at Rocky Flats called "Einstein's Brain," about a journalist who comes to the medical school at Princeton to interview Einstein's brain, to ask him how he felt about unleashing such power on the world. It was a prose poem. I meant it to be funny. Allen liked it, although he said something like "you can't exactly interview a brain." (I was never quite sure if he got any of my poems.) But it didn't matter. He was going to let me read it.

Anne said that if I was going to Rocky Flats to read my poem, I had to sit on the tracks and get arrested like everybody else. She seemed determined to make life hard for me. I was afraid to argue with her. I couldn't imagine winning an argument with someone I thought was so beautiful. But she was an incomplete Venus. She left me clanking my chains, stuck in the same place I always was with her. I decided not to go. A few days before, another Rocky Flats protester had sat on the railroad tracks and the train rolled over him. They had to amputate his legs.

Everyone looked at me like I was a traitor. They left. By the afternoon every teacher at the Kerouac School had been arrested for trespassing on government property. Allen read "Plutonian Ode" from the back of a paddy wagon. At the parents' reception in the shrine room, I realized that all the teachers of the Kerouac School were in jail. I sat at the table by myself. About a dozen parents started asking where their children were.

Gregory came stumbling in. He wasn't even supposed to be

teaching here anymore. Allen had told him to stay away during Parents Weekend. "Why?" he'd asked. "I'm a parent. I have three children by four different mothers." He started to tell me, in a loud voice, how he thought there might be something wrong with him because he couldn't stop urinating. Parents looked at each other and if expressions could have sounds attached to them you would have heard an enormous racket like garbage cans being thrown out of windows. They knew something was wrong.

Pretty soon the word had gotten out that most of the Kerouac School and its students had been arrested at Rocky Flats. I looked down at the display of food and faculty books that had been set up on the table; it looked like the wreckage of a carnival. I saw mouths moving, but I couldn't hear a sound. I had blocked it all out.

A policeman came in. One of the parents passed out. I didn't feel so good myself. I handed out flyers about the activities that were planned for the rest of the weekend. I heard the policeman say something about bail, and then I couldn't hear them at all; the parents and the policeman had moved to another corner of the shrine room. It was very quiet at the poet's table. There was nothing left to do but reach for a cracker and some cheese.

Allen came back from Rocky Flats filled with an almost messianic zeal about closing it down. He started looking for signs in the prophetic books of Blake about Rocky Flats, pointing out sentences like "The Reactor hid himself thro envy. I behold him. But you cannot behold him till he be revealed in his System." Blake, *Jerusalem*, chap. 2, plate 43, lines 9–10. Allen was starting to sound like Oral Roberts on a crusade. I was getting worried.

At one of the evening lectures for parents about Buddhism, Rinpoche's handpicked successor, known as the Vadjra regent, gave a talk about the Buddhist doctrine of Sunyata—all about existence as simultaneously void and solid, empty and real. He spoke to the parents about all-penetrating egolessness symbolized by the Diamond Scepter. He concluded by talking about the Six Realms,

all held together in the delusion of time by pride, anger, and ignorance.

This definitely wasn't Nassau Community College. I could take
it, but I wasn't sure about my friends' parents. I wasn't sure I had
any friends, not after I had bailed on getting busted at Rocky Flats.
I sat by myself in the shrine room and watched these parents who
loved their children and were giving in to them, even though I
could see it was giving them a lunatic headache. From the cradle
to the coffeehouse, they had loved their children and were letting
them in some way forget about life, by which I mean they were
letting them forget about money, how to make it, how to hold on
to it. Even if they didn't believe it themselves, they were letting
them live more outrageously, more passionately perhaps, than
they had ever allowed themselves to live. It made me feel tenderly
toward them. It made me miss my own parents, my parents like
two ocean liners plowing their way through the sea, while I played
shuffleboard on their backs and dined at the captain's table. I
wonder if Allen ever felt that way, or Gregory. No, not Gregorio
Nunzio, he hardly knew his parents. He had accepted himself
right away; he'd had no choice.

51. Carla Redux

It was her faux leopard collar and sleeves that gave her away. I usually took my glasses off when I had to stand up in public and read
my poems. Gregory said he was getting to be an old man (not true,
he was forty-six when Allen first introduced us) and had to wear
glasses to read, but that I was still a young man and should want
girls to sleep with me, because I was a poet and girls loved words.
The only problem with taking off my glasses during a reading was

that I couldn't see the people who had come to listen to the poems. But I knew that it was Carla from the black sweater with those leopard-skin cuffs—she had come to the student poetry reading that Anne had put together for Parents Weekend.

Several months earlier, I'd had a disastrous reading at the Boulder Public Library. I read with Allen as a kind of opening act. It was after I'd been to New York with Allen and Peter. I came back with a pair of tight-fitting leather pants. Allen said they looked good. He suggested I wear them at the poetry reading at the public library. I did.

Whenever it was cold outside in Boulder, the heat in public buildings was turned way up. I started to sweat the moment we stepped inside the library. Before long, my entire waistband was condensing and a veritable inlet of perspiration was beginning to flow down my legs. The tight leather pants that Allen thought looked so cool—even though I was standing behind a wooden lectern—made me feel like being locked into a sauna.

I kept wiping my brow, and at one point I even interrupted my own reading to go into the bathroom to mop up. It was impossible to take off the pants; they would have to be peeled off me like rabbit skin. I thought I was going to pass out.

I was reading a lot of my most romantic poems. I was swooning, but not from my own love poetry, rather from dehydration caused by my Christopher Street–bought leather pants. Did Gerard Malanga ever feel like passing out when he wore his leather pants and did his whip dance in front of the Velvet Underground? Something tells me he didn't. I had no choice in the matter. While I was reading a poem about the death of a flower, I unzipped my leather pants and began to roll them off me until I had them around my ankles, and I furiously started moving my feet up and down until I was able to completely step out of them.

I finished my sad, romantic poem about the flower, standing behind the lectern in my white underpants and ruffled shirt. Only Allen, who sat behind me on the tiny platform, could see what was

CARLA

Redux

happening. Now, how was I ever going to come back from behind the lectern?

Toward the end of my reading, I kept inching the lectern back, closer to the bathroom where at least I could rush in and put my pants back on. Luckily, Allen came up to the lectern to make an announcement about some upcoming event at the Kerouac School, and I was free to step behind him, grab my pants, and make it back in time to listen to Allen start his reading. I know that he had stepped up to the microphone only to help me, to give me some cover, in every sense of the word. He even seemed more attentive to me in the days and weeks following my combination reading and striptease. I had done something Allen liked to do in the old days, only he would have stepped *in front of* the lectern. I had taken off my clothes out of necessity, because I was burning up. Allen liked being naked as a political act. He and Peter were happy as larks when they were nude. They would take off their clothes at an all-you-can-eat buffet if the line was too long. "They like throwing their meat around," Anne said. But only in public.

At the Parents Weekend reading, I spoke to Carla for the first time since our breakup. She said she had come to the reading because she remembered how my poems had drawn us together once before, and that thinking about them had suddenly changed her idea of me. She didn't hate me anymore.

It was hard to know what to make of that remark. Was it something she said as a joke? Was it a profound statement of her real feelings? Was she over the bodily pain, the mental suffering, or was it regret for the past? Was she warning me about the future? The fact that I never really knew this woman was brought home to me by her appearance that night at the library. There were so many different explanations for our love affair that, at the end of it, nothing was ever really explained.

I loved her voice, which was slightly husky and sad. I listened to her words and in my head translated them all into feelings, into pure emotion. I couldn't believe that this was the same woman who had brought down the iron gate that kept me away.

I made the mistake of telling her about my life since we'd stopped seeing each other. I told her how awful it felt to know what she was going through and still not be able to tell her how much I loved her and was concerned about her. But I think I said those things for selfish reasons, to awaken some kind of pity in her. I was staking all my hopes on this moment.

She surprised me. She seemed to encourage these thoughts. When she touched my arm, I was like a sponge in water, absorbing her tenderest feelings.

"I don't want to mislead you," Carla said. "I want to spend the night with you, but that doesn't mean we're going to be together tomorrow and the day after that."

I knew I couldn't do that, which was a novelty for me. In all my time at the Kerouac School, when it came to having a sensation I never thought about it twice. I even had sex with my teacher Larry Fagin's girlfriend, Susan Noel, the one Peter Orlovsky called Susie Christmas. I could never quite figure out why I did it. Perhaps I was secretly angry about all those dinners Larry was charging on my parents' credit card. Or was it contempt for my own shyness around girls? Someone once called youth a glorious beach at the edge of blue water, where women seem to be always available to us, their beauty freeing us from the falseness of our dreams.

I was so serious about poetry, so serious about the world, that I was missing the point. Allen was missing the point, too. Shouldn't pleasure and happiness come first? Why, then, send Carla away? Why do we refuse to be cured of the disease of loneliness?

I didn't know what to do. I felt like dashing my brains against the brick facade of the library. Often, when you are strong enough to think about such things, you wish you could reclaim the words once said to you, just as you wish you could reclaim the people themselves and ask them, "What were you trying to tell me?" I was never smart enough, not then, anyway, to know what was

C
A
R
L
A

Redux

going on. I certainly couldn't keep Gregory away from drugs. Or bring Billy and his father together. Or find out why Anne never really dug me, or make Allen less insecure, despite his incredible fame. Perhaps we all lose our true companions. Allen lost Jack; Gregory lost his youth in prison; Bill lost Joan, the one person who, even in her craziness, probably loved him; and Jack lost them all behind the door of his mother's house. Had I just spent two years in the valley of the lost men?

In the end, I didn't send Carla out into the night. My love for Carla was taking a long time to die. It was Gregory—banished, disgraced Gregory—who told me, "Go after huh" in his New York street kid accent. "Go after huh, don't let huh get away!" I figured everything had already fallen apart. Everything about Carla was mixed up inside my head. Her mixed signals were mixing me up.

Allen always had a broken heart. It helped his poetry. As for Burroughs, I wasn't sure he had a heart at all. He was like those target cutouts you see on a pistol range, the black silhouette of a man. Curiously, it was Gregory who was more reliable on the subject of love. It was Gregory who sent me out after Carla.

"Let me tell you," Gregory said. "Love is the whole ball game. There isn't really anything else."

I ran out of the shrine room after Carla. There was the rain again, the rain that falls alike on the lovers and the lost. I asked her to stay until all the parents had left, until the rain stopped, until I could lean her against a tombstone in the old Boulder cemetery and, stealing a line from Gregory's great poem "Marriage": "woo her the entire night the constellations in the sky." I thought you could talk like that, then, when you were young and in love with the weird, sweet complications of your own heart.

Carla stayed. I went home with her. She put Brian Eno's *Before and After Science* on the record player, ambient music for the pretty sleep that comes after love.

The Kerouac School was finally up for accreditation. A team of about seven men and two women from the Association of Middle Colleges arrived in Boulder to observe the Kerouac School during a typical week. They started their work the day that all my teachers in poetics, the administrators, and most of the students were to be arraigned in Jefferson County on the Rocky Flats trespassing charge and for interfering with government activities. The special prosecutor rode to the courthouse from the airport with Allen, who had come back that morning from a poetry reading in the Pacific Northwest.

Attendance was pretty sparse that semester anyway, so Peter had the idea to recruit some of the vagabonds from the mall to sit in the classrooms and look like they were taking notes, five dollars for every hand that went up with a question. Thank God, Allen overruled him.

Accreditation would finally come, though the Kerouac School would have to wait.

52. Graduation and Beyond

I walked back to my apartment, remembering how my father had helped me set it up two years earlier. I couldn't even think about dismantling the apartment and moving back to Long Island. Yet slowly, in the days leading up to graduation, I started carting home empty boxes I'd gotten from the giant liquor store and filling them up with books. Those dozens of books reminded me of the many reasons for my coming to the Kerouac School in the first place. I kept Balzac's Lost Illusions, one of the first books we read in Allen's class, on my shelf as long as possible. It was the story of a young man from the provinces who comes to Paris to become a poet and a great man of letters. Abruptly, I stopped thumbing through it and put that book, too, in a half-empty box. That's when my apartment really started to have the odor of departure. I had never used the kitchen very much, but now it looked like I had never even boiled water in it.

It would be hard to leave. I thought of my father, how he and his brother had shared a tiny, one-room apartment in New York City on 178th Street in Washington Heights after their parents had died shortly after coming to America. Seymour had been only fifteen at the time. It was strange to think of him living in the shadow of the George Washington Bridge, the great bridge named for the father of our country. My father lived in that room with my uncle until his wedding day.

My parents used to ask me about Allen's mother and father, almost as if they wanted to be reassured somehow that Allen's parents were like them, that maybe they shared with Allen's parents the suspicion that America was still a dangerous place, and not the paradise it seemed.

I couldn't take being alone with my thoughts anymore, the wreckage of my half-packed apartment all around me, so I bolted and headed toward Pearl Street. It felt good to be with people who didn't just commune with the dead like so many of my relatives. "Is Allen a self-hating Jew?" my father once asked me when I was back home briefly between semesters. They were always suspicious of his Buddhism and his Hindu chanting. Having written "Kaddish" wasn't enough for them. It was the only poem of his they would recognize.

In a used-book store in Boulder, Allen and I had once found a discarded page from an old Hebrew prayer book. It was sticking up out of a spy novel where someone had used it as a book marker. When Allen saw it, he called it to the shopkeeper's attention. I remember being a little embarrassed, but he and Allen searched the entire shop to restore the page to the book it belonged to. I was secretly proud of Allen that he wanted to find a home for the page of Jewish prayer. When they couldn't find it, Allen's eyes filled with tears.

I told Seymour this story. I wanted him to know that, beyond Allen's Buddhism, beyond that river was the ancient village of Allen's Jewishness. He knew it; I know he felt it. He always cried when he recited "Kaddish," written for his unfortunate, schizophrenic mother, Naomi. He knew the wellsprings of his Jewishness as he knew an old friend. Allen Ginsberg, this *om*-chanting Buddhist meditator, gave me a sense of my own Jewish faith in a way that no rabbi, Hebrew teacher, or bar mitzvah lesson ever did.

The day of graduation arrived. The ceremony was to be held at night, in the shrine room, which made me realize that I still hadn't really meditated. Despite Allen's warning me to "start sitting or I wouldn't graduate," I'd managed to avoid the banner-lined room for two years, except for a dance or an occasional talk by Rinpoche.

As the shrine room filled up with students, faculty, and proud parents, I looked around and noticed there weren't many poets graduating with me from the Kerouac School. A poet named Dan Goldstein, however, was one of them. Besides being a devoted poetry student, Goldstein was an incredible thief. He could steal anything. Allen used to say, after telling him it was wrong to steal, that Dan was "the reincarnation of Neal Cassady." In fact, his parents were Jewish furniture salesmen in Toronto. He came from money, but he liked to steal. He was the official thief of Naropa. He stole things for Jubal and for Gregory. Books were his specialty. He single-handedly cleaned out the University of Colorado bookstore. Not surprisingly, his favorite poet was François Villon. Now we were graduating together, about to receive our official diplomas from the Jack Kerouac School of Disembodied Poetics.

Rinpoche was late. Very late. He gave the shortest talk of his career. "Ladies and gentlemen," he said, "when you go out into the world, have a little dignity." He told us to be brave, to have courage, and to conduct our lives like a samurai sword: with straight backs made of impenetrable steel and, as in the edge of the sword, with hearts sharp as a razor but open enough to be moved. He then took out a samurai sword and waved it around. I saw Anne duck; she was sitting with Allen and Gregory and Bill on the stage of the shrine room. Rinpoche then turned to Allen, who called out my name. I was going to receive the first diploma, which stated that I was graduating in the Year of the Earth Horse. Rinpoche offered me his good hand to shake. He looked crocked to me. He had a big Little Red Riding Hood basket full of diplomas. Anne gave a short talk. She said something about how we now had to go out and do the Jack Kerouac School proud by becoming great poets. She said we had a tradition to live up to.

As she said this, I suddenly felt a chill, as if a great wave of oblivion had just passed over me. I didn't particularly like Anne, I wasn't going to miss her, but when she started to cry as she gave her talk, I felt guilty. I thought Anne was wasting her time saying farewell to people she had never talked to in the first place. Then the band Oregon played some music, which involved endless drumming. Next there was a dance recital which Barbara Dilley called a dance about fire and water. I wanted to throw myself into the water and let the current carry me away. I felt the knot in my throat pushing at the knot in my necktie.

Allen stood up in his linen suit and read two poems, one by Rinpoche and one of his own. His was a poem I had always loved. He had asked me what he should read at my graduation, and now he was reading it, and so I felt he was reading it to me:

> Because I lay my head on pillows, Because I weep in the tombed studio . . . Because I get scared—because I raise my voice singing to my beloved self, because I do love thee my darling, my other, my living bride, my friend, my lord of soft tender eyes . . . seeking still seeking the thrill—delicious bliss in the heart abdomen loins and thighs Not refusing this 38 yr. 145lb. Head arms & feet of meat . . . Nor one single Whitmanic toenail contemn nor hair prophetic banish to remorseless hell, Because wrapped with machinery I confess my ashamed desire.

Approaching the dais to receive my diploma was like stepping into a spotlight as the last light of the day fell across the stage. When they called my name a few hands started to applaud. Feeling a sense of occasion, I bowed deeply from the waist toward Allen, who put his hand over his heart and bowed back to me. Whatever distance there had been between us (the distance of love unrequited to the nth degree) seemed suddenly to melt away.

I sat back down with my diploma unfurled like a napkin on my lap, my eyes brimming, Allen's voice cracking up in the void, the big shrine room full of its bright banners hanging from the ceiling, the floor covered with rice as if a wedding had taken place. I thought of all the lunatics I had known at the Kerouac School and how I would miss them. And Gregory—where was he?

Suddenly I could hear a howl from outside, like Quasimodo in the bell tower. It sounded like someone was yelling "Penguin dust!" It reached us in the shrine room while Allen was finishing his poem. It was Gregory's voice, shouting from outside the shrine room: "*Herald of the Autochthonic Spirit!* That's it! Tell Sam Kashner—that's the title of our book!"

Allen, when he reached the end of his poem, wrote down the title as casually as if Gregory had been sitting across from him at tea.

Of all the lunatics, I would miss Gregory the most. I had come to the Kerouac School, had come to knock on Allen's door so that he would teach me to write and to become a poet. But Allen was a famous man who had other famous men around him, and others still who depended upon him and clung to him like a life raft, who sapped his energies and often left him too exhausted for his own work. There was a kind of terror in the way Allen insisted on being the one who held everything together. In our nuthouse, Allen was king.

But it was Gregory who had become my courage teacher, who had pulled over to the side of the road and made me watch the last few hours of sunlight going down through the mountains. He saw his own youth slipping away, but he wasn't sorry. He was grateful. "I wish I could stop being young," Gregory said to me the last time

C

O

O

L

we were together. "To watch youth walk away would be a beautiful thing, to see it for what it's worth, its vanity, and to take a final look at it and then cross to the other side of Time."

That's what Gregory had to say, but they wouldn't let him say it at graduation. They didn't even let him in the room. "For only the lovers of life are fit to die," Gregory shouted through the high windows of the shrine room. And then again, "Penguin dust!" That was the last thing I heard him say. I ran out of my graduation ceremony and around the side of the building to find him, but there was no one there. You'd have a hard time talking me out of the idea that he was never really outside at all. Perhaps I just heard him, the one who made me laugh, roaming around inside my head. After the ceremony I dashed home and looked up autochthonic: "he loves the earth on which he walks."

Later that night, Dan Goldstein threw a graduation party in his apartment. It had a couple of thousand books in it, a table full of expensive wine, and fabulous food—a great spread, all stolen. I don't think my teachers knew what a beggars' banquet it was.

Allen and Peter and I left the party early. Allen said he had something to give me—my last job as an apprentice. Allen handed me a piece of paper. He said it was his latest poem. He said he was up half the night writing it. He wanted me to type it up. Peter said it was best if I read it at home. I opened up the piece of paper, which was folded into thirds like a letter. I couldn't believe I was going to have to type another poem for Allen on the same day I had graduated from the Kerouac School!

The poem was in Allen's by now familiar, tiny notebook handwriting. It was called "Forgotten Birthday: Sammy's Lament." My last assignment was a poem Allen had written for me. It was about how sad he felt now that Peter was often missing from the house, now that Peter was sleeping with Juanita, and how he had forgotten Peter's birthday for the first time in twenty years until I'd reminded him, and then he realized he'd forgotten my birthday, too. The poem went on to say how he was glad we were both born and knew each other and had become friends and that, even if we wandered away from each other, we would have a home in each other's hearts. It was pretty sentimental for an Allen Ginsberg poem. But I already knew that about Allen, his sentimental streak, his schoolgirl crushes.

It's hard to tell you what that meant to me, to have this poem from Allen, this incredible gift that gave me my passport into this world I had willed myself into, as if in a dream from which I refused to wake. I'm sure it didn't mean as much to him. I doubt he had stayed up half the night writing it. He dashed it off. I had seen him do it. It didn't matter. It was the moon and stars to me. I would carry it in my pocket and, when it grew too fragile for my pocket, keep it in my wallet. Then one day, while taking it out to read on the subway, incredibly, I left it behind. I never even bothered to memorize it because I wanted it always to seem new.

I hated my life when I lost it. I'm older now; I don't see the weight, the tragedy of it. I don't let such things stab my joy anymore. I can't afford to. Once I left the Kerouac School, I had no choice. I had to put their books away: *Howl, Kaddish, Naked Lunch.* I had to take Sal Paradise at his word, that it was time to "go out, dig the river, the people and smell the world."

Coda

I would see just one of them again.

After ten years of trying to become a poet in America at the end of the twentieth century, I moved into an apartment on Lafayette Street in New York City. The statue of Puck looked out over the street. Carla tried living there, too, while I spent most of the time out on Long Island working for my father in the window shade business. I took Carla to the Mudd Club on weekends. She didn't need me. Every time we went there, she seemed to know more and more people. Eventually, the gatekeeper let her in as soon as he saw her. She had a secret life while I was with my parents. Her old boyfriend, the violinist, came back into her life. I didn't like it. I asked her if she was seeing him, if I should consider it "official dating" of an old boyfriend.

"You can't tell me who to fuck," she said. "You don't control me." I think that's when I realized the relationship was really over.

We went out one last time, to see the Feelies on Washington's birthday. They were a rock band that, in the beginning, performed only on national holidays. The lead guitarist, with his oversized glasses and curly hair, looked just like a young Allen Ginsberg. I never saw Carla after that. I wanted my James Dean plastic life mask back. She wouldn't give it back. For a while, I was haunted by the memory of this love affair.

I *would* get married. I *would* be good. I didn't astound the girl next door . . . as Gregory wrote in "Marriage." But I met a woman named Nancy in a poetry writing class. She was the teacher. She wore pearls and a red sweater. I thought she was beautiful. She worked for an outfit called the Academy of American Poets. She arranged the readings and raised money. Nancy worked for an old, rich woman named Mrs. Bullock; when she stepped down it was taken over by a younger rich woman named Mrs. Chase, who turned out to be Chevy Chase's stepmother. She liked Nancy and was kind to me, and she threw us a big engagement party at her Park Avenue apartment. The Academy poets were everything the Beats were not: they wore suits, they won prizes, they had readings—not in church graveyards or coffeehouses but in places with fancy zip codes, like the Guggenheim or at the library across the street from the Museum of Modern Art, even the Morgan library.

Nancy wore her hair like Louise Brooks, the silent screen actress who played Lulu, the prostitute who gets murdered, "the girl in the black helmet." Nancy came from a Southern family. Her mother and father grew up in New Orleans; they lived on opposite sides of the Audubon Park Zoo. At night, they could each hear the lions roaring in their cages. I liked Nancy's stories about her parents. They seemed so exotic. Nancy's father had been a test pilot in the navy; back in the 1950s, he broke the sound barrier for a living. He's a very quiet and very nice man who looks like John Wayne. He's tolerated my social dissonances for fourteen years. Nancy's mother was a homecoming queen at LSU, whereas my mother had enrolled in Stern College for Women, but had to drop out when the war came. (She had to be home, she later explained, to hide the mail. She didn't want her parents to know that her brothers had been sent overseas to fight. It was a full-time job to keep the war from my mother's parents.) That's how different our parents were.

Nancy and I got married. We had a small reception at a French restaurant on East Eighty-third Street, Le Refuge. I took refuge in marriage.

I didn't invite Allen. I didn't invite Gregory. I regretted it. More time passed.

Nancy got a job at the College of William and Mary in Williamsburg, Virginia, teaching creative writing. That's what poets did at the end of the twentieth century. Poetry was turning out to be a mug's game after all. Whoever said that—I think it was T. S. Eliot, the most successful poet of the century—was right. You wait around for your SASE (self-addressed stamped envelope) to come back, your poems rejected from *The New Yorker* in your own handwriting. You see the fiction writers getting all the attention.

You get used to a certain kind of poverty. When Jack Kerouac wrote, "Because I am poor everything belongs to me," it was the 1950s, maybe earlier. Allen would often write that line on the blackboard at the Jack Kerouac School. But this wasn't the '50s anymore, it was the end of the 1980s and nothing belonged to you if you were poor, or even if you were middle class. They never told you that at the Kerouac School. I used to want to be like Allen and Gregory; now I wanted to be like Jayne Anne Phillips and Paul Auster. Jayne Anne used to be a poet; she even studied with Richard Hugo when he was a visiting writer at the University of

Colorado in Boulder. "Poets don't have any glory," she told me, "it's the novelists who make all the money and have all the fun." I went to a Paul Auster poetry reading when I first got out of the Kerouac School. It was held at the St. Mark's Poetry Project where Anne Waldman reigned supreme, even during her increasingly infrequent trips back to New York, only Auster didn't read any poetry that night; he read from a work-in-progress, something he called "a metaphysical detective story." It made him famous. Now he makes movies. I was beginning to get the picture. I stopped writing poetry. I'd write novels instead. I studied the field. I'd start at the top. I'd call my first book, *The Latest Novel of Joyce Carol Oates.* It would be a little like science fiction. Joyce Carol Oates would be in it. She'd get caught in some kind of nuclear compressor with Stephen Hawking. He wrote best-sellers about black holes and things going on behind our backs in outer space. Their molecules would get all mixed up, like in that movie *The Fly.* When they emerge from the compressor, Joyce Carol Oates would write hundreds of books about serial killers hiding out in black holes that all sound as if they'd been written by a mechanical voice. Stephen Hawking would be able to take up boxing. My novel would be a best-seller. It would make me famous. I'd be cool again.

As a poet you become bitter, so you hold on to a lousy job at a college, where your colleagues don't think creative writing is a worthy thing, even though they're teaching Beckett and Shelley and Faulkner and Keats; their whole existence depends on creative writers! Your students feel sorry for you. They think teaching is another form of social work. You help them get through their phase of writing poetry. Then you realize their "phase" is how you have spent your life. This makes you even angrier. It's a bad idea all around.

You sting yourself like a scorpion and poison your life with the thing you once loved. You know you'll never again have the joy you once found in it.

I wanted some of that old magic. I wanted to feel drenched in the importance of poetry again. I wanted to look into the past with my own brown eyes and see Allen Ginsberg standing in front of me, with a sheaf of poems for me to type. I had to see him again, or everything would be lost.

So I invited Allen to come to Williamsburg to give a reading. I was teaching a class or two, so as not to go crazy in Virginia, where I felt like I was in the witness protection program, talking to my neighbors about crabgrass and the weather.

I was teaching a course on the Beats. I was taking students away from the other teachers, even the ones with tenure. I had to keep the enrollment down to thirty or forty students, as so many wanted in. They hung on my every word about Allen and Gregory and Bill. They talked about Rimbaud like he was Rambo. They brought in CDs of Tom Waits reading Kerouac. I made them read "Sunflower Sutra" and "Howl" and "Kaddish," *On the Road, Vanity of Duluoz,* and *Visions of Cody.* They talked about Neal and Jack and Allen like they were living with them in their dorms. I saw myself in these kids, these young hipsters.

Allen was older now. There was a lot of gray in his beard. We picked him up at the airport in Norfolk in the fall of 1991 and brought him to our house, a Dutch Colonial on a tree-lined street just off campus. As soon as he arrived he wanted to lie down. He always had the happy capacity for taking naps in the middle of the day, wherever he was. His secretary had faxed from New York a list of all the things Allen needed for his travels, what kind of salt-free meals he had to have because of his blood pressure, the brand of chamomile tea he liked to have onstage. The fax made a big deal of the microphone, and how to arrange the prayer scarf on the table where he kept his books and finger cymbals. It also listed the med-icines he was taking, in case he lost them or ran out. He had liver trouble now, and his stomach sometimes gave him a hard time. He'd never quite lost the slight palsy in his face.

We tried to have everything ready.

When Nancy and I first met him at the airport, in what passes

C
O
D
A

for autumn in that part of Virginia, I wanted to cry. I kissed him on the lips. He said I had gotten even skinnier. While I was getting skinny, Allen was getting old. He came to life, however, whenever he was around students. They started hanging out at our house at all hours over the weekend that he stayed with us. Allen, who had seemed so tired, so wrung out, still had never abandoned that wonderful ability to appear interested in everything. Maybe it was meditation, all those years of Buddhism. Maybe he really did come to see the world as holy.

Then, just as easily, he could turn it off and seem very far away, or fly into a fit or a rage. Here was a man who had been to some of the most interesting and exotic places in the world: China, eastern Europe, Cuba, the Ganges, Paris and London in the 1950s and 1960s. But he almost never went there as a tourist. So I wasn't about to show him Colonial Williamsburg. I didn't think he'd be interested. But he wanted to see it, so I took him to watch the colonial-era reenactors, the village smithy, the barber who bled you, the wigmaker. Allen said that next we'd be paying to see Robert Frank's America—photographs of Americans drinking Coca-Cola and shoving quarters into jukeboxes. (He was right; a few years later, Disney tried to develop a theme park in northern Virginia, which would contain as an exhibit an actual family farm. To me, that sounded like the beginning of the end of America as we knew it.)

Allen put his arm around me and we walked into the house. He didn't seem too interested in my marriage. Suddenly we were above sea level again, back in Boulder, where the women in Allen's life seemed as distant and as interchangeable as clouds.

I wondered about Peter and Allen. I had heard things, but I never said anything to Allen. I had heard that Peter was drinking heavily, despite the fact that he was still taking antidepressants. I heard that he was back in Bellevue, not as an orderly but as a patient. He would fly into psychotic rages after drinking. I heard that he'd run down the street naked, wielding a knife. I even heard that poor Allen had to sign the papers committing him. But mostly

I was worried about the reading the next night; would there be enough people? The reading was to be held in an old movie theater that had been around since the 1930s. It held about five hundred people, and it had had one night of glory sixty years earlier: the premiere of a Judy Garland film. That theater was the only place in Colonial Williamsburg where I felt an authentic sense of history.

Many of Nancy's friends were poets she knew from the Academy; they were very presentable. She didn't know the Beat poets very well. Just before the reading, Allen panicked. He said he'd forgotten his harmonium and he couldn't perform without it—he needed it for the reading that night. Nancy said she would run back to the house and look for it. She took a long time. She came back empty-handed.

"I looked," she said. "I'm sorry. I couldn't find it."

"It's a big wooden box with stickers on it from around the world," Allen explained, sounding desperate.

Nancy turned red with embarrassment. She had been looking for a copy of Wallace Stevens's first book, called *Harmonium*. Their two worlds had collided.

We went back to get it.

It was an unforgettable night. A line of people stretched for almost a mile outside the theater. I didn't know there were so many hipsters in Williamsburg. Two hundred people had to be turned away; some had come from as far away as Washington, D.C. The ones who got in sat in awe.

I stepped onstage to introduce Allen. My psychiatrist and my internist sat in the front row with their wives. The table had been set behind me, according to Allen's instructions, with a stick of incense just starting to burn from the stage. I had prepared an introduction but I was too nervous to read it. I acknowledged the fact that Allen was in Williamsburg, Virginia, by introducing him as "the father of my country." The audience gave him a standing ovation when he appeared in front of the curtain. He played a few songs on his rhythm sticks, some of the ones he had written in Boulder, under the watchful eye of Bob Dylan on the Rolling Thunder Revue tour.

C
O
D
A

C

O

O

L

He launched into "Don't Smoke, Don't Smoke, it's a thirty billion dollar capitalist joke . . ." Everyone laughed and applauded, but when he got to the part about where he urged people to smoke pot instead—or at least suck cock—I saw one of the oldest members of the English faculty get up to leave. I thought he was going to have a heart attack.

I was ecstatic. I was glad Allen hadn't lost his gift, his ability to offend. I wanted him to become again the frantic, demonic poet of his youth. We were together now, and Allen was rolling back the years for both of us, attempting to prove that neither one of us had really changed. I knew that it wasn't true, but it was such a wonderful lie.

Then he read the poem about giving Neal Cassady a blow job, the one he'd asked me to finish for him a million years ago. A few more people walked out. But most of them stayed, and cheered, and loved it. They were standing up now, and hollering their support back to Allen.

Later that night, they wouldn't let him leave the College Delly, where I had taken him for a midnight snack. He was the King of May again. A girl took a flower she was wearing from behind her ear and put it behind Allen's ear. They were rushing around, spreading the word that Allen Ginsberg was here, sitting at a table outside! A hundred glasses of beer seemed to be sloshing around our table, encircling Allen like golden candles. He defied the strict dietary laws sent down from New York. He had a hamburger, a pitcher of beer, and bummed a cigarette. He looked happy.

I never let Allen know I had stopped writing poetry. I knew no one was reading it, not my poetry at any rate. Only the magazines that the Kerouac School put out, like *Bombay Gin*, Trungpa's name for the school's literary magazine, or *Rocky Ledge*, put out by Anne Waldman and her husband, Reed Bye, were publishing me with any regularity. A small press called Hanging Loose in Brooklyn had put out a book of mine. It was called *Driving at Night*. It included poems I had written as far back as junior high school. I remember how excited I was when the editors told me that they had just gotten an order for six thousand copies, an extraordinary number for a book of poems by an unknown poet. But then they had to give all the money back when it turned out that the orders had come from a driving school in Iowa. They thought the book was a manual on how to drive after dark.

I couldn't buy a break as a poet, so I started writing prose. I wrote a biography and a novel and some journalism. I felt about my jumping ship from poetry to prose the way Oscar Levant felt about Milton Berle when he announced his conversion from Judaism to Christian Science. "Our loss is their loss," Levant had said. My poetry didn't set the world on fire, but that's all right with me. The world's on fire enough as it is.

It was close to three A.M. when we returned home. We tried to get back into the house, but for some reason Nancy's keys didn't work in the lock. A student of Nancy's—a kid from an old Virginia family who spoke French and loved the Beats—tried putting his shoulder to the wheel and forcing the door open. Nothing happened. I couldn't believe we were locked out of our own house, with a tired Allen Ginsberg, exhausted, in the middle of the night in Colonial Williamsburg. I had dreams like this that ended better.

A police car saw the four of us trying to break down the door of our house and stopped to investigate. He couldn't get the door opened, either, so he used his police radio to call a locksmith. We found one in Toano, about twenty miles away, who would take the job, but it was going to take a half hour at least before he could get to us—he'd been getting ready for bed when we'd called him. We had no choice but to wait.

Finally, the locksmith arrived. He was a stout, middle-aged man, a retired Vietnam War veteran, who brought with him a metal device for forcing the doorjamb. The locksmith apologized for taking so long. He said he usually goes to sleep early because there wasn't much call for a locksmith after the sun goes down. Allen admired the locksmith's strength when he finally forced the

C
O
D
A

C

O

O

L

door open with a loud pop. I thought of the epigraph Allen had placed in *Howl and Other Poems*: "Unscrew the locks from the doors! / Unscrew the doors themselves from their jambs!" It was from Whitman.

The rug had apparently become caught up under the door; Nancy said she must have accidentally kicked it in her haste to get out of the house after searching for Allen's harmonium.

The locksmith said that he owed his strength to tai chi. Allen asked him to show him some moves, so out on the front lawn, close to four A.M., Allen Ginsberg and the heavyset locksmith practiced tai chi, while the policeman shone the beams of his headlights on the front lawn.

When we were finally back in the house, Allen wanted to stay up for a while and talk. He wanted to discuss the reading. He was full of insecurity about it: did he read too fast, did he read the right poems? His concerns were endless. He couldn't get settled with the idea that he had done a great job. He had given a wonderful performance.

Allen left the next day. A car picked him up; I still couldn't drive, so I could not take him to the airport myself. Upstairs in the guest room, he'd left a copy of his *Collected Poems*. He wrote in it, "This is from my heart to yours, still young old friend. Love, Allen."

I looked for the Neal Cassady blow job poem. It wasn't there. Not that particular one, anyway. (Allen loved writing about giving head.) I searched for my birthday lament. That wasn't in there, either. Immortality denied!

I never saw him again.

Allen sold his papers, all those files, even the one he kept on Gregory's cat, titled "CAT—CORSO, GREGORY. ANIMALS POET PLAYED WITH," to the University of California at Stanford for some real bread. He was able to buy a loft with an elevator in New York City—all those stairs on East Twelfth Street had finally become too much for him. He moved his father's second wife, whom he revered, into the same building. He was finally able to afford health insurance. He needed it. Liver trouble was one of the things on Allen's list of ailments. Whenever he got hysterical and over-whelmed he would say, "I have Bell's palsy, high blood pressure, spastic bowel, and liver trouble. I can't deal with this now." So you'd back off, take your problem elsewhere. But "liver trouble" was really hepatitis C, which became liver cancer, which meant the end for a worn-out body, even one as stout and indefatigable as Allen's. Wasn't it Allen's father who blurted out that weird couplet in the middle of dinner with Rinpoche at the Flagstaff House in Boulder so many years ago: "Is life worth living? It depends on the liver."

Trungpa was the first to go. He died in Nova Scotia in 1987. He was forty-seven years old, pretty young for an old soul. His doctors wouldn't say what exactly was wrong with him, except that his liver was shot. Too much sake. His students said that he just wasn't attached to his body in the way nonenlightened people are. Some of Trungpa's students said that he knew he was wearing out his body, but that he didn't care. It was, they said, the ultimate act of crazy wisdom.

I was jealous. It's not that I wanted to die, I just didn't want to be afraid of death. Allen wrote songs to death; he wasn't afraid. Not when it counted, anyway, at the end. I think life is just too damn short. I want to be late for my death. I want the people I love to live forever, and the people I hate never to be born. It's too late for both: the hours and years mow us all down.

I started meditating after I heard about Trungpa's death. I'd heard that several monks had come just to prepare Rinpoche's body for cremation. They handed out small glass vials of the salt they used to preserve his body until the ceremony. His followers said that if you developed a serious illness, you could always break open the bottle and swallow the contents. It was supposed to have curative powers. Allen and many of Rinpoche's students meditated with the body around the clock. I thought about going, but I wasn't feeling so great myself.

I finally told my parents I was meditating after all those years of having successfully avoided it at the Kerouac School. "You can't beat the Judeo-Christian ethic," my father reminded me, "especially the Judeo part." He and my mother certainly didn't try to talk me out of it. Their paths were different. I think, though, that as a result of meditating, I've quit judging people so harshly. Now I believe in every religion. I'm not taking any chances: I meditate, therefore I am not.

Burroughs died in August 1997. He never got the Nobel prize that Allen had tried to nominate him for. He died in Lawrence, Kansas, buried among the other bad hombres of the American frontier. His secretary and assistant, his guardian angel, James Grauerholz, kept him alive longer than any doctor. James was like Ron Howard to John Wayne's dying gunslinger in *The Shootist*. He came into Bill's life after Jubal. Bill was lucky—luckier than his son, whom he outlived by many years. Billy Jr. got placed on a list for a liver transplant, had one, and to celebrate its success, went on a two-week bender. He didn't want his father coming to the hospital or riding home with him in the car. He made a lot of sad jokes and disappeared with his new liver and a few of the Westies into the dark old bars of Denver. Billy died of a heart attack right after that.

It's funny the things you think about when you first hear about the death of someone you cared about. Allen Ginsberg died on April 5, 1997, at 2:40 A.M. His obituary in the *New York Times* ran beside the reminder: "Daylight savings time resumed at 2 A.M. today," the kind of detail Allen would have put into one of his poems. When I first heard of his death, I thought, Now he'll never get the chance to go on MTV's *Unplugged*, which he really wanted to do, with Dylan and Beck as his special guests. He also wanted to have sex with Johnny Depp. Allen had plans.

I wondered who would have the job of packing away all his files. Allen was the most anal-retentive, revolutionary, bohemian poet you could meet. Burroughs said that the only man who loved files more was J. Edgar Hoover, Allen's bête noire and the man whose agency, he thought, had planted a spy at the Kerouac School.

No one ever did uncover a spy at Naropa, though for one brief moment Allen actually thought it might have been Trungpa Rinpoche himself. The Kerouac School finally got its accreditation. It's a permanent part of Naropa University now, the first accredited Buddhist college in America. I went to see it recently. It had become something fine and good—a place of sanity and noble thought. I even saw Anne Waldman there, still teaching, still famously beautiful, still unable to be still. She's going to hate this book, but then, come to think of it, she never liked my poetry, either.

Gregory Corso wrote in his poem "Ode to the West Wind" how he had no home, no income, no status as a poet in America. Well, that's not entirely true. A wealthy benefactor did come along at the end of his life. So at least he didn't have to worry about where his next meal was coming from. But other than this generous handout, there wasn't much in the Corso bank account. He died in his daughter's home in Minnesota. Robert Frost, the only establishment "old poetman" that Gregory, alone among the other Beats, really liked, said that "Home is the place where, when you have to go there, they have to take you in." That's where Gregory went, and he was taken in. A recording of Gregory's poems was made at the end of his life, read by him and by Marianne Faithfull, who had started coming to the Kerouac School in the early nineties.

When Gregory, who "lived by the grace of Jews and women," had stood at Allen's bedside as he died, he was himself dying of prostate cancer. When he passed away in January 2001, I read about it in the *New York Times* on the same day I agreed to write this book. I opened the paper and there it was. *The Happy Birthday of Death.*

Gregory used to refer to himself as a toothless old man when I first met him, but he was only forty-six then. He'd lived long enough to see some of his contemporaries win major accolades, like the poet John Ashbery (whose poems Allen didn't understand), who went on to win the Pulitzer Prize, the National Book Award, and many international prizes for his life's work. Gregory, whose poems you can find in the *Norton Anthology of Literature*, still didn't have very much after all those years of poesy. "But I have walked in mine integrity," Gregory used to say. It was the only time I heard him quote the Bible.

I heard that someone in Gregory's family planned to take his ashes to Italy and scatter them in the English cemetery in Rome, where Keats is buried and where Gregory had found his cat, Horace, which he'd brought to America and left on my doorstep, along with his manuscript of poems.

When Gregory's book *Herald the Autochthonic Spirit* finally came out—Allen had sent it to me—I eagerly opened it and looked for my name. Gregory hadn't thanked me, not anywhere, for all those months of baby-sitting him. All I could do was laugh.

Allen, by the time he had come to Virginia, was already a great man; at least, he was accepted, and he wasn't being kept out of the academies, or the anthologies, any more. He had his pin from the Academy of Arts and Sciences. And, like W. B. Yeats in Auden's memorial poem, Allen had survived it all. For Yeats it was Ireland, for Allen it was his mother's madness that had hurt him into poetry.

As for me, I had eaten the luminous cake of Allen's poetry. It was still there, glowing inside me.

I wonder if he can still see it after all this time.

Author's Note

I would like all readers to note that many of the names in *When I Was Cool* have been changed to avoid embarrassing people involved in events that took place many years ago, and who would not have known that their exploits might end up in a book someday. The following is a list of pseudonyms: Carla Fannetti, Linda Louie and Mickey Louie, Hadrian, Bonnie and Nanette, Simone, Kitty, Monica, Barbara the Barber, Jubal, Felice Duncan, and Dan Goldstein. Peace.

Acknowledgments

How good of Diane Reverand to let me grow up and write this book when she was an editor at HarperCollins and of Jeff Kellogg to adopt it after Diane's departure. As the editor of *When I Was Cool*, Jeff gave shape to this book and saved it from drowning, more than once. Jeff satisfies all the laws of friendship and remains indispensable. I'd also like to express my appreciation to David Hirshey and two other early readers at HarperCollins, Emily McDonald and Kate Travers; their sharp eyes and ineffable hipness helped things along. And thanks to Andrew Proctor, whose enthusiasm and erudition sent this book on its way. To the three graces of Nineteenth Street: Anna Bliss, Catherine Crawford, and Jenni Lapidus, my deepest gratitude. Thank you to Gordon Ball, Allen's Boswell, whose sweetness can be seen in those wonderful pictures he was kind enough to let me use. Praise be to Nat Sobel, my friend and the literary agent who tolerates my social dissonances and is there to pick up the pieces. And to Johnny Depp, who wears Jack Kerouac's old raincoat through the streets of Paris.